WALTER RIEZLER

BEETHOVEN

With an introduction by
WILHELM FURTWÄNGLER

WALTER RIEZLER

BEETHOVEN

With an introduction by
WILHELM FURTWÄNGLER

Translated from the German by
G. D. H. PIDCOCK

NEW YORK
VIENNA HOUSE
1972

Originally Published by Atlantis Verlag G.m.b.H.
Berlin & Zürich, 1937.
E. P. Dutton & Company Inc. New York, 1938.

First Vienna House edition published 1972

International Standard Book Numbers:
(Cloth Edition) 0-8443-0075-6
(Paper Edition) 0-8443-0076-4

Library of Congress Catalogue Card Number: 72-80708

Manufactured in the United States of America

TO
THE MEMORY
OF MY MOTHER

BEETHOVEN

An Introduction by Wilhelm Furtwängler

THERE is perhaps no other German whose name is held in such reverence throughout the world as that of Beethoven. His music is not popular in the sense in which Wagner's or Schubert's is popular; but in it there is a spiritual force unique in German music, and by no one has the power and greatness of German feeling and character been more cogently expressed than by him.

In an age that seems little favourable to a true and thorough understanding of Beethoven it is desirable that this should be specially emphasized. The average current interpretation of his works suggests perplexity and embarrassment. Some see in him the 'Classic', a composer long since dead, and now of purely historical interest, whose works are to be performed, if at all, as museum pieces—that is, in a manner strictly conformable with their 'style'. Others, following the Romantics, insist upon seeing in him the 'Titan', the first entirely subjective composer, whose works justify, or even call for, personal interpretation of every conceivable kind. Others again—those of the modern 'objective' school—hope to gain access to him by means of a jejune and colourless fidelity to the letter of the score. All these methods of approach, carried to their logical conclusion, simply result in caricatures; and it may be said that even a moderately satisfactory rendering of Beethoven's works is very much rarer than the public realizes.

And what of the verbal interpretation of these works? Here, it must be admitted, we are faced with special difficulties; and in this connexion it is not amiss to recall something that Wagner once said: ". . . since it is impossible to discuss Beethoven's music without immediately going into ecstasies . . ." Only those who do not really know Beethoven will take this as mere hyperbole. But whither do these "ecstasies" lead, seeing that they are the purely personal reaction of the commentator? Assuredly not to the attainment of understanding! Nor, it is true, shall we attain understanding by an attempt to approach Beethoven's works (incomparably clear and unambiguous as they are in their own language) along roads that are unconnected with music; or to find poetic keys for the unlocking of his compositions; or even to interpret them in the light of some theory of 'style-criticism' or some purely formal analysis that has never emerged from the domain of the abstract.

Here one thing, and one thing alone, will help: to hold fast to the musical reality of Beethoven's works. In them Music and Soul are one in a manner that is only possible in the works of a truly great musician. Even to attempt to separate the one from the other is an offence. Not through literature, and certainly not through psychology, but only through music, shall we gain access to the soul of this great man; nay, more—it is only in full awareness of our humanity that we shall fully grasp the tremendous reality of his music.

PREFACE TO THE ENGLISH EDITION

THIS book, the fruit of forty years' study of the problem of Beethoven, contains no 'discoveries' such as have been announced to the world several times during the last score or so of years. No keys are provided for the 'unlocking' of the compositions, nor are the 'fundamental laws' of Beethoven's creative work proclaimed. Even purely historical research is not furthered to any substantial degree. The book makes one claim, and one only: it attempts to answer the question "What is the essence of Beethoven, and what do his works mean?" In many respects my answer to this question may perhaps be new; but generally speaking it is intended merely to explain what the open-minded musical listener dimly feels without being able to account for it. And it may therefore be that my answer will help him to hear more and to hear better, and so to understand and appreciate more deeply the inwardness of those works. This is the type of reader that I most desire; but I also want all those who 'do not know what to make of' Beethoven, and who think they are justified in setting up other great composers in opposition to him.

The whole book is built upon a deep conviction of the autonomy of music. Music is itself a language, whose field of expression comprises all Nature and all Humanity. What it has to say it says outright, without need of help from the literary and visual arts, though it can enter into close and very mysterious relations with these. But, in the last analysis, it is music and nothing else. Therefore all talk about music in which we try to translate its 'expression' into words is pointless. If we cannot understand its language without the help of words, we shall never learn it. What words have it in their power to do is something much more modest, though not therefore superfluous: they can reveal the purely musical facts, and so help us to understand the organic structure of a composition. With this, however, we have reached no more than the starting-point whence we may set out upon further investigations whose object is to bring to light the affinity between music and the other spiritual and intellectual manifestations of a given age, a matter that can here only be referred to in passing. None but those who have grasped the true essence of Beethoven's creative work can give a conclusive answer to the question to what sphere in the spiritual life of his age Beethoven belonged.

This book is, I fear, like a painting of which parts are finished and parts only sketched in, the different degrees of completion having no relation to the importance of the respective parts. I should need thousands of pages to deal in detail with every one of Beethoven's major works; and to confine myself to generalities or to a few short hints would mean that I should merely scratch the surface or, indeed, be entirely incomprehensible. I have therefore given in the Appendix a detailed analysis of one symphonic movement. In it I have tried to show the kind of analysis that in my opinion is necessary to get to the bottom of the musical facts. If this analysis is read before Part III, many allusions in that part of the book that otherwise might be obscure will be understood. As books on the plastic arts can necessarily tell only half their story without illustrations, or at least without adequate knowledge and a vivid memory on the part of the reader, so a book on music must, as it were, 'talk into the void' unless every detail of the work under discussion is fully present to his mind. Purely aural knowledge, however exact and complete it may seem, rarely suffices; the reader must have the music before him, though in the case of an orchestral work a piano score will serve. Unfortunately it is impossible to avoid the tiresome task of counting the bars. (In the Miniature Scores published by Eulenburg and Philharmonia the bar numbers are given.) The few music-type examples in this book are not to be regarded as a substitute for the scores; their purpose is merely to indicate individual passages of special importance, or to make clear thematic or structural similarities. They are therefore purposely kept within these bounds, and make no claim to structural completeness.

In this translation effect has been given not only to certain corrections made in the second German edition of my book, but also to a number of further additions and alterations that seemed to me of importance. I take this opportunity of thanking the translator for the great care and pains he has devoted to his difficult task, and for his readiness to comply with the various wishes I expressed during several weeks' collaboration with him. My especial thanks are due to Mr Alan Bush, A.R.A.M., Professor of Harmony and Composition at the Royal Academy of Music, for his valuable help in the rendering of a number of technical terms—in particular of certain words that are the same, but have a different meaning, in English and German, and are, indeed, not always free from ambiguity in either language. I hope and believe that it has been possible in each case to render precisely the meaning I attach to these terms.

WALTER RIEZLER

March 1938

CONTENTS

13

14 CONTENTS

APPENDIX
THE EROICA SYMPHONY
An Analysis of the First Movement, p. 247

LIST OF ILLUSTRATIONS

PART I

LIFE

LUDWIG van Beethoven was of Flemish descent. The 'van' is not, like the German 'von', a mark of nobility, but, as in 'van Gogh', of origin. The name means 'of the beet-fields', and thus points to peasant stock. (There is a village called Bettenhoven between Liége and Limbourg.) As early as the fifteenth century the name was not unknown in various Flemish towns. The family seems to have been of a roving disposition, for in the registers of births and marriages at Malines many persons of this name are to be found, but few seem to have died there. In 1684 Michel van Beethoven was born at Malines; he made a considerable fortune as a 'master baker', but lost it through his dealings in lace, pictures, and other *articles de luxe*, which he carried on in addition to his main business. In 1741 he fled from his creditors to Bonn, where his two sons, Cornelius and Ludwig, had been living for some time. Of these the former was a tradesman and the latter, the grandfather of the great Beethoven, was a singer attached to the Elector's choir and orchestra. This Ludwig is the first musician we hear of in the family. He had no creative gifts, but was evidently a capable executant artist. When he died, in 1783, he was court *Kapellmeister*, and a highly respected man. His portrait, which was among the property left by his illustrious grandson, shows a calm, harmonious face of distinctly Flemish type, different in every feature from that of his grandson. As a side-line he is said to have made use of his father's business connexions to engage in the wine-trade. It is known that he had much domestic unhappiness: his wife, a native of the Rhineland, *née* Poll, had to be removed from the house and cared for elsewhere on account of a serious disease, which, according to rumour, was chronic alcoholism. Of his children, his son Johann, born about 1740, was a musician like himself, also a singer attached to the *Hofkapelle*. This son caused him much anxiety; but the stories that would brand him as a drunkard are authentic only as regards the latter years of his life. Things cannot have been so bad in earlier years, for he was much in request among the better-class families of Bonn as a music-teacher. None the less he was weak and unprincipled, and was not always over-scrupulous in his efforts to improve his financial position. Even his excellent wife could not influence him in this respect. She was not, as is often said, of low birth, but came of a respected and originally well-to-do family. Her father, Heinrich Keverich, was Inspector of the Kitchens at the palace of the Elector of Trier; some of the ancestors of her mother, a Westorff of Coblenz, were senators and councillors. A few years after the death of her first husband, an official of the court, she married Johann van Beethoven. Her father had died young, and her marriages were evidently a source of great anxiety to her mother. After apparently sacrificing her fortune to secure her daughter's happiness, the old lady of sixty-three developed some sort of mental disorder, to which her daughter's experiences may have contributed. We are informed of this in an official document: "The guardian appointed for her on account of the decline of her fortunes calls her weak-minded; but it is not for a God-fearing man to judge this woman's habits and conduct, for she was always endowed with a sane and vigorous mind. Lately, however, she has imposed upon herself a life of such severe and unusual penitence that it is hard to understand how she can survive, living as she does in this unnatural manner, taking little food, and that of the worst quality, and sometimes lying almost the whole night through in the bitterest cold, wind, and rain, outside the churches in the open air." She died the same year, 1768, six months after her daughter's fateful marriage. It was said of the latter that "nobody had ever seen her laugh", the result, no doubt, not only of a life of care and trouble but also of inherited hypochondria.

She took her duties with great seriousness, was a good house-keeper, cared for her children, and did her best to prevent her husband from squandering their none too ample means.

Such was the world into which the great Beethoven was born, on or shortly before the 17th of December, 1770. He was the second child; the first had died soon after birth. (He was one-sixteenth Walloon—one of his great-great-grandmothers had been born a Gouffau—three-sixteenths Flemish, and twelve-sixteenths German. Thus he was fifteen-sixteenths of Teutonic blood.) Of his childhood we know but little. He seems to have been perfectly normal in his games and pranks; but side by side with this we are told that at times he would sit lost in thought, and that he was often shy and taciturn, and even sulky, in the presence of others. He would often lie by the window "busy with deep and beautiful thoughts", which made him forget the world around him; or he would go and sit in the attic, from which with a telescope he could see "seven hours away." Late in life he still remembered the charm of his native countryside. His musical gifts seem to have shown themselves very early. His father made him play in public on the 29th of March, 1778—that is, before he was eight; but he announced, whether intentionally or by accident, that the child was only six. Probably he had in mind the fame of another infant prodigy, Mozart. But Ludwig was not a second Wolfgang. His gifts were of a different nature, and matured more slowly; his father, moreover, completely lacked the gift that Mozart's father had so conspicuously possessed for developing latent genius. Johann van Beethoven's musical knowledge, and his ability to impart it, were doubtless good enough for the Electoral choir and the amateurs of Bonn; but, himself a capricious and undisciplined man, he failed entirely to understand his talented son, and attempted to curb the boy's obstinacy and strength by violent means. We are credibly informed that Ludwig often wept during his music lessons; and it seems also to be true that sometimes his father would come home at night from the inn, waken the boy, and force him to practise. Johann himself evidently did not set too much store by his own teaching, for at about the time of Ludwig's first appearance in public he entrusted the boy to other musicians for instruction, among them a monk, Brother Willibald Koch, to whose organ-playing Ludwig would listen spellbound. The boy seems to have learnt so much from him that he could take his place at early mass in the Minorite monastery.

But the real teacher of Ludwig's early years was Christian Gottlob Neefe. A Saxon by birth, and originally a lawyer, Neefe had appeared in Bonn shortly before 1780, as conductor of a touring opera troupe. There he stayed, for, though a Protestant, he was given the post of court organist. In 1780 Johann entrusted his son's musical education to him. For the first time the boy felt the touch of a firm hand and the influence of a cultivated mind. As a composer Neefe was only moderately talented. But he was familiar with the mysteries of song and sonata, which then occupied the minds of musicians; he knew the works of C. P. E. Bach and the Viennese school; and though he had not acquired all the strict and rigid rules of the old masters, and was therefore not in a position to impart them to his pupil, yet he was so fully alive to the greatness of Bach's *Well-tempered Clavier* that he based his method of teaching upon it. Evidently he was in no sense a mere musical craftsman; he took pains to grasp the intellectual and spiritual principles, and even wrote essays on the aesthetics, of music. Like the young Goethe, he had moved in Oeser's circle in Leipzig, and so was familiar with other matters that stirred the minds of his contemporaries; and we may assume that he spoke of these things to his young pupil. He was a serious and thoughtful man, as can be seen from his portrait, which shows the strained expression characteristic of those with a deformed body. We have no detailed information as to his methods; but we may take it that they were thorough, since for one thing his pupil seems to have learnt from him to form his notes carefully and neatly. Beethoven's ordinary handwriting, though full of character at an early age, was clumsy and uncouth. This suggests that he did not learn much at school, which, however, he did not attend for long. Neefe helped him most by employing him as his assistant at church and, for a short time, to play the harpsichord in the theatre orchestra, where it was his duty to conduct at rehearsals. In this way Ludwig early acquired a first-hand knowledge not only of the orchestra but also of contemporary operas and operettas. He was also engaged to play the viola, but apparently he had little talent for this instrument, for he was not given solo work. Nor, as was evidenced by a boyish prank in which he gave an astonishing proof of his harmonic invention, was he unconscious of his own genius. In Holy Week of 1785, as a lad of fourteen, when accompanying the "Lamentations" at a church service, he indulged in such bold modulations that the singer broke down. This provoked the admiration and astonishment of the performers and the indignation of the singer, who complained to the Elector. The latter, evidently much amused, confined himself to a mild rebuke.

Though the boy had made good progress under Neefe, the latter's instruction was in no way equivalent to that of a great master. When he was sixteen, therefore, Ludwig was sent to Vienna—we do not know at whose instigation or expense—to study under Mozart. But the journey was ill-starred. He arrived in Vienna at the beginning of April, 1787, and found Mozart immersed in the composition of important works and distracted by his many troubles, so that he was little inclined to give regular lessons. Nevertheless, Beethoven was deeply impressed by the famous Master, though what impression he made upon Mozart we do not know. The remark Mozart is supposed to have made after listening to one of Beethoven's improvisations: "Keep your eyes on him; some day people will talk about him!" is of doubtful authenticity. Barely a fortnight later Beethoven was summoned home: his mother was seriously ill. By the 25th of April he had reached Munich, where he had spent the night of the 1st of April on his outward journey. On arrival home, he found his mother still alive, but without hope of recovery. In June she died of consumption, and now, after a childhood and adolescence that had been far from easy, he found himself faced with life in real earnest. Not only had the death of his beloved mother deprived him of the only spiritual support that any member of his family had ever given him, but he had to look on helplessly while his father, never a man of any strength of character, sank lower and lower. Johann now gave himself up to drink, and in less than two years matters became so bad that he could no longer do his work. One evening Ludwig had to rescue his drunken father from the police. Influential friends saved him from expulsion from Bonn; but he was declared no longer capable of managing his affairs, though through his son's efforts he was spared too great a humiliation. Ludwig was paid the greater part of his father's emoluments, and now had to look after his two younger brothers. (Four children had died in infancy.) Of the brothers, the elder, Johann, was intended for an apothecary, the younger, Karl Kaspar, for a musician. Thus a heavy burden was laid on Ludwig's youthful shoulders, and to add to this he was suffering at the time from certain ailments, of the details of which we have little knowledge. In one letter he speaks of "constriction of the chest" (asthma?) and "melancholia", and later he once said that at fifteen—for some time he believed himself to be two years younger than he actually was—he had "known how to die." His official duties were strenuous, and his compositions were already taking up a considerable part of his time; yet with admirable self-abnegation he continued to carry out his obligations towards his family. In doing so he showed as much moral strength as practical common sense. In those days he was capable of coping with life; and if later he was less successful in this it was due solely to his deafness. Yet even in those hard times he was not entirely alone, for he found some one who could almost take the place of the mother he had lost. Frau von Breuning, whose children he had taught for some years, received him in her house and treated him like a son. This became his second home; and here he had his first experience of good manners and high culture. In this motherly soul who now befriended him he found his real teacher, a woman, always kind and considerate, who showed a complete understanding of the mind and nature of a genius. A lifelong friendship bound him to her children and to young Franz Wegeler, who later married her daughter, Eleanore. He also had two other faithful friends: Franz Ries, the

BEETHOVEN IN YOUTH
(Engraving by Neidl after Stainhauser. In the
Music Department of the State Library, Berlin.)

violinist and conductor (the father of Ferdinand Ries, who for some time was Beethoven's pupil in Vienna), and Count Waldstein, a true gentleman and a skilled amateur musician, who doubtless often spoke to the Elector about him.

Thus, despite all his hardships, these last years in Bonn were fruitful in the human contacts they brought to Beethoven. Nor were they less fruitful on the artistic side. The fame of his genius spread rapidly: visitors from other parts were already carrying reports of his wonderful playing, particularly of his improvisation. From these reports we learn, too, that there was considerable musical activity in Bonn at that time, and that the music-making was on a high level, particularly in orchestral playing. But in every way the cultural life of the town prospered under Maximilian Franz, the youngest brother of the Emperor Joseph II, who had been made Elector in 1784. Mozart had once poked malicious fun at his limited intelligence, but he had developed mentally to an unexpected degree. Following the example of his brother, the Emperor, he represented, in his capacity as a Prince of the Church, the 'enlightened Catholicism' of the day. He was tolerant towards those of other faiths and not violently opposed even to free-thinkers. The teachers at the Academy, which he raised to the dignity of a University, were 'modern' men, among them Eulogius Schneider, the radical revolutionary, who a few years later was executed at Strassburg, on Robespierre's instructions, as too extreme a terrorist. The young Beethoven, who was a student at the University, attended his lectures; and it was probably from those in his circle that he became acquainted with the 'ideas' of the French Revolution, which moved him passionately, as they moved his great contemporaries Hölderlin, Hegel, and Schelling.

The Elector also encouraged the theatre more than his predecessors had done. Upon the failure and dispersal of another touring troupe, he determined to found a 'National Theatre', which should foster drama, opera, and operetta alike. Although we read in Neefe's prologue, written for the opening ceremony, that the object of this theatre was "to further as much as possible the German mode of life and German art", it would be a mistake to conclude that the repertory was exclusively German. Even in those days they could not do without French and Italian operas and operettas. Nevertheless the people of Bonn heard between 1789 and 1792, the last four years Beethoven spent in the town, the following German works: Gluck's *Die Pilgrime von Mekka* (*La rencontre imprévue*); Mozart's *Entführung aus dem Serail*, *Figaro*, and *Don Giovanni;* and 'Singspiele' by Dittersdorf, Benda, and Schuster. Beethoven played in the orchestra, and thus had an opportunity of becoming closely acquainted with contemporary operas. Yet he was not inspired by this to compose operas himself; indeed his efforts, apart from songs, were directed almost entirely to the composition of absolute music. Apart from this, he wrote only the *Ritterballett* and two cantatas, the more important of the two probably being the composition he showed to Haydn, when in July 1792 the latter spent a few days at Bonn on his way home from London. His young fellow composer must have made a good impression on him, for he encouraged him to proceed with his studies and agreed to take him as his pupil in Vienna. The Elector not only gave Beethoven the necessary leave but agreed to continue payment of his salary, so that there was no obstacle in his way. Beethoven set out from Bonn early in November 1792, and was never to see his native town again. His friend Count Waldstein wrote in his album, as a farewell message, some words that not only indicate the opinion of a sensitive and musically educated man of those days upon Haydn and Mozart, but also what high expectations the youthful Beethoven's friends had of him: "Mozart's Muse has not ceased to mourn and weep for the death of her protégé. In Haydn, the inexhaustible, she found shelter but no occupation; and through him she seeks some one whom she may again inspire. Work without ceasing, and from Haydn's hands you will receive Mozart's spirit."

It was for the purpose of learning that Beethoven, like any other young and aspiring musician, came to Vienna; and there he studied under the greatest master of the day. His course of instruction began with the elements of counterpoint; and his exercises, some of them corrected by Haydn, show that Beethoven knew no more of it than other beginners. Haydn seems to have proceeded in a very leisurely manner, at which his impetuous pupil was not best pleased. Moreover, he was preoccupied with his own work, and his corrections were not too painstaking. Beethoven therefore went to another master, with whom he took lessons in secret at the same time as with Haydn. This other master was Schenk, the composer of *The Village Barber*, who has written of these lessons in his autobiography. Many years later, he and Beethoven often recalled how they had tricked the famous man. There is no doubt that Beethoven did not get what he wanted from Haydn, and in his disgust he said hard things about the man he otherwise so much admired. He also refused Haydn's request that he should let it be publicly known that he was his pupil. On the other hand Haydn laughed at his pupil's pride, and called him, both then and later, the "Grand Mogul." Yet he must have realized the stuff Beethoven was made of; and in spite of the differences between the two of them, they were evidently on fairly intimate terms, for Haydn intended to take his pupil to England with him in 1794. Shortly before this he had heard Beethoven's three Trios, op. 1, played from manuscript. That he dissuaded Beethoven from publishing the third, in C minor, which has long been regarded as the most important of them, was later ascribed by Beethoven to Haydn's recognition that it was better than his own work. There he was certainly wrong, for we know to-day from the sketchbooks that Beethoven polished up the Trio again after that performance, a fact that indicates that at the time he admitted the justice of Haydn's criticism. With Haydn's early departure the tuition died a natural death. His successor was Albrechtsberger, an elderly and respected writer on musical theory; and under him Beethoven spent about a year upon a thorough study of counterpoint. He also occasionally went to Salieri, an Italian, particularly for instruction in vocal writing.

But it must not be supposed that in Vienna Beethoven led the retired life of a student. Thanks to introductions he brought with him from Bonn, his fame quickly spread through the musical society of the city, and he himself did all he could to conquer that society. Immediately after his arrival he took dancing lessons, not so much for the purpose of learning dancing, for though fond of it he was always a clumsy performer, as of acquainting himself with the social habits of the city. It can hardly be supposed that his idea was to adapt himself to them; at all events he did not succeed in doing so. To start with, his appearance did not match his new *milieu*: his thick-set body was surmounted by a rough-hewn head with features that even then were indicative of a sombre and reserved nature. His hair was black, his complexion swarthy, his face pitted with pockmarks, and his small but exceedingly expressive eyes were dark. Upon this aristocratic and ceremonious world the middle-class Beethoven, with his free-and-easy manners and almost revolutionary ideas, must have had much the same effect that Rembrandt, the miller's son, had on the bourgeois patriciate of Amsterdam. But unlike Rembrandt, he had not the qualities of the parvenu, and was not impressed. On the contrary: "It is easy to get on with the nobility, if you have something to impress them with," he once said; and to judge by his own experience he was certainly right. It is true that once he was set to dine among the servants, but he at once got up and walked out. Later, however, he was given ample satisfaction, for Prince Louis Ferdinand of Prussia, who had been present on that occasion, invited both Beethoven and his hostess to dinner a few days later, placing the latter on his right hand and Beethoven on his left. On the whole the Viennese nobility knew how to treat a genius; they allowed themselves to be "impressed" and did not take offence even when their own canons of good form were violated. There are innumerable stories of Beethoven's uncouth or even offensive behaviour in society, though this was often due to thoughtlessness or lack of attention to music on the part of others. But it was for the love of music that the nobility bore with him and his rough manners, for they cultivated the art with an almost fanatical devotion. At the same time they realized that Beethoven was a force to be reckoned with, not

only as a musician but as a man; they acknowledged his outstanding personality, intellectually so far above that of other
musicians; and they gave him their friendship despite the
difference in their social standing. Thus these nobles, Lobkowitz, Lichnowsky, Esterhazy, Kinsky, and others, honour-
ably deserved the immortality that Beethoven's dedications
conferred upon them.

The impression made by this man of genius was evidently
enormous even in those days. "He is not a man, he is a devil!"
said the Abbé Gelinek, the most celebrated exponent of improvisation, after he had been defeated by Beethoven in a com-
petition. Beethoven's playing of Bach's *Well-tempered Clavier*
created a profound impression; but his improvisations were
something altogether new to his audiences. He plumbed hitherto unplumbed depths, and raised what in the case of other performers was a mere social entertainment to the level of the
highest art. But in other ways also his playing was something
entirely new, not so much for its virtuosity, in which indeed he
was surpassed by many others, as for the undreamt-of possibilities of expression that he revealed. His technique was evidently
more than adequate, though perhaps it showed too little discipline, for many of his listeners called his playing "rough and
hard." That this was not due to lack of technique, but was
intentional, is proved by a well authenticated story: he once
competed with Sterkel, a pianist of the 'elegant' type, and suddenly, without hesitation, began to play in Sterkel's style. His
legato was famous, and such as had never been heard before,
even from Mozart. (He admired the delicacy of Mozart's playing, but found it wanting in true legato.) He was probably the
first to make piano technique subservient to expression—the
expression of new spiritual worlds.

As a composer also his star was soon in the ascendant. It was
not indeed till 1795, after two unimportant sets of Variations,
that his op. 1, the three Trios, was published, but the eagerness
with which it was awaited is shown by the subscription list.
Beethoven had concluded an agreement with the publishing
house of Artaria on very favourable terms, and in spite of the

high price of a ducat a copy, nearly two hundred and fifty were sold. The great majority of subscribers were, of course, members of the nobility; but the middle classes were not behindhand, for musical culture at that time was by no means the preserve of the aristocracy alone. It is significant that hardly one fourth of the subscribers bore German names; the better class of Viennese—the most fertile soil for the propagation of great German music—contained a strong international element, though this did not affect the character of the music that was loved and practised there. Indeed this cosmopolitan section of Viennese society was more faithful to Beethoven than the native bourgeoisie, which some years later deserted him in favour of Rossini. At the time, however, there was no public audience of any size for a composer of absolute music, as there had long been for the composer of opera. London was the only city in which things were different, and was the first in which even Haydn was given adequate public recognition. For this reason Beethoven rarely played in public during his early years in Vienna. He only did so eight times between 1795 and 1799 and then always as a 'supporter' of some other performer—on one occasion Haydn—or at a charity concert. He generally played only one piece, not always of his own composition. But those who attended the private concerts given by the nobility could often hear him and the works he was now pouring out in quick succession. The Viennese nobility maintained a number of orchestras, several of which must have been of high quality; and chamber music was played, by both the nobles themselves and the cultured bourgeoisie, with a considerable degree of skill. Beethoven's rapidly growing fame was founded entirely on this private music-making and not on public concerts. His reputation soon spread beyond Vienna. In 1796 we find him in Prague, probably in the suite of Prince Lichnowsky, and shortly afterwards in Berlin, where he often played before King Frederick William II, a highly cultured musical amateur. It was for Duport, a cellist attached to the King's private orchestra, that he composed the two Cello Sonatas, op. 5. He later told Czerny that his improvisations had impressed the King so much that he had been invited to remain at the court. He refused, he said, because he could not live among "spoilt children", who wept with emotion instead of applauding. Later he once said to Bettina Brentano, irritated by Goethe's mute emotion, "Music must strike fire from a man's mind!" It is said that sometimes after playing he would burst into roars of laughter to break the spell he had cast upon his audience.

These successes were only the first stage in the young genius's unobstructed rise to the highest summit of fame. The demands society made on him might have been dangerous for any other. He was protected by the inexhaustible wealth of his creative power and the unshakable will that enabled him to devote his whole strength to his work. Whenever he felt the danger of distraction he fled to the country, there to live for his work alone. It early became his rule to spend the summer in the country, a rule from which he hardly ever departed. Nowhere was his creative imagination so fertile as when he was in the midst of nature. On long walks his compositions grew—though at the cost of violent inner struggles, to which his sketch-books bear witness—towards their final shape, to be elaborated and polished at home. The passionate love of nature was not with him, as with many of his contemporaries, a matter of mere sentiment, but virile and fruitful. "Nature was to him food and drink. He seemed actually to live on it," said an Englishman who visited him in the country. He felt himself one with all that was elemental. This fact may help us to understand an odd eccentricity, which annoyed so many of his landlords and those he lived with: during his morning ablutions he would begin to compose and, singing and humming, pour bucket after bucket of water over himself until the place was flooded. Contact with the eternal, primitive element of water brought the ideas swarming into his mind.

His love of country life was not in the least due to a longing for solitude or the avoidance of his fellow men. The lonely Beethoven seeking solitude is a popular myth. His duties in aristocratic society may often have been a burden to him; but intercourse with fellow musicians and enthusiasts of his own class he always welcomed. Here he relaxed, was "unbuttoned", as he called it, and full of jokes. He also made new and lasting friendships, among others with Amenda, a man of high intelligence, to whom he wrote a number of admirable letters, which have fortunately been preserved. It must be admitted however that the course of these friendships was not undisturbed by serious misunderstandings. Even before he became deaf, he was at times suspicious and would heap violent abuse upon his friends. But he was equally ready to acknowledge himself in the wrong, and would show a touching eagerness to make up the quarrel.

"Things go well with me; I may even say, better and better," he wrote, in May 1797, to his friend Wegeler in Bonn. So we must think of him during those years as an inspired artist, blessed by good fortune, who succeeded in all he undertook, but whose success was always a fresh spur towards perfection. Three years later he wrote the following beautiful words to the same friend: "This much will I say: that when you see me again, I shall be greater; not only will you find me greater as an artist, but better and more perfect as a man, and if there is greater prosperity in our fatherland, my art shall be shown only for the benefit of the poor." It is dangerous, no doubt, to take impulsive expressions of this sort too literally; yet we may guess that the wealth and exclusiveness of the society for which he created made him uneasy, though at the same time he was not sorry to see his income steadily increasing. He was glad of the security of his material existence, and it is characteristic of him that he did not forget the obligations he had undertaken in Bonn. As soon as his finances improved he sent for his two brothers, and continued to assist them. This he did though he had little in common with them, and certainly had small esteem for them.

The second letter to Wegeler referred to above, and another written at the same time to Amenda, gave them the first intimation of the calamity that was to darken his life. For several years already Beethoven had realized that his hearing was affected. He had consulted physicians, but had hidden his fears from his friends and acquaintances. No definite cause can be assigned to the trouble, a disease of the inner passages of the ear.

Medical men consider it possible that it had some connexion with other diseases from which he had suffered; it is at any rate advisable to take into account only the illnesses that Beethoven is known, or at least believed upon some definite grounds, to have had. A French doctor originated the theory, to which Romain Rolland has given publicity, that Beethoven's deafness was due to congestion of blood in the head, caused by his almost superhuman concentration. Whether there is anything in this the experts must decide. Distinct traces remained on his face of small-pox, which he had had as a boy. Early in life he suffered from painful abdominal complaints, which were probably the result of typhoid and continued almost throughout his life. Like Goethe he combined a very strong constitution with a pre-disposition to disease, but unlike Goethe he did not come of a long-lived family. As can be well understood, none of his ill-nesses caused him so much mental suffering as his deafness. Yet this did not hinder his productive work; indeed his compositions show no trace of it. But as a musician, who "knew no greater pleasure than to let his art be heard", he must inevitably have suffered acutely under his disability. "But for my hearing I should long ago have travelled over half the world, and I must do so," he wrote to Wegeler, and he proposed to Amenda that the latter should accompany him. Evidently, under the first shock of his discovery, he regarded his ear trouble as worse than it was, at any rate for some time. For years he was still able to play and conduct in public. But it was the threat of loneliness that most haunted him. This is shown by his letters, and par-ticularly by that pathetic document written in the summer of 1802, known as the *Heiligenstädter Testament*. Into this, which he addressed to his brothers but never despatched, the sick man poured all the grief and despair that had gathered in his soul. Having spoken in it of the likelihood of an early death, and hav-ing taken leave of the world and of his fellow men, he disposed of his possessions; and from this it has been assumed that behind it lay the intention to commit suicide. That is untrue. It is the despairing cry of a man who sees no future but a life of isolation, who fears he may not have the strength to bear such a fate; the

c

cry of a heart, overflowing with love for mankind and a longing for fellowship, but tormented by the fear of being misunderstood. The care with which he provided for his brothers, with whom he had so little in common, is truly touching. At the age of seventeen, he had "known how to die"; and so, now, he knew it again—he who was capable of living life to the full, and who was only eager to hold it fast. His much-quoted phrase "we must grip fate by the throat" shows how little it was his intention to bow before his misfortunes. If we read the *Testament* in its proper relation to all we know of him at that period, we see it as the instinctive reaction of a fundamentally healthy nature against an impending evil, which he meets by giving way for a moment to his horror of it. In this he resembles Goethe, except that Goethe purged his soul of his fears of threatened dangers by pouring them into his writings, whereas Beethoven's works contain no trace of his terrors. It is almost certain that, in the very months during which the *Testament* was written, he was working intensively at the completion of the Second Symphony, in which no trace of any cloud is to be seen. And a glance at the list of his compositions shows that in these years particularly he wrote a number of serene and cheerful works. In other ways, too, he was by no means low-spirited. Hardly had he rid himself of the worst of his depression by writing the *Testament*, than he began again to poke fun at his friends both in letters and in musical jokes. It would be entirely wrong not to take him seriously in each of these manifestations; it was the great-hearted breadth of his nature that made him capable of these contrasts and contradictions. He felt both with the same intensity; and however abruptly and harshly contrasts succeeded one another in his daily life, we should guard against the temptation to seek the same lack of harmony in his work. In this he exercised the strictest discipline and self-control, qualities that were almost entirely lacking in his mode of life, in which he submitted to no discipline and so was compensated for the almost unbearable severity of self-control that he imposed on himself for the sake of his work. But however much we may deplore this lack of discipline and moderation, and whatever suffering it may have caused those around him, yet the grandeur and nobility of his nature is throughout apparent. It is not every great man who exhibits in his moments of relaxation and repose so little that is undesirable; and above all it is not every creative genius that takes life, apart from his work, as seriously as Beethoven did. His nature was to a rare extent guided by moral principles. Beneath statements like that already quoted from his letter to Wegeler—there are many such in his letters—was a serious ethical will. When he underlined the passage in Sturm's *Betrachtungen über die Werke Gottes* ('Reflections on the Works of God'—a book that interpreted morals on rationalist lines, which he constantly read): "Only this one thing I ask of Thee, O God: Cease not to work at my improvement!" he was in deadly earnest. Another underlined passage (in the 'Reflections on the Sun and its Benefits to Mankind') is significant: "In the state of life to which I have been called I will distribute among my fellow men those benefits that I have received from God. Without self-seeking I will give help to all that need it: to this man instruction, to that comfort, to that strength and nourishment." That is how he felt towards humanity, and his remark on another occasion: "I judge people by what they do for me; I regard them as mere instruments on which to play what pleases me", is only apparently inconsistent with it. There were, no doubt, individuals who were only "instruments" to him: publishers who, he thought, only wished to do business with him, "friends", like his amanuensis, Schindler, who were inferior to him in one way or another and whom admittedly he often made use of without scruple.

The years during which the first signs of deafness made their appearance were particularly fruitful, and he was rapidly becoming famous. On the 2nd of April, 1800, he at last gave a concert on his own account, in the *Burgtheater*, with the following tremendous programme: A "Great Symphony" by Mozart, two vocal numbers from Haydn's *Creation*, a Piano Concerto of his own, which he played himself, the Septet, an Improvisation for Piano, and a work that was doubtless eagerly awaited, a "Grand New Symphony for full Orchestra", the first symphony of Beethoven's ever to be heard. The Viennese press ignored the concert altogether; and the Leipzig *Allgemeine Musikalische Zeitung* printed a colourless account of the works performed. This is of no significance as regards the esteem in which Beethoven was held, but only proves how slight public interest was in purely instrumental music. With a few exceptions there was as yet no informed and responsible musical criticism in Germany, and therefore an article that appeared as late as 1805 in the same Leipzig journal is of no importance whatever. In it Beethoven's First Symphony was said to be "Haydn exaggerated from *bizarrerie* to the point of caricature." Two years later, however, after the first performance of the same work in Paris, a French critic underlined its dissimilarity to those of Haydn, and wrote that the style of the symphony was "clear, brilliant, and *rapide*." From this it is evident that his contemporaries understood his music well enough. Beethoven's fame could not be obstructed by unintelligent criticism. Its rapid growth is shown by the publisher's demand for his new compositions, which now appeared in almost unbroken succession. And these were not only published but also sold—a proof of how highly both the technical skill and the understanding of musical circles were developed in those days, for we need only remember the demands that all these works made on the technique and intelligence of the performers.

We must not at this period expect much information as to the impression made by Beethoven's music. It was not until various friends from Bonn, such as Stefan Breuning, Anton Reicha, and the younger Ries, came to Vienna, at about which time Czerny and the last named became Beethoven's favourite pupils, that we begin to get more detailed information. From their reports it is clear that even then Beethoven was the almost undisputed central figure of the musical scene, so far at least as it was laid in private houses and the concert hall, and not in the theatre. Only once at this time did Beethoven come into contact with the theatre, again with a ballet, as in Bonn in 1790. In 1801 his *Prometheus* was performed twelve times. Every serious music lover must have known even then that his chamber music and sym-

phony were infinitely more important; but great things were
expected from him in the theatre as well. Schikaneder, who was
still running the *Theater an der Wieden*, engaged him as opera-
composer and provided him with rooms in his theatre. In 1803
a concert was given there, confined this time to Beethoven's
music: the First and Second Symphonies, the C minor Piano
Concerto, and an oratorio, *The Mount of Olives*. This was the
first performance of the Second Symphony and the Concerto.
The new symphony seems to have made a deeper impression
than the oratorio, and rightly so. Beethoven himself fully realized the weaknesses of the latter work: he had not yet completely
mastered the technique of vocal composition. The same applied
to opera, as was proved shortly afterwards when, in November
1805, the first performance of *Fidelio* took place, and was a failure. This was not entirely due to the inauspicious date of the
performance, which took place immediately after the occupation of Vienna by the French, so that the audience consisted
almost entirely of French officers. Even his friends could not
regard the work in its original form as anything but a failure. A
few weeks later an historic scene took place in the house of Prince
Lichnowsky: Beethoven's friends, the Prince and Princess—
the latter at the piano, playing the opera from the score—urged
him to agree to the alterations that every one was convinced
were essential. Beethoven, who had grown very fond of the work,
fought for each bar and it was only after seven hours' hard work
that he was persuaded to sacrifice three numbers from the first
act and a few other minor details. It is difficult to understand
why, when after further revision it was produced again the
following year, it did not have an immediate and lasting success.
Beethoven petulantly withdrew it after a few performances. Its
day was yet to come; that it is immortal has long since been
proved.

Meanwhile an event of a different kind and of crucial importance had happened. Six months before the ill-fated pro-
duction of *Fidelio*, a work that once for all proved Beethoven to
be the master of a new age had been given its first public performance in the same theatre: the *Eroica* Symphony. The

name had not yet been given to it, and the work was announced simply as "a Grand New Symphony." The public probably knew nothing of the title Beethoven originally intended for it, viz. *Bonaparte*. It already bore the dedication to Prince Lobkowitz, at whose private concerts it had several times been performed during the previous year. The audiences could therefore listen to it with open minds, which was not the case later on, when they were tempted by the name and history of the Symphony to look for something new beneath it. Nevertheless, even at Prince Lobkowitz's concerts its hearers felt that it was "unique." Prince Louis Ferdinand was present at one of these, and so deeply was he impressed by it that he had the Symphony repeated. At one of these performances the orchestra, which was conducted by Beethoven, broke down at the great syncopated passage in the first movement; such things had never before been demanded of an orchestra. The critics too, who like many professional musicians had been foolishly mistaken in their first opinions of the work, gradually realized the truth. In 1807 the Leipzig *Allgemeine Musikalische Zeitung* discussed the score, which had now been published, and wrote of the astonishing mastery with which, in spite of its length, the first movement was "held together and welded into a homogeneous whole." On its first performance in Paris in 1811, the Symphony was received with "frenzied applause", to quote Proud'homme's own enthusiastic report.

Beethoven composed many works of prime importance at the same time as, and shortly after, the *Eroica*. Nevertheless he could not rid himself of his longing for the theatre. When in 1807 the Imperial Theatre was placed under the direction of a committee of nobles, some of whom, particularly Lobkowitz and Esterhazy, were Beethoven's closest friends and patrons, he applied for the post of opera-composer. (The contract with the *Theater an der Wieden* had come to an end through Schikaneder's retirement.) He undertook to write an opera, an operetta, or some other smaller pieces, every year, although he fully realized, to quote his own words, "what expenditure of time and energy is required to write an opera, since it prevents the com-

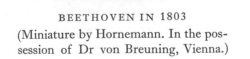

BEETHOVEN IN 1803
(Miniature by Hornemann. In the pos-
session of Dr von Breuning, Vienna.)

poser from undertaking any other mental work whatever."
What can have caused him to make this application is a mystery,
unless it was financial worries. Yet at this time these cannot have
been very oppressive. It is not surprising that his application
remained unanswered. ("I shall never get on with this 'princely'
theatrical rabble," he wrote to Count Brunswick in Hungary.)
Even his friends evidently did not take it seriously: they knew
well enough that the operas would never be forthcoming, and
also that, in view of Beethoven's growing deafness and his difficult temperament, there could be no hope of harmonious co-
operation. It is impossible that he should have intended to compose only operas; he was, in fact, engaged on the Fourth and
Fifth Symphonies and other great works. Yet he still brooded
over his operatic plans. He was negotiating for a libretto with
H. J. von Collin, the poet, for whose *Coriolanus* he had written
a magnificent overture. He thought seriously of *Macbeth*, and
went so far as to draft preliminary sketches for it. But Collin,
ignoring Beethoven's evident eagerness to undertake the work,
gave up the idea altogether, and chose another composer,
Reichardt, with whom to collaborate on other operas. At this
Beethoven was deeply hurt; but Collin was probably influenced
by the theatre authorities' doubts regarding Beethoven's punc-
tuality and his suitability for operatic composition. So once
again he gave up his operatic plans. Yet that queer composition,
the *Choral Fantasy*, which he composed about this time, and
which is one of the few works from his hand that must be regarded as failures, proves that the composition of purely instrumental music could not fully satisfy his need for self-expression.

In 1808 Beethoven was faced with an important decision.
Jérome, by the grace of Napoleon King of Westphalia, offered
him generous terms if he would accept the post of principal
conductor at his court. This proves either that nothing was
known outside Vienna of his deafness, or that Jérome's sole
object was to add lustre to his court by the acquisition of a
famous name. But Beethoven hesitated; and to ensure his remaining in Vienna, three of his noble friends and patrons, the
Archduke Rudolf, who for some time had been his pupil, Prince

Lobkowitz, and Prince Kinsky, agreed to allow him four thousand gulden a year and so to free him from all financial worry. "Now you can help me look for a wife", he wrote to his friend, Ignaz von Gleichenstein, in Freiburg, "if you can find in F. a beauty who will reward my harmonies with a sigh . . . then prepare the way for me. But she must be beautiful. I cannot love anything that is not—otherwise I should have to love myself . . ." Whether his friend had any suggestions to make is not recorded. We do know however that not long afterwards Beethoven made his own choice: Thérèse, the niece of his physician Dr Malfatti, a black-haired Italian girl of seventeen. Early in 1810 he proposed to her, but was rejected, for what reasons we do not know.

This was neither the first nor the last time that he wished to marry and was unsuccessful in his suit. Once—we do not know who the lady was—it was years before he brought himself to give her up. Who would make bold to say whether fate did well or ill in denying him his wish? There is no doubt that a happy marriage would have spared him much of the misery that as a bachelor, with his increasing deafness, he had to suffer. Perhaps, too, if he had had some one to care for his health he would have lived longer. It can be proved that during the years when his devoted friend, Frau Nanette Streicher, looked after his domestic affairs, and engaged faithful servants for him, he suffered less from those disorders from which the fatal disease developed. But apart from all this, it must be said that Beethoven's creative work was obviously quite independent of his health and physical comfort. During several bouts of severe suffering he produced an unusual number of important works, whereas the years 1813–1816, when his health was better, were relatively unproductive. His compositions were rooted in depths that were beyond the reach of health or sickness, domestic comfort or discomfort.

Yet love seems to have been essential to him. "Beethoven was never out of love; and as a rule he was deeply affected by his passion", said his friend Wegeler; and he added: "In Vienna, at least as long as I was living there, he always had a love affair on hand. Sometimes indeed he made conquests that to many an

Adonis would have been difficult if not impossible. I should add that, as far as I know, all the women he loved were of good social standing." This testimony, which by no means stands alone, must prevail against the opinions of other writers, who would have us believe that Beethoven led an entirely celibate life, or who maintain that "the erotic played no part, or a very small part, in his life," with the result that the power of Eros "went to increase his intellectual vigour." (W. Krug.) The modern theory of 'subliminal eroticism' as the root of artistic creation applies as little to Beethoven as to any one else. In his affairs of the heart he was entirely normal, and as ardent and impulsive as in all other directions. He was very open to emotional influences, and himself admitted that he was inconstant in love. He himself was surprised when one of his mistresses held his affections for seven months. But he was far from being licentious. He even thought ill of Mozart for composing operas whose libretti contained such improprieties as did *Don Giovanni*, *Figaro*, and *Cosi fan tutte*. We know the names of only a few of the women with whom he was connected in one way or another. Some of these, however, whose names are historical, call for mention here. He had a short but ardent love affair with a pupil, the Contessa Giulietta Guicciardi, with which, however, his dedication to her of the *Moonlight* Sonata has no connexion. (Years later he spoke of her in anger.) At about the same time he became closely attached to her cousins, the Countesses Brunswick, who had recently arrived in Vienna from their country home in Hungary, and whose brother Franz was one of his greatest friends. One of the sisters, Thérèse, who never married and is believed to have burnt all Beethoven's letters to her, was a woman of unusual intelligence. The other, Josephine, a young widow whose marriage had turned out unhappily, found comfort and support in her sorrows in her friendship with Beethoven and in his music. Miniatures of her and Giulietta were found among his belongings after his death. As in this case, the bond between Beethoven and his women friends was generally music. He appeared at concerts with Christine Gerardi, the singer, who came from Tuscany and whom he greatly admired. The young Countess

Erdödy, a great invalid, in whose house Beethoven lived for some time, was an excellent pianist. To her he wrote a number of beautiful and tender letters. Maria Bigot, an Alsatian, whom Haydn had also known and admired in his old age, seems to have been a still more brilliant pianist. One day she played the *Appassionata*, which he had just completed, from his heavily corrected manuscript. Baroness Ertmann, a colonel's wife, was also a fine pianist; and he wrote to Frau Marie Pachler-Koschak: "I have never known any one who plays my compositions as well as you—not excepting the great pianists, who are mechanical and affected. You are the true foster-mother of my mind's children." With Anna Milder, who created the part of Leonora in *Fidelio*, he was very intimate, and even more so with Amalie Sebald, who was gifted with an "enchanting voice." To judge by the tone of the letters he is known to have written to her, it is unlikely that it was to her that he addressed the famous and very beautiful letter to the "immortal beloved." But on this subject we can only grope in the dark, for we do not even know whether the letter, which was found after his death in a secret drawer of his desk, was ever sent, or whether it had been returned to him. The impression made by Beethoven on a young girl is shown by the diary of Fanny del Rio, whose father owned the school to which Beethoven sent his nephew. This tells us much of value concerning the human attributes that were so strong a part of Beethoven's nature, and is at the same time a moving record of a young girl's love growing gradually out of admiration for an older man's genius.

One girl, with whom his relations were perhaps less romantic than with others, is a valuable source of information regarding Beethoven's life. This was Bettina Brentano, who was less than twenty when he first met her, in 1810. She was gifted with unusual intelligence and temperament, and a power of sympathetic understanding that amounted almost to genius; and evidently Beethoven responded more freely to her ingenuous and open-hearted confidence than to other women. Unfortunately this quality in her was combined with a too lively imagination, for she found it difficult to distinguish fact from fiction. It is necessary therefore to beware of believing everything she tells us about him. We know that of the three famous letters of Beethoven to Bettina, only the second, that of the 10th of February, 1811, is genuine; and unfortunately we must regard as fictitious the greater part of Beethoven's utterances as recorded in Bettina's letters to Goethe, and also Goethe's alleged replies to her. Some of Beethoven's sayings, however, are genuine, as for instance the splendid words already quoted: "Music must strike fire from a man's mind." The remark: "My nature is electric" may also be accepted, for we know that Beethoven felt himself in close sympathy with the elemental. But most of Bettina's records only have value as the poetic reflection of Beethoven's personality in a mind that was youthful and romantic, enthusiastic, and had indeed a touch of genius. As regards actual facts, her statements are of little value. Of these the best known is the story of Beethoven's meeting with Goethe in Teplitz, and of how the two met the Emperor and Empress on the Promenade, when Goethe stepped aside with a courteous bow while Beethoven strode ahead through the company with folded arms, ignoring their greetings. No doubt there is a germ of truth in the story, for we know from his letter to the publishers, Breitkopf and Härtel, that he was irritated at Goethe's courtly manners: "The air of the court suits Goethe—more so than is seemly for a poet." But for all his uncouthness it is certain that he would not have acted so churlishly. Happily there are other and more trustworthy witnesses of the historic meeting of the two great men. Goethe wrote on the 19th of July, 1812, after they had first met, "Never have I met an artist of such spiritual concentration and intensity, such vitality and greatheartedness. I can well understand how hard he must find it to adapt himself to the world and its ways." Thereafter they were together almost daily. On the 21st of July Goethe notes in his diary: "He played delightfully." After a temporary separation, caused by Goethe's departure, they met again in Karlsbad in September. Goethe was doubtless often irritated by Beethoven's uncouth manners, but there was no question of a serious quarrel. This is also proved by Goethe's well-known letter of the

2nd of September to Zelter: "In Teplitz I made the acquaintance of Beethoven. His talent fills me with amazement, but his
temperament is unfortunately quite uncontrolled. I can well
understand his finding the world detestable, but he fails thereby
to make it pleasanter either for himself or for others. He is to be
excused much, however, and deeply pitied, for his hearing is
failing him, which perhaps is less disadvantageous for the
musical side of his being than for the social. He is naturally
laconic, and is becoming doubly so as a result of his deafness."
It would be highly interesting to know more of what Goethe
thought of him; but taking into account the evidence of others it
is fairly certain that, despite the indifference Goethe may have
shown now and then, he was well aware of Beethoven's greatness, rarely though it was that he heard his works performed.
It is hardly surprising that the C minor Symphony, which Men-
delssohn as a young man played to him when he was eighty,
seemed strange and even incomprehensible. But he appreciated
the greatness of the music, and for a whole day he remained
under its influence. Nor was Beethoven's admiration for
Goethe, of which he had given a token two years before by the
composition of the *Egmont* music, diminished by their meetings.
He read Goethe's works as much as ever; and the innumerable
marginal notes in his copy of the *Westöstlicher Divan*, which has
been preserved, show the close attention with which he read it.
Goethe was one of the four cornerstones of Beethoven's intellectual culture; the others were Shakespeare, Homer, and Plato.
Any one who calls Beethoven "uneducated" has a strange idea
of education. Similarly it is incorrect to say that he was "incapable of expressing himself, either orally or in writing" merely because he was not fond of writing, and, lacking any proper
academic training, was arbitrary in his handling of the German
language.

A few days before his meeting with Goethe he wrote from
Teplitz the following letter to a little girl of ten, who had sent
him a pocket-book embroidered by herself. This speaks as much
for his mastery of language as for his breadth of sympathy:

"My dear, good Emilie, my dear friend,

"The answer to your letter to me is late; a mass of business and constant illness must excuse me. My presence here in search of health proves the truth of my excuse. Do not rob Handel, Mozart, Haydn, of the laurels that are theirs and not yet mine.

"Your pocket-book will be kept together with tokens of respect from many other persons, which I am far from deserving.

"Keep on; do not merely practise art, but penetrate its innermost depths; it is worth it, for only art and science can raise mankind to the divine. If ever you should want anything, my dear Emilie, write to me with confidence. The true artist has no pride; he sees, alas, that art has no limits. He feels dimly how far he is from his goal, and while perhaps he is admired by others, he realizes with sorrow that he has not yet reached the place to which the better spirit lights the way before him like a distant sun. Perhaps I would rather come to you and yours than to many a wealthy person who reveals his poverty of soul. If ever I come to H. I will visit you and your family; I know of no good qualities but those that entitle one to be counted among the better men and women; where I find these, there is my home.

"If you would like to write to me, dear Emilie, address your letter to me here, where I shall spend another four weeks, or to Vienna, it does not matter. I am your friend and the friend of your family.

Ludwig van Beethoven"

When Beethoven thus revealed to a child his true humility, which generally and for good reasons he concealed, his life's work had come to full fruition. Behind him lay almost twenty years of tremendous creative activity, during the last ten of which his mastery was almost unmatched in the history of music. He had had many triumphs. In 1808 the Fifth and Sixth Symphonies were heard for the first time in public, together with the G major Concerto, which he himself played. In 1810, he wrote in a letter: "Sometimes I could almost go mad at my own unmerited fame; fortune seeks me out, and for this reason I almost fear some new misfortune." In 1812 he completed the Seventh and Eighth Symphonies. The last Trio, the last Violin Sonata, and the String Quartet op. 95 had been finished at the same time or shortly before. His fame was not only secure in Vienna, but had reached England and France. Since Haydn's death he had been accepted almost without question as the greatest master of instrumental music. It was only the members of a certain coterie of musicians, among whom for some time, strange to say, were budding geniuses like Weber and Schubert, who doubted his greatness or considered that he was on the road to disaster. In 1813 the tide seemed about to ebb; in the next few years he completed little, and it soon began to be said that Beethoven's creative power was exhausted. He was not, of course, entirely forgotten by the fickle Viennese, for his works were repeatedly performed; but his figure lost something of its earlier glory. The charm of novelty—for year after year he had pampered Vienna with new compositions—was lacking. Shortly before this time he had enjoyed one of the greatest of his triumphs, though its occasion was a composition that was unworthy of him—*The Battle of Vittoria*. Maelzel, a court mechanician and the inventor of the metronome, had persuaded Beethoven to compose a 'battle-piece' to celebrate Wellington's victory at Vittoria, which Maelzel was anxious to take with him to England. Strangely enough, Beethoven agreed to the proposal, and, when the journey fell through, scored the composition for a big orchestra with a profusion of wind and percussion. He himself conducted the work at a concert arranged by Maelzel for the benefit of wounded soldiers. The greatest musicians of Vienna gave their services—Salieri managed the 'cannonades', Hummel played the big drum—and the success of the composition exceeded anything in Beethoven's experience. The Seventh Symphony, which had its first performance at the concert, was also loudly applauded, though some members of the audience doubtless looked upon it as an appendix, so to speak, to the 'battle-piece', and so of secondary importance. Yet the second movement of the sym-

BEETHOVEN IN 1812
(Life Mask by Klein. In the Krieg
Collection. Photo by Hürlimann.)

phony had to be repeated. (The third item on the programme consisted of two Marches, by Dussek and Pleyel, performed on Maelzel's 'Mechanical Trumpeter' with full orchestral accompaniment!) Spohr, who played the violin in the orchestra, tells us that even at that time Beethoven's conducting was unsatisfactory. Early in 1814 the *Battle of Vittoria* was twice repeated, and on the second occasion the Eighth Symphony was given as well as the Seventh. Towards the end of the year, Beethoven gave two benefit-concerts with the same programme, the first of which was the greatest social triumph he ever enjoyed: among the audience were two Empresses, the King of Prussia, and many other royalties. The programme also contained a cantata composed in celebration of the Congress of Vienna, *Der glorreiche Augenblick*.

Meanwhile he had had another success, which undoubtedly meant more to him: he took *Fidelio*, the Cinderella of his works, in hand again, rearranged the music with the intelligent and sympathetic assistance of Treitschke, the librettist, and had the satisfaction of at last seeing it score a triumphant success. This time, also, he conducted it in person, though this was only rendered possible by the regular conductor, Umlauf, standing behind his back and straightening out the confusion caused by the deaf composer. About the same time he played once more in public, taking part in his Piano Trio, op. 97. If we may believe Spohr, who attended a rehearsal, it was "no longer a pleasure." Spohr adds: "It is bad enough for any one to be deaf, but how shall a musician endure it and not despair? I was no longer surprised at Beethoven's almost perpetual melancholia." But this last statement gives a false impression. "Perpetual melancholia" is entirely inconsistent with Beethoven's unflagging energy. Moreover, we have plenty of evidence, dating from the same period, that he had by no means lost his old humour. He was still often in his "unbuttoned" mood, as was said of him in an account of a banquet given by a physician, Dr Bertolini, in the house of Dr Malfatti. It was at this time also that his connection began with S. A. Steiner and Co., the music publishers. To one of the partners in the firm, Haslinger, Beethoven took a

liking. ("God preserve you, the devil take you!" is the conclusion of one of his letters to him.) His correspondence with
this firm is full of harmless and high-spirited jokes, which, so
far from being the outcome of that embittered humour that is
often characteristic of unhappy people, show a spirit of true
cheerfulness, and a delight in verbal jests both good and bad.
It is also full of puns, a form of humour that has always been
specially popular with German musicians down to the present
time, not excepting Wagner, Pfitzner, or Reger.

Is there any explanation for the unfruitfulness of these years?
It has been suggested that Beethoven's mind was distracted by
the social obligations connected with the Congress of Vienna.
But the tide had already begun to ebb before that; and the same
objection applies to another, more serious and fateful distraction that has often been cited as the cause. In November 1815
Beethoven's brother Karl died, and left him guardian of his son,
also named Karl, who was a minor. This obligation imposed a
heavy burden on Beethoven, and for years cost him much time
and energy. He took it very seriously. It must be remembered
that there was no real bond between him and his brothers. Had
it not been that he felt his responsibilities towards them to a
degree unusual in a creative artist, they would have meant
nothing to him, for his brothers were men of mediocre education and equally mediocre moral qualities. This feeling was not
sentimental but essentially ethical, as was proved by his behaviour in 1787 after his father's breakdown. Thus was the
child the father of the man. Apart altogether from the question
of blood-relationship, he regarded as sacred a duty once
undertaken—though he also saw in blood-relationship something inescapable, and moreover his childlessness was evidently a cause of suffering to him. In his copy of *Othello* he
put three question marks against Brabantio's observation, "I
had rather to adopt a child than get it", so absurd did the idea
seem to him. When his dying brother left him this charge, he
saw in it not a disaster, but compensation for what had been
denied him. He acted like a father towards his nephew, unworthy as the latter showed himself. He fought to keep him

from his mother, whom he considered both incapable and unworthy of bringing up a child; he wrote long applications to the
courts, carried on law-suits, and won them and lost them; he
took touching pains with his foster-son's upbringing, and sent
him to a school, with which he was continually in touch; and
later he himself attended for a time to the boy's education,
though for this neither his temperament nor the material circumstances of his life rendered him suitable. Indeed he showed
the boy more love than the latter, who though not ungifted was
entirely thoughtless and ungrateful, deserved, and certainly
more than he repaid. At the same time, it must not be forgotten
that his famous uncle's educational talents were by no means
outstanding. Many of Beethoven's friends were not satisfied
that he had acted rightly. He had shown once before a certain
moral obstinacy, not to say presumption, when in 1812 he not
only interfered, as if by right, in the matrimonial projects of his
brother, Johann, who had long been his own master, but even
stirred up the spiritual and temporal authorities of Linz, where
his brother lived, against the girl. In this, however, he only defeated his own ends. (Yet during the weeks when he was carrying
on this struggle in Linz he finished the Eighth Symphony!) He
showed the same lack of adaptability in the education of his
nephew. "Your intentions are excellent, but not always in
accord with the views of this wretched world," wrote an unknown writer in Beethoven's conversation-book in 1819. In the
task he had undertaken, his sense of duty was admirable; the
intensity of his paternal feeling most moving; and his violent
opposition to his sister-in-law, who was obviously a very du-
bious person, quite comprehensible. Yet in the end he failed, for
he succeeded neither in permanently alienating his nephew
from his mother, nor in instilling into him any idea of his own
high conception of life. It is pathetic to observe this great man's
unceasing struggle to gain his worthless nephew's heart, as, for
instance, when, at the end of a letter, we find these words of
entreaty: "Do come—make my poor heart bleed no longer!" or
when we read an account of how, after his nephew's attempted
suicide in 1826, Beethoven, now stone-deaf and ill, came in pro-
d

found agitation to the hospital to which the young man had been brought.

And yet any attempt to explain the apparent failure of his creative power during those years by reference to such worries and distractions is to misjudge the depths from which the procreant force of a great artist draws its nourishment. Though the creative stream had ceased to flow in full spate, openly, before the eyes and ears of men, it had by no means dried up; it was flowing on beneath the surface, deriving from the depths a new strength that was soon to reveal itself in the greatest of all his works. It was during those years that two compositions slowly formed and ripened, compositions in which the world rightly sees the twin peaks of Beethoven's creation: the Mass in D and the Ninth Symphony. Work on the latter began in 1817. He intended to compose another at the same time, as he had previously composed the Seventh and Eighth; and he hoped to have them ready by the beginning of 1818, so that he could take them with him to England in response to the invitation of the Royal Philharmonic Society. The English had not borne him a grudge for their disappointment, a few years before, when he had sent them three unimportant overtures, which, moreover, were not even new. Now began those regrettable practices in his dealings with publishers, which can only be explained by the unfounded fear of poverty that haunted him after his appointment as his nephew's guardian. Nothing came of the journey he had so seriously planned. In 1818 he decided to write a great Mass to celebrate the enthronement of the Archduke Rudolf as Archbishop of Olmütz, and for a while put the Symphony aside. Although he had two years in which to complete it, the work grew to ever greater dimensions and was not finished for another two years. And it was still nearly two more years before the symphony, now definitely intended for England, was complete. Meanwhile, however, other works of importance were written, in particular the last four Sonatas and the *Diabelli Variations*.

He still appeared now and then in public as conductor of his own works, but to what extent he could manage without the help of others we do not know. We do, however, know that in spite of his friends' warnings he made a last attempt at conducting, in 1822, when *Fidelio* was revived. But at rehearsal the task proved too much for him. The stricken master left the hall and went home. Once again he put himself in the doctors' hands, for still he had not given up all hope of regaining his hearing; not till this treatment was proved fruitless did he resign himself to his fate. For some time his deafness had made it impossible for him to cope even with everyday matters. His domestic affairs were in a bad way, and he had endless quarrels with his servants, who cheated him, or at least so he believed. It was like a sigh of despair when he underlined the words of Penelope in the Odyssey, which he constantly read: "So my handmaids betrayed me, jades without a trace of feeling."

He became more and more suspicious, and quarrelled more and more frequently with his friends. He was unjust even to those who wished him well, as was shown by his unedifying quarrel with his patrons, whose allowance was discontinued for a time owing to the collapse of the currency. Yet nearly all his old friends remained true to him, and indeed he made several new ones, so that even now he was not entirely alone. Nor had his humour deserted him. The strength and essential soundness of his nature seemed incorruptible, in spite of the often terrifying attacks of his illness.

There are numerous descriptions of his spiritual seclusion while at work on his great compositions. Schindler wrote of the year 1819: "Towards the end of August I went . . . to the Master's house at Mödling. It was four in the afternoon. Immediately we went in we heard that the two maids had left that morning. After midnight there had been a scene that had disturbed every one in the house; apparently after waiting a long time both of them had fallen asleep, and the food they had prepared had become uneatable. In one of the living-rooms, the door of which was locked, we could hear the Master working on the fugue of the *Credo*, stamping, singing, and shouting. Having listened for a time to this appalling noise, we were on the point of leaving, when the door opened and Beethoven stood before us with a wild expression on his face, which caused us the gravest anxiety. He looked as though he had been through a life-and-death struggle with the whole tribe of contrapuntists, his sworn enemies. His first remarks were confused, as though he were surprised and displeased at having been overheard. But soon he began to speak of the day's events, and said, with remarkable calmness: 'A nice business! They have all run away and I've had nothing to eat since midday yesterday!' ..."

Stranger still is the well-known affair a year or two later, when he was taken for a tramp and arrested one evening in a suburb of Vienna. He had set out in the morning, hatless and wearing an old coat, had wandered about all day, and by evening had completely lost himself. It was midnight before the suburban *Musikdirektor* identified him, and the mayor had him sent home in a carriage. Never probably has a great work of art been composed under more distressing conditions than the *Missa Solemnis*. And yet at this time of terrible affliction, when he had withdrawn himself almost entirely from the world, the fancy took him to write some dance music for a village band at Mödling; and this while he was working on the *Credo*!

He still wanted to see performed the works he had created. Immediately after the completion of the Ninth Symphony he planned a performance of it together with the Mass. This time his mind turned to Berlin, for the Viennese had deeply disappointed him by their enthusiasm for Rossini. But as soon as his intention became known in Vienna his friends and admirers joined, under the leadership of Count Lichnowsky, in writing a letter assuring him of their admiration and begging him to emerge from retirement again and let them hear his new works. This had its effect: Beethoven declared himself ready to arrange a concert. But all was not yet well. Beethoven's suspicions nearly brought the whole project to the ground, and the three men who had charge of the preparations, Count Lichnowsky, Schuppanzigh, the violinist, and Anton Schindler, had much to put up with before all difficulties were finally overcome. Infinite pains were taken to make the concert a success. The orchestra was augmented and the soloists carefully selected; but the choir

was insufficiently rehearsed. (The first properly rehearsed performance of the symphony was probably the one that took place
in Paris in 1835. According to Wagner, it had had three years'
preparation!) Yet the impression made by the performance in the
Kärntnerthor Theater on the 7th of May, 1824, was tremendous.
The concert opened with the Overture *Zur Weihe des Hauses*,
then followed 'Three Hymns', (the *Kyrie*, *Credo*, and *Benedictus* of the Mass) and finally the symphony. Every seat was
sold—only the court was absent!—and the applause was over-
whelming. Beethoven, who according to the announcements
"took part in the direction of the concert", stood watching in the
orchestra, deep in thought. Frau Unger, the singer, turned him
round so that he could at least see the applause he could not
hear . . . He was bitterly disappointed at the smallness of the
takings and there were angry scenes with his friends. A repetition three weeks later actually resulted in a deficit, for it took
place on a fine Sunday. It had not improved matters—perhaps
even it had done harm—that as a bait for the public a tenor aria
by Rossini had been inserted between the *Kyrie* and the
symphony. All the press notices were enthusiastic; but that was
rather an echo of the artistic success of the concert and a token
of homage to Beethoven personally, than a sign of true understanding.

After completion of these huge works, Beethoven allowed
himself hardly a day's rest. As is shown by the sketch-books,
he concentrated on an overture, 'B-A-C-H', and on his Tenth
Symphony. There is no indication that the latter was not to be
purely instrumental. A Mass in C sharp minor occupied his
mind so much that he was already negotiating with publishers
about it. He was also considering a Requiem, an oratorio (*The
Victory of the Cross*, among other texts, was discussed), and
music for *Faust*—"for me and for art the highest of all" is
written in his own hand in a conversation-book; with Grillparzer he was discussing in detail the plans for an opera,
Melusine, and with Rellstab material for another opera. His
mind was teeming with plans. His imagination was working
more feverishly than ever; he felt within him the energy to

complete all these works, but was only doubtful whether his days on earth would allow him the time. ("If only I had a thousandth part of your strength and determination!" the young Grillparzer wrote in a conversation-book in 1826.) Between about 1813 and 1816 his health had been relatively good; but since then it had grown gradually worse. In 1820 jaundice, a premonition of the liver disease to which he finally succumbed, made its appearance. In 1825, an inflammation of the intestines tormented and frightened him. During his recovery he composed the "Convalescent's Thanksgiving to the Divinity", in the A minor Quartet. Before he had finished the Ninth Symphony he had begun a string quartet, and though all his other plans remained unrealized, he wrote five quartets during the three years before he died, all of them works of the greatest importance and consummate skill. The first three were written to the order of Prince Galitzin, of St Petersburg, a young man who greatly admired him. But the fact that Beethoven persevered with this work shows he was urged by some inward impulse. If we did not know that they had been commissioned, it would never occur to us that these quartets were not the inevitable product of his creative mind. It is true, indeed, that this product was the outcome of his superabundant inventive power, which showed not a sign of exhaustion, but rose to a spiritual level that, as in the case of Bach, may well be called unsurpassable. It is astonishing that certain of these last works, which are by no means 'easy', at once made a profound impression on their hearers.[1] Schuppanzigh and his quartet performed them, Beethoven himself helping at the rehearsals. Only the Great Fugue, the Finale of the B flat Quartet, was found too abstruse—a fact that need not cause us any surprise.

The disease from which Beethoven died was cirrhosis of the liver, a complaint that frequently results from alcoholism. It has therefore been assumed that this was the cause in his case; but though one of the physicians who treated him expressed a similar opinion, this is not so. It is true that Beethoven was fond of wine and drank it regularly, as Goethe did too, and in considerable quantities; also he often took part in lively drinking bouts, particularly towards the end of his life, with the violinist Holz, who for this reason has often been called his evil genius. But we can judge from Beethoven's remarks after participating in a real carousal how rarely such things happened. That his drinking bouts with Holz did him considerable harm is fairly clear, for at that time—he met Holz in 1825—his disease must have been far advanced. It can be well understood that he felt more cheerful in the gay atmosphere of the Viennese wineshops than at home, for there he could forget his troubles, and be his old merry, even boisterous, self. Like all those who, though deaf, do not retire into themselves—and nothing was further from his mind—he talked a great deal, and, to judge by the conversation-books, on a great variety of subjects.

He still had a large circle of friends, and his need of companionship was as great as ever. Towards the end a new interest came into his life, for foreigners arrived more and more frequently to visit him. Before long, in fact, it was much the same with him as with Goethe in Weimar: the 'devout' made their pilgrimage to him in Vienna. It was less easy to obtain admittance to Beethoven than to Goethe, who in his last ten years gave audiences with Olympian majesty; but many people managed to do so, and it is only rarely that we hear of a visitor being ungraciously received. Many of them, indeed, enjoyed the "delightful friendliness" spoken of by Neate, an Englishman—a friendliness that was something more than formal courtesy, for it came from a heart that was still filled with love of humanity. One of the best records of such a visit is that of Stumpf, a German harp-manufacturer, who had long lived in London: "When the door opened I trembled as though I were about to enter the presence of some supernatural being . . . Beethoven's face only occasionally brightened up; when it did, it seemed as though the sun were penetrating a huge black bank of cloud, burning its way through with its fiery eye . . . All the news we were able to tell him seemed to cheer him up . . . 'Yes, I'm in good spirits to-day. How do you like old Vienna? Where one eats and drinks, sleeps and . . . Ah, but here every one lives in his own way, and plays and sings what he has made for himself . . .' Like Napoleon, Beethoven was below the average height; his figure was somewhat thick-set, with a short neck and broad shoulders, upon which were set a big round head with a thick, disordered growth of hair . . . Beethoven enjoyed talking and spoke a great deal. He had an exaggerated opinion of London and the high culture of its inhabitants . . ." A surprising number of visitors had this feeling of veneration—a proof of the extent of Beethoven's fame. Yet widespread as it was, it was only dimly that the world realized his greatness, for during his life-time he was regarded almost as a fabulous being endowed with the power of influencing the minds of men who knew little, or at least understood little, of him as musician. This is true particularly of his professional colleagues, who, unlike amateurs, had long been doubtful or reserved, if not actually hostile, in their attitude towards his music. Yet even they could not escape the magic of his humanity. Hardly ever did they receive anything but kindness and friendship from him. He would talk to young composers about their work with kindly encouragement and genuine modesty; and he not only acknowledged the good that he found in his contemporaries' work, but even extolled them as though he were no greater than they. He unreservedly admired Cherubini, and had nothing but praise for *The Barber of Seville* when Rossini called to see him. Weber, who for a long time had shown no understanding of Beethoven's works, was delighted with his reception, as was Zelter, whose description of his visit gives no indication of his dislike of Beethoven's music. That Schubert, the greatest of the younger men, who moreover was an inhabitant of Vienna, never came into contact with him, is doubtless due to his shyness; he is said once to have turned back at Beethoven's door. It was only during his last illness that Beethoven discovered Schubert's songs. He examined them for hours and said, "Truly Schubert is gifted with the divine spark!" What would he have said if he had known Schubert's major works?

We have a number of detailed accounts of the time of Beethoven's last illness. Having spent the whole summer of 1826 in Vienna, contrary to his usual custom, he allowed himself to be persuaded by his brother Johann to stay with him, towards the end of September, at his country house at Gneixendorf, near Vienna. He must already have felt ill and helpless, for otherwise he would certainly have refused the invitation, as he had often done before. Apart from his ill-health, it was for him an unhappy time; among other things his nephew had attempted to commit suicide, and this had been a serious shock to him. Judging by the conversation-books, his brother and sister-in-law seem to have looked after him to the best of their ability; they even offered to take him permanently into their house in return for a modest sum. Nor does his sister-in-law appear to have borne him any grudge for his previous hostility. But quarrels soon broke out, especially on the subject of their nephew, who had also come to stay in the country to recover his health, and who found an idle life much to his taste. Johann very reasonably advised his brother to put the young man into some regular employment. It must have been a strange life that they led during that autumn. Beethoven had retired more into himself than ever. When he accompanied his brother on visits or business errands, he sat in a corner silent and unobserving, so that people took him for a lackey, or even an idiot, and treated him accordingly. Or he would wander, as of old, through the fields, thinking and composing. His mind still worked indefatigably. During these two months he completed the last of the five String Quartets, op. 135, and wrote the new finale for the op. 130 Quartet, to take the place of the Great Fugue, which his publishers had rejected. Often, as he walked through the countryside, he was thinking out new works that he was destined never to finish.

He still remembered his friends and, as often happens towards the end of life, would have liked to pick up old threads that had long been broken. Thus he wrote from Gneixendorf to the friend of his youth, Wegeler, in Bonn, replying to a letter he had received a year before:

"My old and beloved friend,
    "I cannot express the pleasure your and your Lorchen's

.etter gave me. An answer should have followed quick as an arrow, but I am always neglectful about letter-writing, for I think that my true friends know me in any case. I often compose the answer in my head, but when I come to write it down I generally throw the pen aside, because I am unable to write as I feel. I remember the affection you have always shown me, for instance how you had my room whitewashed and gave me such a pleasant surprise. It is the same with the Breunings. Our separation was in the natural course of events. Each of us had to follow his destiny and try to attain it; but the fixed and eternal principles of virtue still bound us firmly together! Unfortunately I cannot write to you to-day as much as I should like, for I am confined to my bed, and therefore will do no more than answer some of the points in your letter.

"You write that it has been said somewhere that I am a natural son of the late King of Prussia; I was told about this some time ago, but I have made it a rule never to write anything about myself, or to answer anything that has been written about me. I therefore gladly leave it to you to make known to the world that my parents, and particularly my mother, were people of the highest repute. You write of your son. I need not say that if he comes here he will find in me both a friend and a father, and if I am in a position to serve or help him in any way I shall gladly do so.

"I still have the silhouette of your Lorchen, from which you will see how all that was good and dear to me in my youth is no less so now.

"Of my 'diplomas' I write but briefly, that I am an honorary member of the Royal Society of Science of Sweden, also of Amsterdam, and have been given the freedom of Vienna. A certain Dr Spieker recently took my last big Choral Symphony with him to Berlin; it is dedicated to the King, and I had to write the inscription with my own hand. I had applied earlier to the Embassy for permission to dedicate the work to the King, and this permission was granted. On Dr Spieker's instructions, I sent the King the manuscript with corrections in my own hand, as it was to be placed in the Royal Library. It has been hinted to me that I may be given the Order of the Red Eagle, Second Class; whether this will be so or not I do not know, but I have never sought such honours, though for many reasons it would not be unwelcome to me at the present time.

"It has always been one of my rules: *Nulla dies sine linea*, and if I let the Muse sleep it is only in order that she shall wake up the stronger. I hope to bring into the world a few more big works, and then to finish my earthly career like an elderly child, somewhere among kind people.

"You will soon receive one or two pieces of music from Schott's in Mainz. The portrait I am enclosing, though no doubt an artistic masterpiece, is not the latest that was made of me. As regards my honours, the thought of which I know gives you pleasure, I must tell you also that a medal was sent to me by the late King of France, with the inscription: 'Donné par le Roi à Monsieur Beethoven', and it was accompanied by a most amiable letter from the 'premier gentilhomme du Roi', the duc de Châtres.

"My beloved friend, let this be enough for to-day; the memory of the past takes hold of me and it is not without many tears that I write this letter. The beginning has now been made and soon you will receive another; and the oftener you write the more pleasure you will give me. About our friendship there is no need of question on either side, and so farewell. I beg you to embrace and kiss your dear Lorchen and your children in my name and to think of me the while. God be with you all!

"As ever your loyal true friend who honours you,

Beethoven"

At the end of November he decided, either because of the quarrels with his brother and sister-in-law, or because he was impelled thereto by the threat of illness, to leave Gneixendorf. He departed on the 1st of November in an open carriage, spent the night in an unheated village-inn, and arrived in Vienna, shivering with ague, on the 2nd of December. His constitution, which was still powerful, quickly threw off the ensuing inflammation of the lungs; but the dropsy, of which the first traces had already shown themselves in Gneixendorf, developed rapidly. On the 20th of December he had to be tapped for the first time, and three other tappings followed at short intervals. Even during these weeks of suffering his care for his nephew was not relaxed. At last the young man seemed to have settled down to a regular life, for he had entered the army. His uniforms and equipment cost a considerable amount, both in money and trouble; and in this, Johann, who visited the patient immediately after his arrival in Vienna, assisted. On the 11th of January the doctors held a consultation, in which, at Beethoven's request, Dr Malfatti, whom he had known years before, was invited to take part. Dr Malfatti suggested a new treatment, "punch ice", which at first seemed so efficacious that the patient began to regain hope and to show something of his old humour. He even wanted to begin composing again. His mind was busy with his Tenth Symphony, and possibly also with an oratorio, *Saul and David*. His brain was as active as ever: he despised the light reading ordered by the doctor and took refuge, as Schindler tells us, "in his old friends and teachers from Hellas—Plutarch, Homer, Plato, and Aristotle." Many things still happened to cheer him: from London came a present from Stumpf—the big edition of Handel; the Royal Philharmonic Society sent him a hundred pounds at his request, for he considered himself poor, regarding his savings as his nephew's property; and he also received many visitors, among them Hummel, who came several times to see him with the fifteen-year-old Ferdinand Hiller. His first visit was on the 8th of March, only fourteen days before Beethoven died. According to Hiller's account of this occasion, Beethoven was not then in bed. When he saw Hummel, "the expression of his eyes became very friendly and bright", and for some time he discussed a variety of subjects with the greatest vivacity. He repeated his old complaints about the superficiality of the Viennese and about Austrian politics; but neither his natural kindness nor his respect for the greatness of others had left him. He showed them a picture that had been given to him of Haydn's birthplace: "It gives me a childish pleasure—the cradle of such a great man!" The son of Gerhard von Breuning, the friend of his youth, spent all his time out of school with the sick man. His entries in the conversation-book are touching in their boyish freshness.

The doctors' care and attention were now unavailing, though it was not until the last day or two that his mind began to fail. Hummel and his wife visited him on the 23rd of March, but he did not say a word; yet on the same day he made his will in favour of his nephew. When the doctors had left him he quoted to his friends the words of the dying Augustus: "*Plaudite, amici, comoedia finita est!*" (Applaud, friends, for the comedy is finished.) On the 24th of March he received the last sacraments with composure and piety. On the same day some wine arrived that Schott had had sent to him from Mainz. He realized what it was, and said: "What a pity! Too late!" Those were his last words. On the evening of the 24th began his death agony, of which we have grim evidence in the shape of two drawings that Teltscher, the painter, made of the dying man—an incomprehensible proceeding! Breuning and his son, Schindler, Beethoven's brother and sister-in-law, and Hüttenbrenner, from Graz, who was a devoted admirer of his, were round his death-bed. But when at last, two days later, the hour of release came, his friends had gone to make arrangements for a suitable grave. Only Hüttenbrenner and—the irony of things!—his sister-in-law were present. Beethoven died on the 26th of March, 1827, at about six in the evening, while a snowstorm, accompanied by thunder and lightning, was raging over the city. Hüttenbrenner writes, and his words bear the stamp of truth: "A dazzling flash of lightning lit up the death-chamber, at which Beethoven opened his eyes, raised his right hand, with his fist clenched, and for several seconds looked upwards with a grave and threatening expression, as though to say: 'I defy you, hostile powers! Away, for God is with me!'—or as though, like the leader of an army, he would hearten his faint-hearted men: 'Courage, soldiers, forward! Trust in me, and victory is ours!' When his raised hand dropped back on the bed, his eyes were half closed. My right hand was supporting his head, my left was on his breast. Not a breath, not a heart-beat! The spirit of the great

Master of Music had fled from this world of lies into the realm of truth."

On the 28th Danhauser, a young sculptor, took the death-mask. Although the post-mortem examination, at which the temporal bone was sawn through, had already been held, the mask gives a noble impression of his magnificent face. The funeral was at three in the afternoon of the 29th of March. Over twenty thousand people are said to have attended it. The schools were closed. Eight musical conductors acted as pall-bearers, and among those who accompanied the coffin, carrying torches, was Franz Schubert. At the entrance to the Währinger Cemetery the actor, Anschütz, spoke a fine funeral oration, composed by Grillparzer. At the grave itself no one was allowed to speak. On the 3rd of April a memorial service was held in the Augustinerkirche; Mozart's *Requiem* was sung at this, and Cherubini's at a second service, in the Karlskirche.

Beethoven's old friend Stefan von Breuning administered his estate; but the emotional agitation this caused him affected his health, and a year later he followed his old friend to the grave. Beethoven's property was officially auctioned on the 5th of November. It realized little more than a thousand gulden, the priceless treasures in the way of manuscripts and sketch-books fetching less than a single page would command to-day. The world still had little respect for this first-hand evidence of his work, for after all he himself had carelessly thrown aside his manuscripts as soon as a composition was safely through the press. Only gradually did the mysterious force that emanates from these pages begin to have its effect. To-day it is not only on account of our veneration for a genius that we collect them; we now know also that much is to be learnt from the manuscripts. The archives in which relics, once scattered over the face of the earth, are now collected and cared for—particularly those of Berlin, Vienna, and Bonn—are not only shrines, but places of research. There we are nearer not only to the man but also to his work. Light has been shed upon many an enigma by these pages, whose crabbed characters bear witness to his wrestling with his angel.

BEETHOVEN IN 1814
(Engraving by Hoefel after Letronne.)

PART II

BEETHOVEN AND ABSOLUTE MUSIC

FOR more than a hundred years now Beethoven's music has been heard by millions of rapt listeners.[2] Hardly touched by change in taste or the shifting of the intellectual viewpoint, it sways humanity like an elemental power; and in our veneration of its mystery and our conviction that it is both natural and necessary, we accept it as such. The awe and the misgivings that the predominance of this great spirit occasioned in his contemporaries have long since given way to a close familiarity, derived, if not always from a true understanding, at least from a sense of the 'naturalness' of his music. To-day as in the past every work of Beethoven's is accepted by men of open mind as 'music' as much as that of other composers; that it is more powerful and more universal there can of course be no doubt; but in its essence there is no difference between it and the 'absolute' music of Bach, Haydn, Mozart, or any of the later instrumental composers. So it is felt by executant musicians, amateur and professional alike, no less than by the purely receptive listener; and only so far as they do feel this is it vouchsafed to them, each according to his capacity, to approach the mystery that lies hidden in Beethoven's music.

To a large extent, no doubt, writers on Beethoven do not share this view. Again and again for nearly a century now, voices have been heard, from out of the huge mass of literature on the subject, crying that Beethoven's music is not absolute music in the sense of a Bach fugue or a Haydn or Mozart symphony, but something essentially different. Since 1859, when Adolf Bernhard Marx, in his book on Beethoven, formulated the con-

e   65

ception of *Idealmusik* and illustrated it by reference to the *Eroica* Symphony, the opinion has again and again been expressed that Beethoven's music, at any rate that of his maturity, beginning with the *Eroica*, is no longer to be understood as absolute, but as expressive of extra-musical ideas. Wagner had already given utterance to still more radical views; looking at things from the point of view of Music Drama—that is to say, from that of his own personal and entirely unique gifts —he regarded Beethoven's later instrumental music as an "Irrtum"—a mistake. Thus, in *Oper und Drama* (1851): "He transgresses the bounds of absolute music—any kind of music, that is, in which there remains some recognizable trace of song or dance tunes—and speaks to us in a language, entirely inappropriate to the purely musical world, that is only held together by a poetic conception. But it is just this poetic conception that cannot be expressed clearly in music, as it can in poetry." In his youth Wagner thought differently. In a tale written in Paris in 1840, *Ein glücklicher Abend*, two friends are discussing the question of the poetic programmes of Beethoven's symphonies, and agree that any such programmes are impossible, since what comprises the actual content of the music can only be expressed "in the infinitely varied incentives inherent in those characteristics that are proper to music alone, but which are foreign to and incapable of expression in any other language." Not for thirty years did Wagner revert to this view. Then, in his admirable and profound *Beethoven* (1870), he gave to the world a very beautiful description of the musical quintessence of his subject, in whom, though even now he was not entirely free of subjective bias, he did see the one true Master of absolute music. Yet the other view is urged again and again. In about 1910 Paul Bekker based his voluminous and successful book on the idea that Beethoven was "first a poet and thinker, and only in the second place a musician," and defended himself against the resulting strictures of Hans Pfitzner and others by maintaining that Beethoven's form as such was "often crude and arbitrary." And twenty years later this opinion, now grown to grotesque proportions, is repeated from a quarter whence we should have expected something very different. For Arnold Schering, one of the foremost leaders of musical science, has presented us, in *Beethoven in neuer Deutung*, with an "Interpretation" by means of which he considers that he has once for all ensured the true understanding of Beethoven's music, which, seen by itself, is "dominated by lack of any regular plan and by illogicality." He attempts, though on no factual basis—even in the face of well-established facts—to prove that when composing his sonatas and quartets and so forth Beethoven had in mind certain actual literary works, such as the dramas of Shakespeare, Goethe, and Schiller; and that the Third Symphony was the "Homer Symphony", and the Fourth the "Schiller Symphony". The Fifth, however, was alleged to be the "Symphony of the National Rising". Schering even goes so far as to maintain that the idea of absolute music in general, which was first conceived by the Romantics, was a fatal error, since it stood in the way of a true understanding of instrumental music of any sort.

It is true that there are many writings of a different kind upon Beethoven, concerned only with the knowledge and understanding of the purely musical content of his works; that is to say, principally, with what we are accustomed to describe as 'Form'—a term that is often used without due thought and then misunderstood. In contemporary criticism, already, we are surprised to find here and there, particularly in E. T. A. Hoffmann's famous essays, traces of a genuine understanding of Beethoven's musical conception. In spite of the romantic, not to say poetic, language in which Hoffmann clothes his ideas, these do exhibit a profound comprehension of the musical content of Beethoven's works. Nor has Adolf Bernhard Marx rested satisfied with his thesis of *Idealmusik*, but he is seriously and often successfully concerned in his book to bring to light the organic growth and structure of the music. The same applies to his contemporary, the German-Russian W. von Lenz, a subtle thinker whose books on Beethoven are to-day unjustly forgotten. Of all the 'Analyses' that subsequently appeared, most are, to be sure, entirely superficial, confining themselves as they do to the purely academic aspects of sonata form and so forth. Little is gained by this, still less when, as in the case of Hugo Riemann, the analysis is not so much concerned with increasing our knowledge of the compositions as with confirming the commentator's own theories. It is Heinrich Schenker that we have to thank for the most thorough insight into the essence of Beethoven's music. His exhaustive analysis of the Ninth Symphony, the later sonatas, and other works is, in the light it throws on their organic growth, so far unexcelled. It must be admitted that in his efforts to discover this organic growth, Schenker is not in his later books—especially that on the *Eroica*—guiltless of a certain measure of hair-splitting and over-refinement. This danger threatens all who try to unveil the last mysteries of a work of art; and other writers also, such as Fritz Cassirer (in *Beethoven und die Gestalt*) and Walter Engelsmann (in *Beethoven's Kompositionspläne*), in spite of the valuable information they impart, have come to grief as a result of it. It must be remembered that no work of art, not even a piece of music, can ever be fully apprehended as a living thing by means merely of conscious cerebration. What the 'analysis' of music can do for us, and what makes it valuable—even indispensable—is this, and this only: it can sharpen the ear of the unperceptive listener in such a way as to enable him to appreciate the music's organic growth; and it can therefore teach him to hear better, and so to intensify his impressions of what he hears, and not to substitute for an adventure of the living spirit a process of conscious thought.

But the only way to accomplish this task is to confine the analysis strictly to the musical facts, and to try and explain them by reference to the inner laws of music. Unfortunately, however, analyses of this kind are of little value to any but professional musicians, for, as we all know, they are usually undecipherable by the average amateur music lover. He believes that it is only with the assistance of a verbal description that he will ever find what he is looking for—that is, that he will succeed in his efforts to grasp the spiritual content of any given piece of music. But, alas, to translate that spiritual content from the language of music into that of speech is utterly impossible, as Wagner said in the tale referred to above, and as Schumann and other Romantics, who disagreed with the programmatic view of Beethoven's music, very well knew. And yet again and again the attempt is made to interpret in words the content of a tune, a theme, a whole work. Two examples will serve. Paul Bekker says of the opening of the *Eroica*: "The germ of the conflict lies in the Hero himself. Forceful and forward-pushing energy and plaintive, resigned reflectiveness, are juxtaposed . . ." And Romain Rolland, on the opening of the *Appassionata*: "Two in one, one Ego opposed in enmity to the other—now savage strength, now trembling weakness." In such words is the infinite variety of the significance inherent in these motives, which is fully revealed only as the movement progresses, set in a certain fixed direction at the very start; and so the way to a true understanding of the music is obstructed. Even Rolland, who is more musical and knows more than Bekker about Beethoven, for all his efforts to understand the purely musical happenings—that is, the organic growth of a work as a whole—fails to make the hearer realize that this is the very essence of any musical experience. In still worse case is H. Kretschmar's doctrine of 'Hermeneutics', whose aim is "everywhere to seek the soul beneath the body, to demonstrate the pure thought-germ in every constituent element of a work of art." It is confined to expressing in words the emotions or impulses that underlie every single detail, and its adherents are under the impression that by doing so they help us to understand the work in question. To such efforts there is only one thing to be said: if all these phrases really cannot be done without, then at least it should be made clear that they are simply images for the purely musical side of the matter; and as such they can be to the point only if and so far as this side of the matter is rightly understood. The road must lead from the 'word' to the 'music', and not from the music away into other domains of spiritual expression.

Though the conception of absolute music is only a hundred years old, the thing itself has been in existence for three hundred. It is true that during the thousands of years that music has existed there has here and there been pure instrumental music. But this is either merely the expression of some inward stimulus, as in the case of primitive peoples (some of whom are musically highly gifted), and is therefore purely subjective, though by no means wanting in form; or else, as in the case of Asiatic and, clearly, of classical civilizations, it is connected with definitely extra-musical ideas through the agency of ritual or other conventions. But what we to-day understand by absolute music is something else, something that exists only in the West and even there has existed only since the end of the sixteenth century. It is music that has been divorced from words and from which all reminders of the dance have been obliterated, music that can produce, from itself alone and in accordance with its own inherent laws, an infinite variety of shapes and forms, and so has need of no external support. It was not by chance that this evolution took place at the same time as the change in our harmonic consciousness; that is, at the time when we turned our backs upon the old Church Modes and developed the new, and in the narrower sense 'tonal', system of major and minor. The consolidation of the harmonic structure thereby attained, and in particular the securing of the basic harmonic relationships within one tonality, i.e. the relations to each other of the three primary triads, the tonic (on the first degree of the scale), the dominant (on the fifth degree), and the subdominant (on the fourth degree), were discoveries of far-reaching importance. The opinion, still widespread, that music before 1600, or indeed any other system of music that has grown up outside our civilization, was 'primitive', is erroneous. On the contrary, the monody of 1600 and thereabouts is itself primitive in comparison with the vocal polyphony that preceded it. But what grew out of it was unparalleled in any other musical system in the density of its harmonic texture and its wealth of forms that were at once free and disciplined. This formative power that harmony acquired now permeated not only melody but the whole of the musical structure, and gave to music a significance hitherto unthought of, with the help of which alone it attained full confidence and independence. Now only was it able to germinate and develop, freely and spontaneously; but it is remarkable to observe how, in the course of a century or so, the confidence and boldness of its growth and formation increased, until, with Bach and Handel, it first attained the everlasting heights. Bach's last and perhaps least comprehensible work, the *Art of Fugue*, represents the sudden close of the pre-classical epoch of music. The noble words that Goethe wrote to his friend Zelter on the subject of the *Well-tempered Clavier* are almost more appropriate to the *Art of Fugue:* it seemed to him when listening to this music "as if Eternal Harmony were conversing with herself, as we might think happened before the Creation, deep in the heart of God." This indeed shows how profoundly he understood the essence of this music: its magnificent, almost superhuman, objectivity, and—its own secret—its independence of time. As in God's heart, before he spoke the words "Let there be", all that ever "was to be" was already complete and present, so also Bach's music is complete from the very beginning, and in essence remains unchanged, whatever may befall it as it runs its course. The theme of a passacaglia, a fugue, or any apparently freely constructed composition of Bach, is fixed and constant in form from the very first, and is, in its essence, unchanged even by inversion, augmentation, and so forth. It is ever-present, even when it seems to have disappeared; in a double fugue, for instance, the two themes are so closely bound up together that each is inaudibly accompanied by the other. And what happens round about the theme is predetermined by its shape and kind. This is 'static' form—form that is a fixed condition and not a process—even though we require time in which to realize this. And the feeling that is in this music is also static. The time when a Bach fugue was regarded as a dead thing—a mere playing with form—is now finished and done with. It is true that the fugue, as a musical species, was the result of conscious, calculating, synthetical work; and necessarily so, just as any other species, or indeed any other legitimate system of music, rests upon a rational basis. But neither a fugue nor any other kind of musical composition can be said to live unless, besides this rationale, the spiritual stimulus without which man would never have invented music is active in it. A theme like that of the *Art of Fugue* might well have been hit upon by a musician of no genius, and among the theorists there were many who could compete with the great Bach in sheer mechanical ingenuity. But only to a man of genius was it given to build up out of a theme of this kind, and all that happens to it, a world of lofty feeling and wealth of inspiration. This feeling has, it is true, nothing to do with the human emotions; the music it inspires is superhuman, and less susceptible to verbal illustration than music of any other kind. And if we look deeper, we shall find that it is the same with the 'expression' of Bach's music, even when it is apparently entirely subservient to a text; from evidence collected by Schweitzer and Pirro, we know that in his vocal and choral works Bach often depicted in his music every word of the text. This does not mean that the object of music is the interpretation of words; on the contrary, the word is only the occasion—the starting-point—for the music, whose expression, even where, as in the aria *Erbarme Dich!*, the text is charged with spiritual ecstasy, is raised to the level of the superhuman and thus rendered objective. In particular this expression is superhuman in its static self-sufficiency, which is as complete here as in Bach's absolute and superficially more formal music. As in the case of a fugue, an aria of Bach is determined by what happens in the first few bars. The emotions do not glow and fade like the human emotions; and the amazing way in which the sense of individual words is rendered in the music does not affect the static unity of the whole. A single example will serve for many cases: when at the end of the middle section of the aria *Blute nur!* in the *St Matthew Passion*, the word *Schlange* (serpent) is depicted by an uncannily expressive musical figure, this figure is perfectly dovetailed into the context, just as the form and expression of the whole aria are determined by its first few bars. And nothing essential is wanting to give the hearer the desired impression, if he has not heard the word, for the figure 'means' something much more general, though not therefore necessarily less definite. On the contrary, the expression of this music is far more precise and definite than any words can be. True, only those are capable of hearing this to whom the essence of each and every musical form, be it a simple melody or the most highly complex structure, is revealed.

And now we come to music to which Goethe's words do not apply. It is no longer a case of "Eternal Harmony conversing with herself", and the Creation has long been an accomplished fact. Music has descended into the rough-and-tumble of human existence. Not that it was secularized, for secular music there had always been, and it flourished, indeed, with particular exuberance in the days of baroque art. And to say that it became more 'natural' implies a failure to remember that the *Art of Fugue* is also natural within the meaning of its age and its creator, though indeed its nature is very near to God. The truth is that music now drew nearer to mankind; it became more human than hitherto any but folk music had been. It was the conception of nature held by Rousseau and by the *Sturm und Drang* movement that was now pushing its way into the domain of music. According to those who held this idea, music hitherto had been altogether too artificial, not to say rarefied. "This is for far too learned ears!" wrote the youthful Haydn over a passage in one of his early symphonies, and proceeded to simplify it. Only what was simple and immediately comprehensible was regarded as 'natural'. "Truth of human expression" was the aim that Gluck and the Classicists passionately pursued; but they found it not only in the limpid world of the Greeks, but also in the untamed, visionary North. And it is typical of the way in which people in those days looked upon music, that a fantasia of Carl Philipp Emanuel Bach should have reminded its hearers of *Hamlet*.

None of the forms that had until now held sway could be preserved in their original shape. There was no room for 'static' form in music whose object was the direct expression of human feelings. Hitherto the supreme principle had been unity and uniformity of feeling; but now the change had come, and must be taken seriously. The time was ripe for 'dynamic' form; emotion had come into its own, and could 'glow and fade' according to its nature. The orchestral crescendo, first used by the Mannheim School, had a sensational effect; it is said that the audience could hardly keep their seats for excitement. Now that the dominance of a single voice—the melody—had taken the place of rich polyphonic texture, rhythm, as the most important emotional stimulant, regained a significance that had long been lost to it. In particular we now find contrast inside one piece of music, against which the diehards, scenting in it a danger to the unity of the whole, carried on a long but losing struggle. Previously contrast had been admitted only into music of a freer form, such as the fantasia, or the toccata, in the latter of which the sharpest contrasts were often immediately juxtaposed. For the rest, the law still held good that every composition should express one emotion and one only. Such at least was the teaching of the *Affektenlehre* ('Doctrine of the Emotions'), which was attacked first by Rousseau in his later writings, and then by the *Sturm und Drang* movement. Emphasis was now laid in particular on the alternation of the emotions. C. P. E. Bach had already said in 1753: "Hardly has the executant musician stilled one emotion than he excites another; thus does he juggle with the passions." And some twenty years later Neefe, then Beethoven's teacher, meditates in his *Dilettanterien* on the question of what it is that gives instrumental music an inner meaning: "a fervid imagination, profound penetration into the inmost sanctuary of harmony . . . exact knowledge of various characters, of humanity in its physical and moral aspects, of the passions and their external symptoms and effects . . . True, we express emotions such as Joy and Sadness, but only in their full and final manifestation; we do not follow them step by step, from their first germination, throughout their subsequent progress. Least of all do we observe their nuances or the points at which one passion gives place to another; here we leave lacunae, which are repugnant to nature."

No form expresses as well as the sonata the new thought that had come into being. As formerly the fugue, so now the sonata is the form in which the new style most truly and completely fulfils itself. The name is ambiguous. Very early it was given to works in several movements that differed from the suite in the greater regularity of the number and sequence of those movements, and by a tense inward relationship between them such as the suite never knew. 'Sonatas' in this sense, however, include not only those compositions for one or two instruments that are commonly known by that name, but also other chamber music works, such as trios, quartets, etc., and orchestral symphonies. A symphony does not differ from a piano sonata in kind but in degree; in the symphony each form—whether sonata form, song form, rondo, or whatever it may be—is expanded, proportionately to the means employed, to greater dimensions than those of the sonata. In such works the first movement is usually the most important; and this is almost always in sonata form, the word being used here in its more important sense. Like the other forms, such as the minuet, the scherzo, and usually the slow movement also, this has developed from the old 'song form' (a-b-a); in it, too, the first section is repeated after the second, in the 'recapitulation'. But contrast, now expected almost as a matter of course, is generally provided not by the second section, (b), but inside the first, which almost always has a second subject—often a broad melody that contrasts with a highly significant first or principal subject. The middle section contains the working-out of the first; that is, the thoughts are developed with full freedom of imagination, not as in a set of variations, in which the structure is on the whole left unaltered, but in such a way that the composer plays freely with the themes, dividing them up, altering them, and creating new growths from them. And when the principal subject reappears at the opening of the recapitulation, it is, as August Halm rightly says, "in a different frame of mind from when it first appeared." As a consequence of this, the recapitulation is more or less different from the first section, or 'exposition'. (C. P. E. Bach had already written "Sonatas with Varied Recapitulations.") And when yet another development took place, whereby the closing phrase grew into an independent fourth section, the coda, hardly anything remained of the old 'cyclic' character of the movement. It is a dynamic form, which does not, like the static fugue, merely unfold what was already there, but gradually develops its own essential substance, travelling a road whose end was not to be foreseen at the beginning. Proof of the growing predominance of sonata form is to be found in the fact that the coda, and elements of working-out, began gradually to find their way into the rondo as well, which, since its various themes return several times in essentially the same guise, retains more purely the character of cyclic form.

The new form developed gradually, and not without a hard struggle; and it was years before this new 'species', which was striving to come into existence with organic inevitability, arrived at maturity. First the strict structure of the old forms disappeared, and it is not difficult to understand the contempt with which the adherents of the old régime looked on the upstart. (In the preliminary note on the first edition of the *Art of Fugue* (1753), Marpurg, a great admirer of Bach, speaks with contempt of the "spread of effeminate song", and bewails the disappearance of "the masculinity that should rule in music.") How often, too, were the newly discovered seas embarked upon by lesser talents, by semi-amateurs, who however helped on the development of the new form just because they were blind to, and therefore had no fear of, the rocks that lay ahead of them! So it was, round about 1600, with the Florentine 'dilettanti', who, in their efforts to substitute monody for the old polyphonic vocal style, had a decisive effect on its development; and so it was later, when the Mannheim School, the Stamitzes and others, laboured with passionate zeal for the new dynamic form in the composition of chamber music and symphonies. And though their talent was too small for their compositions to live, yet they deserve their niche in history for the good work they did.[3] Among the compositions of even C. P. E. Bach, a far more talented man, there is little that we to-day can call perfect. For this a still greater man was required, and there can be no doubt that he appeared in the person of Joseph Haydn. It is remarkable to observe how he seized upon the growing form and played with it; and how in his hands—for that they are his and not those of any lesser spirit is obvious—it gradually gained firmness and developed, true to its organic laws. The complete and intimate knowledge, and the surpassing comprehension of art, with which he went to work, are generally as much overlooked as his truly passionate nature. (The notion of "Papa Haydn," which probably arose from the touching personal appearance of the aging Master, who liked his younger friends—not excluding Cherubini—to call him by that affectionate nickname, is one of those myths of musical history that will never be eradicated.) Faced with the same problem of form in piano sonata, string quartet, or symphony, to mention only three main classes of his compositions, he attacked it with the unfailing sureness of style that the task demanded of him: the piano's monologue, which permits great freedom of improvisation; the fourfold community of the string quartet, in which each member strives to maintain his own rights; and the many-headed orchestra, whose minds are ruled by one man's will; although in each case Haydn's music is homogeneous in feeling at every moment of its growth, he is always conscious that the different means call for a different style. His mastery was not easily gained, especially since he never underwent a strict course of study. The works of his youth, to-day unjustly neglected, show of course more promise than accomplishment, though they abound in life and inspiration; in their freedom they are true children of *Sturm und Drang*, and in their simplicity, often their primitiveness, they are witnesses to the new thought. Haydn was nearly fifty before he achieved perfection. In about 1780 began that glorious series of sonatas, chamber music, and symphonies, in which for the first time 'classical' style came to full fruition in absolute music. Now at last those who for years had patiently striven to fashion a new mould for the sonata were rewarded: the new form had become reality. It was built up on contrast; and it achieved perfection by means of a development that was at once free and disciplined: free because there was no limit to what *could* happen to the thematic material; and disciplined because nothing was *permitted* to happen to it that was not subservient to the growth of the themes, and, moreover, because it was the duty of the composer to choose one of those alternatives that would ensure the perfect—i.e. the organic—development of the whole work. Only when this duty has been faithfully carried out do we get the satisfying impression that what we hear must sound just so—not because man has willed it but because it is part and parcel of nature itself.

In the decade that followed 1780 Haydn was not alone in his achievement. Side by side with him walked the young Mozart, who, though perhaps Haydn's superior in his divinely inspired genius, was profoundly influenced by the strength and confidence with which the elder man shaped his thoughts and material. And the latter on his side felt the full charm of the younger man's grace and harmonious spirit. The one influenced the other; and both were deeply affected by their new acquaintance with the works of the great Bach. All the sonatas, chamber music, and symphonies that Mozart composed during the ten years of life still left to him, are equal in the richness and perfection of their growth to those of Haydn. Yet we may be allowed to see in Haydn the greatest master of classical form, not because he was the elder, but because to him form as such was more of a problem, and the relation of the parts to each other and to the whole was less a matter of course, than to Mozart, who accepted form as it was handed on to him and poured into it all the wealth of his feeling and invention.

Has ever a man existed who, given a sound ear for music, has felt impelled, when listening to these works, to think of anything but what he was 'hearing',—music that fills the heart full to overflowing and enriches the world with harmony and melody? Yet Haydn himself is said to have observed that every theme in his symphonies represented some moral attribute! With that he does not, of course, hold himself out as a bold innovator or as a man that disavows 'absolute' music. Of such cases there were enough in the baroque period, so far as music was under the influence of the 'Doctrine of Emotion'; thus, Rameau gave to various movements of his harpsichord 'Concertos' titles such as *L'agaçante*, *La timide*, *L'indiscrète*. If Haydn was an innovator, it is rather because he kept such titles to himself, well knowing that they would only serve to determine in advance the hearer's impressions. It is lucky indeed that we have no more exact knowledge of his intentions, for it would not increase our understanding of his music by one iota; and probably if we had we should never recover our mental image of those 'moral attributes'.

This music has long outgrown everything that was once perhaps its *raison d'être*; it has attained quite different dimensions, and has freed itself of every tie that bound it to its age. How little it depends upon the spirit of that age is never so clear as when we listen, say, to a Haydn or Mozart symphony at one of the beautiful Festival Concerts in the castle at Würzburg. In the wonderful late baroque apartments there this music suddenly becomes again an 'event' of the social circles for which they were built; but, strangely enough, it does not draw nearer to us but recedes from us—recedes almost as far as some of the uninspired music of that day, which has no life in it outside its setting. It is this mysterious gift of unceasing growth that distinguishes a truly inspired work of art and gives it enduring life, or at least the possibility of repeated resurrection, independent of life's changes or of knowledge of the conditions under which it was conceived. It is not the feeling—the human emotions that moved the artist when he was creating the work—that is made 'objective', and therefore eternal, but the living organism, to whose final and complete realization the artist's efforts were directed. The emotional content is ever subject to transmutation, not determined once for all by what was originally perhaps some extra-musical impulse. On the contrary, it is only made the richer, and the organic structure of the work, as a living thing, only speaks the more impressively, when it has cast off everything temporal and therefore limited and incidental.

And what of Beethoven? Does not all that has been said apply equally to him? Is his creation not as much music as Haydn's and Mozart's—music of hitherto unexampled power and depth of expression, it is true, but none the less music whose meaning is to be found in itself alone? Is some kind of mental bridge really necessary to give access to the secret of his works? Or does not all thought, all effort to discover extra-musical 'ideas' in it, only lead us away from a true understanding of its content?

Beethoven's occasional remarks on these questions do not on the whole allow of any far-reaching conclusions. It is true that during his last illness he discussed with Schindler a plan to give poetic titles to his compositions, though Schindler himself doubted whether he would have agreed to their publication. He tells us, moreover, that some years previously the Master had expressed himself decisively against attempts to provide his works with poetic programmes, on one occasion in a letter, which has unfortunately been lost. To questions about the meaning of one or other of his compositions he was accustomed to reply: "that can only be answered at the piano"; and to say that if people really wanted to invent titles, these must merely be descriptive of the general character of the music. For some of his compositions he even considered this desirable; for in his later years he found that the audiences were not always able, as they had previously been, to experience the 'emotions' of a movement, whereas in his younger days everybody had felt that the Largo of the Piano Sonata, op. 10, no. 3, for instance, portrayed "the spiritual state of a melancholy man." Any title that he might have considered possible would therefore have been something on the same lines as those of Schumann, who is known to have added poetic titles to many of his completed works.

Beethoven's remark, also passed on to us by Schindler, about the "two principles"—those of "entreaty" and "resistance"—really tells us nothing that is not already illustrated in Haydn's and Mozart's music. Think for instance of the opening of Mozart's *Jupiter* Symphony, or the first movement of his great G minor. Here we find C. P. E. Bach's and Neefe's theory of the "alternation of the emotions" carried into practice. Beethoven, it is true, gave new meaning to this principle, not however, on a programmatic basis, but in obedience to a new and purely musical creative impulse. The importance of his highly significant remark concerning the 'idea' underlying each of his works will be discussed later.

There are very few works to which Beethoven himself gave titles. Such as he did give hardly go further than was customary in the eighteenth century, and tell us very little that we should not have known without them. That the op. 13 Sonata is 'pathetic' is as obvious as that the Third Symphony is 'heroic'. The 'melancholy' nature of the Introduction to the last movement of the String Quartet, op. 18, no. 6, which is entitled "*La Malinconia*," is quite obvious. The movement of the A minor Quartet, op. 132, entitled "Convalescent's Thanksgiving to the Divinity, in the Lydian Mode", would, even without that superscription, be appreciated at once as concerned with matters relating to the other world; and the episode marked "Feeling new strength" creates that impression without the help of words. That they are here is simply due to Beethoven's having written this movement during convalescence after a serious illness. It would be a complete mistake to seek in this the underlying 'idea' of the Quartet as a whole. The words "*Muss es sein?—Es muss sein!*" (Must it be?—It must be!) over the Finale of op. 135 are no more than a joke—though an ingenious one, for it depicts the mutual relations of the two motives very pertinently, and entirely as the open-minded hearer would anyhow feel them. Nor is the heading to the witty and humorous Rondo, op. 129, *Die Wut über den verlorenen Groschen ausgetobt in einem Capriccio* (Anger at the loss of a penny, given vent to in a Capriccio), anything more than a joke. There remain but two works that have something like a programme: the *Pastoral* Symphony and the Piano Sonata op. 81a. The former does not differ in principle from numerous eighteenth-century works of a similar kind; the difference is in its symphonic character, which is typical of Beethoven. The superscriptions he intended for the first and last movements of the latter, to all three of which the publishers, on their own responsibility, gave the titles "*Les adieux, l'absence, et le retour*", to-day sound faintly comic, and Beethoven himself f can hardly have meant them to be taken too seriously. At the same time they do perhaps describe the outward incentive for the composition of the Sonata. These superscriptions are: "The Farewell; Vienna, the 4th of May, 1809, upon the departure of His Imperial Highness the Archduke Rudolf," and "The Arrival of His Imperial Highness the Archduke Rudolf on the 30th of January, 1810." No one will maintain that these superscriptions give us a deeper understanding of the Sonata as music. The general titles are of more value, even though they only bring out more clearly what the performer or the audience is already aware of, viz. that the monologue of the middle movement forms a contrast with the dialogue of the first and last, and the exultation and relaxation of the last with the stress and strain of the first. There are only two really descriptive passages: first, the *Lebewohl* motive of the opening, which dominates the whole movement in Beethoven's own symphonic style and, in the very long coda, attains a degree of pictorial clarity unsurpassed even in *Fidelio*; and second, the bridge passage leading to the Finale. This sort of thing is unexampled in the rest of Beethoven's instrumental music, just as the *Pastoral* Symphony differs in its musical language from all the other symphonies—by which we are driven to the conclusion that none of his other works has a hidden programme of this kind. It is another matter that Beethoven was doubtless occasionally inspired by poems that had impressed him. His well-known answer to Schindler's question as to the meaning of the Sonatas op. 31, no. 2 and op. 57, "Read Shakespeare's *Tempest!*" should not, to be sure, be quoted as proof of this. Anybody who knows the play realizes that its action has very little to do with the title, and that the genuinely stormy character of both Sonatas has still less to do with the action of the play. The 'tempest' of the Sonatas is intended to be taken more seriously, and is mightier far, than that conjured up by Shakespeare, by which

> ". . . not so much perdition as an hair
> Betid to any creature in the vessel."

And surely in these Sonatas there is no trace of the play's

'happy end'! As often occurred, no doubt, Beethoven here probably wanted to put off his troublesome and unintelligent questioner with an answer that was not intended to be taken too seriously. It was to the same inquisitor that he once said that he had not composed a third movement to the op. 111 Sonata "because he hadn't had time." It is however a different matter when Amenda tells us that the Master had in mind the scene in the churchyard from *Romeo and Juliet* when he composed the Adagio of the String Quartet op. 18, no. 1, for in a sketch of the end of that movement Beethoven wrote the words *les derniers soupirs*. But it is characteristic of him that in the actual composition he omitted these sighs, and finished off the movement in a different, though a magnificent and entirely individual, style. There can now be no question of any connexion with that scene; the growth of the movement is throughout organically in accordance with the nature of its thematic material. Beethoven's aim was perfection of organic growth, not the depiction of an extra-musical occurrence. (Schering, in spite of tradition, does not connect this Quartet, but the later one, op. 74, with *Romeo and Juliet*, as he also ignores the well-founded tradition connecting the *Eroica* with Napoleon.)

If the statement were true that in Beethoven's music the laws of absolute music were no longer valid, then either traces of this would be visible from the start, or else at some point in it we should note the intrusion of a fundamentally new attitude towards music, and not merely of a new style. But neither is the case. Beethoven's genius was slow in coming to maturity. When he left Bonn at the age of twenty-two he had, it is true, composed a considerable amount of music, though he himself regarded none of it as worthy of publication. In those days he was by no means a musical revolutionary; his desire was to write sonatas and chamber music in the style of the day, but he had not yet mastered their form. Only certain themes, of remarkable power and individuality of feeling, were such that he could later make use of them. One of these seems truly to have opened the gate into a new world—the famous tune from the long-forgotten *Cantata on the Death of Joseph II*, of 1790, which later, in his

maturity, he used again in the second Finale of *Fidelio*, and
which has been fittingly called the *Humanitätsmelodie*. In the
Cantata the words "Da stiegen die Menschen ans Licht" are
sung to it, and in *Fidelio* it is heard at the moment when Leonora
frees her husband from his fetters. The way the tune soars up,
taking two successive leaps of a fourth, and sinks again, though

Andante con moto

Da stie - gen die Men - schen, die Men - schen ans Licht, . .

not to rest, and so describes a fine, freely poised curve, is unexampled in contemporary music both in its breadth and intensity and in the freedom and grandeur of its feeling. With this
tune Beethoven joined the "many that are called." Indeed, in
writing it he may perhaps have been inspired by some extra-
musical idea; but it must be remembered that it was a question
not of a whole work but of a single tune. The Cantata as a whole,
with its Choruses, Arias, and Recitatives, was steeped in the
conventional style of the day. And, what is still more important,
this Cantata, another composed at the same time, and the *Ritterballett*, were for long Beethoven's only works of this type. When
a few years later his compositions showed that he was no longer
of the "many that are called" but of the "few that are chosen",
when these works began to follow one another in close succession, as if forces long pent up were now released—then it is
worthy of note that he was no longer writing vocal music, but
only instrumental. Up to the year 1800, apart from unimportant
incidental works, Beethoven wrote nothing but absolute music
—sonatas and chamber music, and later piano concertos and the
First Symphony; and in the following years, up to *Fidelio*, there
is nothing in any other domain of music to compare in importance with his instrumental works. And that was at a time when
in theatre, church, and concert hall, vocal music monopolized
public interest, and when no other composer, not even Haydn,
was so exclusively occupied with purely instrumental music.

That it was Beethoven's mission to break the dominance of vocal music there is no doubt. It was the problem of the sonata that for a whole decade almost entirely occupied his mind; and on comparison of his sonatas—using the term in its widest sense—with those of his great predecessors, anyone with sufficient perception must realize that he was not concerned with destroying, or even loosening, an old and strict form, but that on the contrary—in spite of his youthful impetuosity and the new feeling with which his music was charged—he even strengthened that old form.

What we know of the individuality of Beethoven's creative power during the years of and leading up to his maturity, and of the aim towards which his work was directed, is derived from two apparently contradictory facts. In Vienna, at a time when his compositions were unknown, or at least very little known, he was acknowledged to be the unrivalled master of an art then much practised—that of improvisation; and this he remained as long as his hearing allowed of his playing at concerts or social functions. What in the case of other performers was a kind of musical entertainment or an occasion for the showing-off of virtuosity, grew in his hands into an art of the greatest profundity. The competitions during his early years in Vienna between him and other recognized exponents of the art, must from all accounts have been not only diverting but genuinely exciting. The young Rhinelander's rough manners had already startled society; at the piano he became truly daemonic, for he seemed to have at his beck and call all the genii of his art. It was through his spontaneous and inexhaustible imagination, which never failed him once he had started, that he gave his audiences the impression that he was 'possessed'. But he never started unless he was sure of his 'genie', and it happened sometimes that he would refuse to play. Having announced that he would improvise at a public concert, he noted down a few musical ideas, in order not to be entirely unprepared. There is no recorded case of his improvisation being inspired by any extra-musical idea; but it has often been told how he would ask a member of the audience, professional or amateur, for a subject. On one occasion he saw, lying upside down, the cello part of a piece that had just been played, and from it he took a few notes upon which he proceeded to extemporize for a full hour. His inexhaustible imagination could build up a stupendous edifice out of little or nothing. But he never let that imagination run riot; always he held it under firm control. Musicians have left it on record that his improvisations were never formless; they were always in one of the customary musical forms—sonata, rondo, variation, and so forth. What his audiences found still more remarkable was his coolness and presence of mind, for all that he was 'possessed' of a daemon. It was not mere empty boasting when he said he could play any of his improvisations through a second time, for he more than once proved it by doing so.

One thing seems irreconcilable with Beethoven's gift of extempore yet conscious invention; by far the greater part of his creative work cost him many a valuable hour and many a hard struggle with the form both of the movement as a whole and of individual melodies. This we know from the great number of sketch-books that have been preserved. The genius who, in his free improvisations, could pour forth a wealth of perfectly constructed music, experimented again and again before he had shaped to his satisfaction not only such great works as the *Eroica*, but even a simple melody, such as that of the first song of *An die ferne Geliebte*, which seems to spring directly and naturally from the words. And though those improvisations may be held to confirm the theory of 'inspiration', which Hans Pfitzner has ardently supported in his writings, and upon which, in the first act of *Palestrina*, he has shed the light of both music and poetry, the manner in which, as we know from the sketch-books, this tune and many others came into existence would seem entirely to refute it. There is not the least doubt that they did not suddenly and spontaneously 'occur' to Beethoven. He struggled hard and long before he had shaped and developed them from their first form, which indeed shows no signs of genius, and is often even trivial. The argument is not affected one way or the other by pointing to Mozart's or Schubert's method of composition, under which not only simple tunes but whole works, complete and fully fashioned, were the outcome of one single, spontaneous act of creation, so that they only required to be written down. It would of course be entirely wrong to argue from this that Mozart or Schubert was a greater genius than Beethoven—that they were more 'inspired'. Not by the manner in which it is composed, but by the result, is the value of a work of art to be appraised. And that in Beethoven's case this result—be it a mere tune or a whole symphony—gives an impression of naturalness and inevitability that a creative genius alone can make, is our guarantee that the method of composition is simply the strange but perhaps inevitable 'way round' that a genius must take to reach his ideal, viz. perfection. It is not by any means only Beethoven who worked on these lines, though it is only in his case that so many sketch-books have been preserved. From a sheet of paper in Haydn's hand, which by chance has come down to us, we know that even so simple a tune as that of the Austrian National Anthem (also used for the English hymn 'Praise the Lord, ye Heavens adore him') did not just 'occur' to him. And, in the case of Schubert, the process was not always the same as with the *Erlkönig*, which he finished half an hour after he had first read the poem. Not only in the *Winterreise* songs, but also in some of his bigger symphonic works, such as the great C major Symphony, Schubert made a number of important alterations while he was actually engaged on the fair copies; also there are drafts in existence of several piano sonatas that he later rejected. Neither the one nor the other is evidence of the degree of 'inspiration' involved, for when Beethoven seems to be labouring consciously to shape a melody or a whole work, his efforts could only be successful just because he was inspired, and inspired in the highest degree. Metaphysically speaking, the complete organism was there from the beginning, though latent in his mind; and it only required to be made manifest. What seems here to be purely mental work is in reality nothing but the wrestling of the genius with his 'angel' for the blessing of perfection.[4]

When Beethoven had completed a composition, this almost always meant that he had attained the aim he had had before him, and he very seldom returned to a work to which he had once written *Finis*. A well-known case in which he did so is that of the *Leonora* Overtures Nos. 2 and 3. An earlier case, but one that is of some importance in tracing Beethoven's development, is less well known. An Octet for wind instruments (published after his death as op. 103), a cheerful piece that appears to have been thrown off without much labour, may have been intended for *Tafelmusik* for the Elector at Bonn, though it was probably not composed until Beethoven went to Vienna. Some years later he arranged this as a String Quintet, op. 4. A comparison of the two versions is more instructive than all speculation on the subject of poetic programmes. What distinguishes the later from the earlier arrangement is not just the more skilful part-writing and treatment of the thematic material, nor, with the possible exception of a touch of harmonic daring in the transition to the recapitulation, any greater 'originality'; rather is it a feeling for co-ordination of the whole, of which even then he was possessed. The first subject is given a more prominent part in the movement; a certain amount of dead wood is cut out of the bridge passages; the seams are caulked; and the various subjects and episodes are drawn more tightly together. And with this he occupied himself at a time when, to judge by the works he was pouring out one after the other, ideas were coming to him thick and fast. Thus seriously did he take it, if he considered the composition worth the trouble, when once he had the feeling that he had not attained the aim he had set himself; when, in fact, he had failed to achieve that degree of perfection that at the moment he was capable of achieving.

It is this work, by no means one of the most important of his early ones, to which the frequent assertion that his first compositions were in the style of Haydn and Mozart is most applicable. This is certainly the case, for he was never a revolutionary. Nothing was more foreign to his artistic nature than any desire to break with tradition. Neither the rhythms nor the harmonies of his youthful works are any bolder than was then customary; his lay-out is more regular, often indeed more primitive; his tunes are more homely and often more robust, and undoubtedly less differentiated than in the case, particularly, of Mozart; nor do they always show any great degree of individuality. It is of course not to be wondered at that he did not at once attain the perfection of Haydn or Mozart in their maturity. His contemporaries said that he was a "coarser Haydn"—and were certainly wrong. They merely had a dim notion that with these works an entirely new force was beginning to push its way into music, though outwardly Beethoven's music still seemed to be dominated by the old form.

That Beethoven's music was from the very beginning more impassioned than that of his predecessors is obvious; but it would be wrong therefore to overlook the profound passion inherent in Mozart's music. In the case of Beethoven it would perhaps be more accurate to speak of a new kind of passion, a tense and forward-striving impetus, which, however, as has recently been recognized, is less typical of Beethoven in particular than of the age in general. Motives charged with this same quality are to be found in contemporary French music, which had been pressed into the service first of the Revolution and then of the Republic. The *élan terrible* of this *musique à l'usage des fêtes nationales* seems to have been very much after Beethoven's heart. (There were distinguished men among these musicians of the Revolution, such as Cherubini, whom Beethoven greatly admired, and Méhul, Grétry, Kreutzer, and others.) But it is just because we are aware of this similarity that we can properly estimate Beethoven's achievement. Music would have taken a very different direction if it had been overwhelmed by this *élan*, this unbridled outburst of feeling and emotion. The French tried to ward off this danger by a stern and often rigid classicism; in Germany the *Lied* was the harbinger of romanticism. Beethoven alone dared to raise still higher the marvellous, towering edifice of the classical sonata and symphony. He introduced this new tension into the form perfected by Haydn, which, though expanded by his genius to undreamt-of dimensions, was yet prevented from bursting asunder by the —in the deepest sense—ethically guided strength of his creative will. Only if we understand it so are we in a position to express any conclusive opinion on the subject of Beethoven's 'passion'. This is not confined merely to expression in individual themes or in melodic development; its aim is the realization of the 'whole'. Even in his early works, such as the first movements of op. 1, no. 3, and op. 2, no. 1, this is clearly in evidence. In the former the intensity of the principal subject is continued, undeterred by the pause, into the succeeding passage, and maintained even in the second subject, which is introduced in masterly fashion and intimately connected with what precedes it. Such treatment was then entirely new. (Compare with this the first and last movements of Mozart's glorious and impassioned C minor Sonata.) And no less new was the terseness and concentrated energy with which the whole first movement of the First Sonata is developed from the principal motive. This is true Beethoven. And henceforth he proceeds in unbroken development up to the works of his maturity and his last period.

To be sure, the passion of these early works is, in comparison with many of his mature works, kept well within bounds. Not before he had gained complete mastery over his means did he venture to write movements such as the first of the Fifth Symphony, the Finale of the Seventh, or those of the so-called *Appassionata*. From the point of view of expression alone there is even to-day something almost formidable about these movements, and in this respect they are not equalled, far less surpassed, by any later music, however passionate. This force of expression was, and indeed still is, often misunderstood, for it has been regarded as destructive of form. The truth, however, is that in Beethoven's hands it is always combined with almost superhuman discipline and circumspection, which never leave him even when, as in the Finale of the Seventh, he appears to be furiously raging. But this fury he throughout holds under the strictest control. It is only very seldom that he gives full expression to his feelings in his sonatas and symphonies; and even when he does he never quite gives them their head, but keeps them obedient to the 'law of the whole'. Far more often, in fact, does he go for the sake of this law to the other extreme, and by his reticence disappoint the hearer whom the sudden appearance of a melody of exceptional loveliness has led to expect a few moments of emotional indulgence.

Beethoven was well aware that this law was the power to which his creative work was subject. In 1814 he rearranged *Fidelio* a second time—a piece of work that consisted mainly of the alteration of details, and caused him much trouble. While doing so he wrote to the poet Treitschke, who was helping him with the text, in an attempt to explain why it was taking so long: "In my instrumental music also I always keep in mind the work as a whole." But nine years later he talked to a young musician, Schlösser, to whom as to many others he had shown kindness, explaining in considerable detail his methods of composition. What Schlösser tells us has the ring of truth: ". . . Since I know exactly what I want, the underlying idea never leaves me; it rises and grows upward, and I see and hear before me the image in all its dimensions, complete in itself . . . You will ask me where my ideas come from; that I cannot tell you with any confidence, for they come unbidden, direct or indirect; I could grasp them almost, while I am walking in the open country or in a wood, inspired by the moods that a poet translates into words and that I translate into music; they sound and resound in my ears, they ring out tempestuously, until at last they stand before me in notes."

So, caught at the right moment by a man who could truly understand him, Beethoven spoke words that decide the question once for all—nay, touched the deepest secret of his creative work. Surely it should have been impossible to misunderstand these crystal-clear words. It was not 'poetic' ideas of which he spoke, or he would never have said that they came "unbidden"; the moods that a poet translates into words led in Beethoven's case to musical thoughts that were gradually materialized into notes, that is, into musical formations of the utmost significance. But from the very beginning, fully conscious of his artistic will, he relates these formations to the 'underlying idea', which is not entirely realized until the moment they have taken final shape. There is no doubt that by 'idea' he meant nothing but what he had previously called "the work as a whole". They are purely musical ideas, and there is therefore nothing to be said about them in words except possibly by way of pointing out the purely musical facts. The idea of a movement is never identical with its principal, or germinal, motive; rather does it embrace everything that happens apart from this motive and its transmutations. In many cases we learn from the sketch-books of the existence of these ideas in their most primitive form— ideas in the stage of germination and growth—in which the theme has not yet been found; thus, the sketches for the first movement of the Seventh Symphony adumbrate the idea, although as yet only the rhythm of the actual theme is fixed. The wonderful slow movement of the op. 106 Sonata seems to have come to birth in the same way, for Beethoven had the idea of the movement in his head long before the theme had 'occurred' to him, or rather had taken the shape that from the outset had been latent within him. In particular he had that mysterious digression into G major clearly in view from the very beginning, although the theme as a whole had not yet begun to take shape in his mind. In other cases the course of events seems to have been reversed, and the idea to have been developed from the principal theme; thus the first subject of the G major Concerto evidently occurred to Beethoven while he was engaged on the first movement of the Fifth Symphony, as a 'mutation', so to speak, of the rhythmic shape of the theme of the latter; and it was only gradually that the movement as a whole was built up out of it. It also happened that the idea of a movement only became quite clear to the composer during the progress of his work. Thus it was in the Adagio of the Ninth Symphony, the middle section (Andante) of which was added later; and also in the first movement of the *Appassionata*, which originally had no major theme. The procedure is always the same fundamentally: it is not a question of establishing outer 'harmony' or uniformity—of 'rounding off' a movement—but of giving it true inner, organic unity. The word 'organic' is used here advisedly and in its fullest sense, though admittedly a work of art achieves its *Gestalt*[5]—its organic structure—in a different way to a natural organism. The point is that in both cases a living thing is created, the individual parts of which, though their form is by no means finally and definitely fixed, obey a mysterious 'law of the whole' that decides the place of each in the completed organism. What Aristotle called 'entelechy'—without defining this conception more closely—is nothing more than this; nor, moreover, is the conception of *Gestalt* that was the central point of the philosophy of Goethe in his maturity: the self-contained structure, of which all the parts are welded into a living unity; the structure that in the truest sense has 'entity' (being) and thus is the aim of all 'change and growth' (becoming)—in such a way, however, that this growth itself varies in accordance with the ceaseless transmutations of the living structure and gives reality, in an ever increasing degree, to its true meaning. Thus wrote Goethe:

"Gestaltung, Umgestaltung
des ewigen Sinnes ewige Unterhaltung."
(Shaping and reshaping: eternal pastime of the eternal Mind.)

It is highly significant that during the years in which, in Goethe's mind, this idea—the greatest achievement of the classical spirit since Greek antiquity—was growing both in range and in clarity, in Beethoven's creative work a constructive principle based on the same idea should have been attaining perfection: music that in every theme, every melody, is raised to the highest degree of significance and the highest power of expression of its 'entity', and that at the same time contains within itself the greatest potentiality of growth and change.

It is of course not to be supposed that this organic 'shaping' began and ended with Beethoven. Every true work of art is in one way or another subject to this law of unity, and it applies with particular force in the cases of Haydn and Mozart. In the latter, unity is achieved mainly through the feeling and expression of his melodies—something that cannot be defined in words—which even reconcile contrasts; while in the former it is due more to the wonderfully developed sense of balance that enabled Haydn's co-ordinating artistic intellect to set in their proper place in the structure of a movement those themes, often many-shaped and themselves subject to change, with which his sonatas especially seem to abound. In both cases however the 'whole' is also determined by the structural pattern of the sonata, to which all details must conform and upon which they depend. To-day we see in this pattern—this framework—something more than the occasion for the "trite repetition of florid phrases" that offended Wagner as much as the rule of thumb "half-close" and the "noisy final cadence"; for when it is genius that makes use of these academic elements we can feel the life that is in them. It is true no doubt that through Haydn's and Mozart's acceptance of this structural pattern their works seem to us to be different examples of the same *genre*, the difference lying rather in quality and significance than in kind. It is not by chance, or owing simply to external circumstances, that their sonatas, chamber music, and symphonies so often appeared in groups. In Beethoven we find only one group of this kind, viz. the six String Quartets of op. 18; and it is just these works, in spite of some amazingly mature and characteristic movements, that on the whole are most in the style of his predecessors, particularly of Mozart. To his memory Beethoven may perhaps have wanted to pay homage as Mozart paid homage to Haydn with his famous six Quartets. But though Beethoven published three Trios together as op. 1 and three Piano Sonatas as op. 2, this grouping, especially in the case of the Sonatas, emphasizes not the type, but on the contrary the individuality, of each separate work. Here we see the first and most crucial contribution that Beethoven brought to music. The structural laws of the sonata are no less valid than they were—in a certain sense they even gain in significance: but the formulary elements, the mere scaffolding, now yield precedence to the thematic, or are themselves made use of thematically or even melodically. Though in the case of Haydn or Mozart, in spite of the marvellous unity and balance of their works as a whole, we can still separate the vessel from its contents, or at least see them separately, we can no longer do so in the case of Beethoven. Vessel and contents

are now one. This is especially clear in the bridge passages leading from the first to the second subjects, whose function, as a
rule, was originally simply to modulate from the principal key
to its dominant, or in minor movements to its relative major.[6]
This function still of course exists; but Beethoven either gives
these bridge passages independent melodic expression, which
in its intensity often almost surpasses the principal subject, or
else he links the bridge so closely with that subject that the
second is upon us before we are aware of the transition. In other
cases, again, the second subject leads direct into the concluding
theme, and only there finds its real close. The development section, however, which formerly gave the composer an opportunity for the free exercise of his imagination and for thematic and
figurational play, is now almost always designed so as to point
throughout to the recapitulation, and is as tense as the other
sections. Always it is a new kind of unity that is created; we hear
every work as an organism of a special and very individual nature, not so much because of the variety of its moods—moods
that can be described in words—as of the logical way in which
the form of the movement or of the work as a whole grows in-
dependently out of the thematic material. Beethoven's tunes
are, indeed, tremendously rich and comprehensive in expression and feeling; but that each one of them gives us the impression that it has its own 'personality' is due not to this, but to the
strength and firmness of its construction. Therefore also the
'meaning' of his works is to be discovered from their organic
structure only and not from their emotional content; and what
we call the 'development' of Beethoven's art can only be properly understood provided we realize that this fundamental principle of organic construction remained for him the same through
every period of his creative life, and that the content of his works
up to the very end consists of music and nothing else, so that it
is impossible, by translating it into words, to make its language
comprehensible to any one who is incapable of understanding it
as such. Even his latest works are in as strict sonata form as the
earliest, though now, it is true, they give the impression that
this form is no longer a mere rule of thumb, but has been in-

vented for the occasion, since what is to be said could be said in no other way with such lucidity and perfection, or with such cogent musical logic.

Let it not be said that this individualization is merely the first step on the road that music must anyhow have taken. 'Individuality' in any single composition is by no means distinctive of nineteenth-century music; in the case neither of Schubert nor of Chopin, of Schumann nor of Brahms, has any single work as much individuality as in the case of Beethoven. It is perhaps mostly so with Brahms, as indeed it is in him that Beethoven's spirit chiefly lives. But even so, Brahms's own personality is stronger than that of any single one of his works. This has nothing to do with whether his musical language is more or less subjective—that of the great nineteenth-century masters is undoubtedly more personal than Beethoven's. Nevertheless, in their case, and particularly in that of Schumann and Chopin, the individuality of each separate work is much less strongly marked than in that of Beethoven; with them the quality that impresses the hearer is common to all their compositions. What creates the impression of individuality is the particular nature of the composer's emotional world, which is manifested in his works. In the case of Beethoven this is the 'living structure' of each individual work developed to the point at which its essential character is most clearly defined. Here again we see how near he stands to Goethe. Some words that the latter wrote to Zelter are appropriate: "No one will understand that in both Art and Nature the highest, and indeed the only, activity is 'shaping', or that in the structure—the thing shaped—it is 'differentiation', so that everything may become, be, and remain individual and significant."

Is it not in the separate work as a self-contained 'individuality' raised to its highest significance, that is to be found the one root cause of all the misunderstanding by which the phenomenon known as 'Beethoven' is still surrounded? From all experience it is neither the open-minded listener nor the executant musician, professional or amateur, who, when he listens to these works, is tempted to seek, in some extra-musical domain behind the actual notes, an explanation of the peculiarity of each work; it is not they, but the man with a speculative mind, unless he is guided by a very sure musical instinct. And in this he falls into the same error as those who take Beethoven's personality as proof that his music is not like that of other masters. True, his relations to his age, and to the powerful and wealthy men of that age, were different from those of his great predecessors. Bach was throughout his life dependent on the authorities who paid him and who often treated him as a mere official. Haydn was for years in the employment of Prince Esterhazy, to whose wishes he had to bow; and later he took his orders, as it were, from London society. Mozart never rose to be anything higher than the 'poor musician' who lived by the grace of the wealthy and upon the proceeds of such demand for his services as came from the theatrical managers, and who certainly did not end his troubles when, conscious of his own genius, he took arms against them. But Beethoven, in the same city and in a short space of time, succeeded in winning for himself a position in society that made him independent of it. He soon let it be known that he was prepared to stand no nonsense, and he was treated accordingly. When he accepted a commission, he carried it out as he, and not his principal, thought proper. With a very few exceptions he was the first composer to decide for himself what to compose, and also the first who managed to live almost entirely on the proceeds of his works in the open market. In all this he was the true child of the 'new age'; and in that age his compositions certainly held a different position from those of his predecessors in theirs. It is true that Bach, with his forceful personality, stood head and shoulders above the generality of people around him, and almost every bar he wrote bears the unmistakable stamp of that personality. Yet the whole of his creation is the inevitable fulfilment of historical tendencies. It is as if the spirit of music were expressing through it all the hopes and possibilities that were only half realized in his predecessors' works, and what had to be expressed in order to bring to maturity a growth that had lasted for centuries. This is no less the case with Haydn and Mozart, for their works also have their definite place in their age,

g

and to their genius fell the task of first giving reality to what had merely been hinted at in the work of men of smaller talent. With Beethoven this was much less the case. Apart from his very slender association with the *élan terrible* of French revolutionary music, he troubled himself very little with what went on around him in the musical world, so far as this was not concerned with the perfection of his immediate predecessors, Haydn and Mozart. There was nothing in their works to point to anything beyond themselves: no greater perfection seemed possible. All that Beethoven did for the sonata and the symphony was his own personal achievement; he stood alone, with nothing but his own strength to rely upon. It is easy to read a sociological lesson into all this, to explain Beethoven's work by reference to the political convulsions, and particularly to the social readjustments, of the time. We know indeed how profoundly his humanity was touched by events around him. And it is certainly true that his symphonies—and not only the Ninth—were written for a different audience to those before whom Haydn's and Mozart's were performed. This applies to the outer dimensions of the music as well as to its inner expressional force; but from it we shall never understand the phenomenon of Beethoven's creative power. This was opposed to the existing tendency towards disintegration of the old social structure, or better, it held its own in the struggle with the forces of disintegration that manifested themselves on the surface of things, and so it revealed the existence of forces that lay deeper. It was the reverse in the case of the music of *Sturm und Drang*, in which form became less strict during a period in which society was at least superficially secure. The Mannheimers, as well as Bach's sons, were in the service of Royalty and the nobility, who accepted this music exactly in the same way as they did the purely decorative baroque 'society music' that was still firmly seated in public favour. That Beethoven succeeded, at a time when all culture was menaced with disintegration, in firmly establishing form, was owing to his own creative genius, which was subject only to his own will and was not dependent upon any sociological condition whatever. But in this he certainly stood alone, visible from afar in the greatness and uniqueness of his personality. This superficial critics have often mistaken for sheer arbitrariness, which, they claim, was purely subjective and destructive of form; whereas its efforts were in reality directed, with inexorable consistency and with a moral power that commands our admiration, to realizing the 'objective', and to preserving and further developing organic structure in art. In each new work this structure is achieved afresh, and so firmly established that it has succeeded in making its influence felt ever since.

This mistaking of strength for brutality, and of the uniqueness of his creation for egotism and high-handedness, even today stands in the way of a true grasp of Beethoven's essential nature. And even to-day many people can see only one side of it. It is as if he had written nothing but the popular Sonatas—the *Pathétique*, the *Moonlight*, or the *Appassionata*—or the Third, Fifth, and Ninth Symphonies; or as if it were only these works that reflect his true and essential nature; or, finally, as if the equally numerous compositions that give us a blessed sense of ease and relaxation and are full of unclouded serenity, were mere incidental works. But these are no less important and no less indicative of the true Beethoven. Even the magnificent cast of his face taken in 1812 is often misunderstood in the same way, for in reality the inexorable sternness of his features implies neither melancholy nor the despair of loneliness, but the wonderful concentration of the creative mind. If we did not know Beethoven's face, or anything of his life, if we knew him from his work alone, it is very doubtful whether we should be able to draw a picture of any significance of Beethoven the man, as we should be able to without difficulty in the case of Haydn, Mozart, Schumann, Chopin, and Brahms. Would it not then be almost as with Shakespeare, whose human personality, in spite of all our efforts to grasp it, always vanishes behind his work? The 'handwriting' of the two great men is of course unmistakable, so that doubt as to the genuineness or otherwise of their compositions can at the most arise in incidental or youthful works; and the intensity and depth of humanity are the same in each. But Beethoven's humanity is so entirely merged in his works, so entirely objectivized, and in particular, if we look at his productions in their entirety, so universal, that it is wellnigh impossible to realize that the creator of this world of music was a mortal being endowed with individual characteristics. It is not his many-sidedness alone, though this is amazing enough—witness the three Piano Sonatas of op. 31, which themselves are early works. These reflect not merely three different moods, but three separate and distinct worlds of feeling, between which there is contact in hardly a single bar. And it is only consistent that their structure also should be different. They were composed in one year, that of the three Violin Sonatas, op. 30, which are no less different from each other than from each of the Piano Sonatas. What wealth of possibilities, what power of creating objective images, is inherent in each one of these works!

In Shakespeare, it is true, this power of creating objective images operates in another way than with Beethoven; that is to say, it is not directed, as in the case of the latter, at the self-contained organic form of each separate work, but only at the action and the characters. The form of his plays is more loose-knit, so that it is often quite possible, without affecting the substance of the play, to shorten, transpose, or even entirely cut scenes. With Beethoven the least alteration or omission is out of the question. To find organisms of equal strength and perfection of structure in the realm of poetry and literature, we must turn to the Tragedies of Sophocles. Even in Goethe we find but little: *Iphigenie* and *Tasso*, perhaps, certainly not *Faust*, attempts to compare the general design of which with the Ninth Symphony have recently been made. With Kleist, a contemporary of Beethoven, it is another matter. Here we find a passion for the organic structure of the 'work as a whole' that is directly reminiscent of Beethoven. *Penthesilea*, for instance, is not so much like a symphonic poem in the modern sense, as like a true classical symphony, and his splendid but unfinished work, *Robert Guiscard*, reminds us, in its power and its close-packed tension, of the exposition sections of many of Beethoven's first movements. At the same time we must beware of overlooking one essential difference: in Beethoven's works this concentration of the passions shows only 'one side of the world', and in none of them does he allow us to forget that there is another side. Kleist's world-image is cast in the mould of this passion: he never relaxes, never sits back in peace and quietness; at the most he allows a glimmer of light to shine dimly through the twilight of a dream. In spite therefore of the plastic significance of its form, a drama of Kleist is almost always purely subjective, whereas Beethoven, even when he seems to have unchained all his spiritual forces, far outsteps the bounds of the subjective.

If, as we follow this process of objectivization in Beethoven's sketch-books, we see in it nothing but a passionate and indefatigable striving after perfection, we cannot be said to have grasped it in its full depth. There are many kinds of perfection, and it is to be found in almost all ages; but never in the history of all the ages and all the arts has there ever been such perfection as that of the great theme of the Finale of the Ninth Symphony. It was only after prolonged experiment, which led him after strangely false scents, that Beethoven at last found its true and final shape. The perfect growth of this tune is clear for all to see; but it is impossible to state in words what is the basis of that profound expression that, as Wagner finely said: "inspires us with sacred awe." Absolute simplicity and an unsurpassable, elemental straightforwardness of melodic and harmonic development, like those of certain of Haydn's themes, notably the Andante from the *Surprise* Symphony, are combined with dignity and a sublime spiritual breadth. All individuality, all superfluity, all expression derived solely from poetic ideas, are avoided.[7] Even Beethoven did not always go so far as he did here, where it was a question of music of the utmost nobility and the most enduring grandeur. But fundamentally his object was always the same; he never rested until he had found the simplest, the most 'absolute', and, objectively, the most valid form for each and every musical phrase, even the most specialized and the spiritually richest; that is, until he had eliminated every trace of the individual and subjective. For him perfection meant, primarily, simplicity and inevitability, and not merely homogeneity of growth or unity of structure. "*Immer einfacher!*"—

"Simplify, simplify!"—he once wrote in his sketch-book as a reminder for himself. The wonder is that this simplicity is never purchased at the price of spiritual values: yet the simpler he is, the closer and fuller is the texture, and the greater is the degree of spirituality—witness a theme like that of the middle movement of the *Appassionata*. But it is true that this spirituality is of a special kind; it is just as much objective as the music itself, if for a moment we may venture to divide the indivisible. Perhaps a comparison will serve as an indication of a striking point: in the principal theme of Mozart's G minor Quintet, which portrays the very acme of sorrow and suffering, we hear the lamentation of one who stands bodily before us, distinct and individual; but in the 'arioso dolente' of Beethoven's op. 110 Sonata it is the lamentations of humanity itself that we hear. In spite of its unique form, in spite of its touching pathos and spiritual clarity, this music points to far-off regions whence the cry of no individual being can reach us. Hence the variety of spiritual meaning in most of Beethoven's music, and the possibility of various 'interpretations' in its performance. Haydn and Mozart can only be played well or badly: Beethoven in many different ways, for there is no one 'right' way. Here, and here only, is to be found the secret of the depth of his music. And so it is open to the full depth of the universe, in which everything spiritual is as yet undifferentiated, 'transparent' against the background before which all action takes place. It is the same 'transparency' that we find in Shakespeare's plays: the fateful vicissitudes, and the terrifying reality, that we experience in *King Lear*, are only the foreground through which something greater, wider, and more universal than the actual substance of the play is seen; though, indeed, this substance does not detract from the value of all that happens in the foreground, but on the contrary raises it to its full significance. In Shakespeare as in Beethoven, foreground and background are an indivisible unit; the latter only comprehensible in the former, and the more completely comprehensible the deeper and more intensely we experience all that happens in the foreground.

'Objective' and 'absolute': these words we must also apply to

Bach's music if we want to describe accurately the quality that raises it above the level of common humanity. In Beethoven they have a somewhat different meaning. Bach creates objectively, looking out upon mankind from his safe retreat, and enfolded in the arms of the divine grace. Beethoven stands in the middle of the battle-field of the human passions and joins boldly in the fray; but always his gaze is fixed upon the absolute, and he never rests until he is satisfied that his works are fully imbued with that quality.

From this can be understood the importance or otherwise of the much discussed but often misunderstood contrasts in Beethoven's music. Here too a comparison with Shakespeare is helpful, for he also made something new and mystic out of that age-old artifice, poetic contrast. He is not satisfied merely to place contrasts side by side and so to let one set off the other; he makes them penetrate one another, combines the gay and the serious, the comic and the tragic, often at the same moment and in the same character: witness the Fools, in many of his plays, with their underlying melancholy and thoughtfulness; the grave-diggers in *Hamlet;* a considerable part of *The Merchant of Venice;* and *Troilus and Cressida*, the subject of so many controversies, a play that lies half-way between jest and earnest. Beethoven also found in the music of his predecessors this same artifice. Mozart was indeed a master of contrast, in his operas (especially *The Magic Flute* and *Don Giovanni*) as well as in his symphonies, particularly the last two, the G minor and the *Jupiter*. But the contrasts always stand out clearly against each other; in the operas they appertain as it were to various strata of the spiritual structure, and in his absolute music they create a sense of balance between the different emotions. True to the laws of the sonata, Beethoven also began in this way; but very soon we find in his music contrasts of an entirely different kind, by which balance appears at first glance to be destroyed. When, in the Largo of the op. 7 Sonata, towards the end of a pianissimo phrase, he marks one single, harmonically conspicuous bass chord on the weak beat of the bar with a double forte, this is something more than a mere 'effect' in the style of the humorous

drum beat in Haydn's *Surprise* Symphony; it is as if amid the
solemn peace of the movement a chasm had suddenly opened at
our feet. There are many similar cases, and later we find them to
a much greater degree. A good example is the fortissimo B
natural in the Finale of the Fourth Symphony, which pushes its
violent and baleful way into the cheerful and innocuous playfulness of the semiquaver figures; and still more impressive is the
well-known blustering F sharp minor passage in the Finale of
the Eighth Symphony, which is both dynamically and harmonically startling. It is often a purely harmonic contrast, like the D
sharp in the first movement of the Violin Concerto, which
comes like a bolt from the blue and intrudes upon the clear and
serene D major harmonies. Or the contrast may be simply melodic, like the little oboe phrase during the pause, in the recapitulation of the first movement of the Fifth Symphony. The way in
which the tension is for a moment relaxed, and the hearer is
given a glimpse of the 'other side' of the world is truly marvellous. Other cases will be noticed in Part III, the Survey of the
Compositions. It is always this other side—the background—
that is effective, not indeed that it in any way obliterates the
effect of what has gone before, but that it is like a light shining
from the depths. The various strata, which in Mozart were clear
and distinct, are often to be seen in the later works both in com-
bination and in opposition; and so the 'world-background' becomes visible.[8]

But this also applies to most of those contrasts of a different
kind in Beethoven's music, in which one mood follows another,
apparently in the old way. The greatest example of this is the
opening of the Finale of the Fifth Symphony, which is prepared,
under terrific tension, by the nebulous harmonies and melodies
of the third movement. That it is not in fact a case of two independent parts being merely juxtaposed is at once clear when,
as is sometimes unfortunately done on festal occasions, the
Finale is performed by itself. When played in their proper place,
the first few bars give us the impression of sudden release from
almost intolerable tension; when torn from their context they
have an effect of both brutality and vapidity, although admitted-

ly they usher in something that is entirely new and that logically speaking requires no preparation at all. The sense of these bars and of all that grows out of them is not only injured but completely destroyed by being thus torn from their context, because the third movement is not a mere exercise in 'preparation by contrast', but forms one inseparable unit with the Finale. The past is not dead and done with; it remains as a living background until in the working-out it once more appears as the foreground, when light is shed upon it by the background of the theme of the Finale. No such passages are to be found in Haydn or Mozart, though they also wrote Introductions that contrasted with and set off what was to come, and though in Haydn's early B major Symphony the third movement reappears in the Finale. But here contrast is never indispensable to the meaning of any individual passage. To omit the beautiful Introduction of Mozart's great E flat Symphony would, indeed, be to eliminate an 'effect', and perhaps to destroy the architecture of the work; but it would in no way rob the Allegro of its vital meaning or its depth of expression. But in Beethoven, the true nature of a theme or a melody is very often revealed only by its connexion with the preceding passage. It is therefore proof of complete misunderstanding to reproach Beethoven with being "trivial" in passages like those referred to above, or similar ones, such as the beginning of the last movement of the great B flat Trio, op. 97, or—a passage that should be taken perfectly seriously—that in the Finale of the Ninth Symphony in which the big drum, cymbals, and triangle are prominent. Whoever does so shows that he is incapable of hearing a work as a whole, and, moreover, that he listens superficially. He who really listens cannot fail to appreciate the skill with which, here as elsewhere, Beethoven creates musical images of the highest significance, developing them, building up climaxes, and describing bold curves, and so raising the simplest and most primitive material into the sphere of the highest art. This is what Schumann meant when he said that Beethoven "often finds his themes in the gutter and turns them into universal maxims."

Only from this standpoint can the question that is often

raised—whether Beethoven is to be counted among the Classics or the Romantics—be considered in its full range and import; and only from this standpoint is any definite answer possible. If by 'classical' we understand only 'perfect according to pattern', the answer does not much matter, for we find such perfection in Gothic and Romantic art, and even in the Primitives. But if in the Classics we recognize the very precise *Weltansicht* —that definite view of the world as a whole—that was first given reality by the Greeks during the period of their highest culture, and which is to be found again and again throughout the centuries in the works of the greatest minds, to dominate a whole epoch for the first time in Goethe's poetry and *Naturanschauung* (view of nature), an epoch that we are rightly accustomed to call the 'classical'—then our understanding of Beethoven certainly depends very much upon the answer to this question. He was a contemporary of the Romantics, of the brothers Schlegel, of Tieck, Hölderlin, Hegel, and Schelling; and it was they, through the mouth of Bettina Brentano, who originated the legend of the "Romantic Beethoven," which, as Arnold Schmitz has shown, was current throughout the nineteenth century and coloured people's view of him both as man and as musician. Schmitz exposes the falsity of this legend and gives prominence to those traits in his essential character and his whole mental and spiritual outlook that separate him from the Romantics. Everything that has so far been discovered supports this view. The deeper we delve into the essence of Beethoven's music the more obvious it is that it belongs to the classical world, and the more clearly it is divided from the romantic. Seen from the standpoint of Haydn and his age, it appears as a further organic development, each phase of which can be traced, but which soon led to a world that could not but be alien to that age. None could then foresee the fate of the sonata, in what stupendous structures and dimensions this concept of form was to be embodied. Romantic music has throughout had a different aim. In it the sonata was developed no more than the fugue was developed after 1750. The principal concern of romantic music was melody; not only the vocal melody of *Lied* or opera—not, that is to say, melody as a self-contained form, at any rate to the same extent as in Beethoven—but also melody as the uninhibited expression of all the wealth of romantic 'feeling', even to that complete self-surrender of which Beethoven, obedient to the 'law of the whole', still fought shy. It is easy to show how loose-knit, for all the intensity of their expression, even the loveliest of Weber's or Schubert's melodies are in comparison with Beethoven's. Here too, as after 1750, the old structure was taken to pieces, as we may see principally in the larger instrumental works. The form of Weber's and the young Schubert's sonata movements was primitive in comparison not only with Beethoven's but also with Haydn's and Mozart's. With them indeed form is a mere rule of thumb, whose purpose is to provide some sort of solid ground and framework for melodic 'inspiration'. It is a different matter with Schubert in his maturity. In his later sonatas, chamber music, and the great C major symphony, we find here and there a movement that shows a perfection of growth worthy of Beethoven himself; witness for instance the slow movement of the E flat Trio, op. 100, in which everything that follows the first bar develops strictly in accordance with the rules from the rhythmic germ of that bar, with its last accented quaver. If only this most richly endowed man had not died at the age of thirty-one, the probability is that, with this as a starting-point, the classical sonata would have developed still further. At that time this could have taken place at the hands of none but Schubert. In Chopin's works, sonata form as a problem is of less importance than smaller and freer forms, supreme as the mastery was with which he handled them; and full as Schumann's sonatas and symphonies are of glorious music, we often feel that fundamentally the spirit of the sonata is antagonistic to it. None of the great works of Schumann is as perfect as the C major Fantasy, op. 17, in which romantic feeling, free of all fetters, soars passionately and rapturously upward. Not for several decades did Brahms fight his way back to classical lucidity out of the confusion of romantic 'storm and stress', and embody again in his maturest works the idea of the sonata in a new shape.

The links that, in spite of all differences, connect Beethoven with the Romantics can be easily traced. That Schubert in his later compositions here and there obeys the 'law of the whole' as Beethoven understood it, has already been mentioned. On the other hand, apart from the *Pastoral* Symphony, which is in a class by itself and which here and there anticipates Schubertian effects, there is much in Beethoven's later music that seems almost to be preparing the way for Schumann: motives and melodies charged with vagrant emotions and appearing to lack any definite close, such as in the first movements of the Piano Sonatas opp. 101 and 109, in the Violin Sonata op. 96, and especially in the last Quartets. But the difference will at once be perceived on comparison of a tune like the first subject of the Schumann Fantasy, which from its opening chord—the dominant seventh—to the end seems to be floating in mid air and never touches ground with the tonic, with a similar composition by Beethoven, or of one of the Bagatelles, op. 126, with any of Schumann's smaller pieces. As Arnold Schmitz rightly says, Beethoven tests each detail for its capacity to bear the weight of the building. The style of the structure, in which every part is arranged in due order, is truly classical, and not, as in Schumann's case, romantic. That is to say, here also the aim is still 'organic structure', and not the expression of uninhibited 'feeling'.

But those sudden contrasts, spoken of above, which are only to be found in Beethoven, are also subject to this classical style of structure. They are not known to romantic music—very characteristically, for *its* contrasts arise from changes in the moods and feelings of the 'Ego'. This Ego is affected, now in one way and now in another, by the outer world; and in Schumann it is even split up, according to the manner in which it is so affected, into two beings, Florestan and Eusebius, that alternate in the 'Ego' with more or less gradual transition. But Beethoven sees the contrasts in the outer world as objective entities, and gives them form in his works. They are more abrupt than any romantic contrast, and therefore often seem to imperil the unity of the work. But just as Beethoven includes contrasts in his works because his gaze is directed on *das Ganze der Welt*—the

World as a whole—so, from his devotion to the cause of *das Ganze des Werks*— the Work as a whole—he gathers strength to bend them to his will and to safeguard the unity of that work. Its texture is not destroyed by them, but intensified. He either prepares his contrasts in secret with amazing skill, or causes them to appear in a sudden and arresting flash and to light up the whole work. For the moment one example will suffice: without the sudden fortissimo in the F sharp minor passage, the whole Finale of the Eighth Symphony would lose in both weight and depth, and what was left would be little more than a sort of inspired frolic. But with that sudden outburst a sinister chasm opens; nay, more: a powerful light is thrown on all that has already been heard, and when later it is heard again we find that it has been subjected to some mysterious transmutation.

Those who for this reason dispute that Beethoven is a classic have neither heard him aright nor grasped the true meaning of the classical idea. He has, to be sure, nothing in common with the classicism of his age; but his work in particular proves how important it is to distinguish clearly between the classic and the classicist. The latter attempts, by the adoption of the Greek style which he admires and whose perfection he recognizes, to produce something of his own. His is, as it were, a second-hand style, and this is always found in its pure form where genuine creative power is wanting. This does not mean that results of high artistic merit cannot be arrived at along this road. In the realm of architecture especially, classicism at the beginning of the nineteenth century produced, not only in Europe, works that through their grandeur of conception and their noble proportions are a living force even to-day; and in painting and literature also it has given birth to many great works. If in the case of music it is less appropriate to speak of pure classicism, the reason is that no prototype from the great classical age has been handed down to us. Yet it is hard to believe that Gluck could have written his operas had he not been inspired by his conception of Greek tragedy—false though that conception doubtless is. What differentiates the works of the classicists from those of the true classics is this: the classicist, though conscious of the perfect harmony of the classical world, is unconscious of the background to which this harmony relates. The ideal of classicism is self-contained, and to that extent perfect, form; while that of the true classics is always 'open form'—form that is open to the 'world-background'. The presence of this world-background does not of itself ensure that the work will be truly classical; there are spheres of art in which it is only dimly felt, and in which it does not determine form; and there are others again in which the mystic predominance of the background has the effect even of destroying form. Only in the world of the classics is each figure of the foreground—that which we see as 'real' in a work of art—irradiated by that mysterious light that shines out from the background and so enhances its power and authority. Here foreground and background are one—the 'World as a whole' is given form in the Work.

BEETHOVEN IN 1818
(Portrait in oils by Schimon.
Verein Beethovenhaus, Bonn.)

PART III

THE WORKS

"That can only be said at the piano."—BEETHOVEN

THE ROAD TO MASTERY

WHETHER or no we can say we understand Beethoven depends upon whether we can discern in his early works the original contribution that he brought to music. Something has been said on this subject in Part II, in particular where reference is made to that movement of the Trio, op. 1, no. 3, in which this originality is clearly perceptible. In the early pianoforte sonatas it is still more so. In these works we are conscious of the close sympathy that the master of improvisation felt for this instrument. Here he was free; here those thoughts came to him that gave the most exact expression to all that moved him inwardly. And this it was that, even in those early days, enabled him to compose such a work as the first movement of his first Sonata, op. 2, no. 1.

The economy, the parsimony almost, of this movement, whose two subjects and codetta:

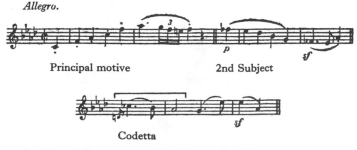

are developed from one motive, is unexampled in all music up to that time.

It must be admitted that the Sonata as a whole does not maintain this level. The slow movement has an entirely uncharacteristic theme taken from a youthful work, and the Minuet is insignificant. The last movement—the first of Beethoven's 'stormy' finales—has, it is true, some magnificent moments, especially the masterly passage in which he prepares for the recapitulation; but the middle section, which takes the place of the normal working-out, is, in its schematic, square-cut structure, simpler than any we should find in the works of his great predecessors.

No greater contrast can be imagined than that between this Sonata and the second, in A major. The first movement of this is loosely knit; and the second subject, which seems to be inserted as an improvisation, has no definite close. (This is not an innovation; a similar tailing off is often found in Haydn's pianoforte sonatas.)

The third Sonata, in C major, is again of a different type. It is brilliant in the sense that, say, Clementi's compositions are brilliant; and in the superficiality of many of the bravura passages we overlook the excellence of certain other parts. This is particularly the case in the development section, in which the principal theme reappears, with a new and unexpected intensity of expression.

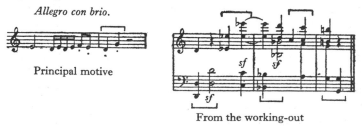

Allegro con brio.

Principal motive

From the working-out

It is, indeed, in the development sections that the new tendency shows most clearly. That is to say, instead of merely playing freely with his thematic material, Beethoven presses forward steadily and clear-sightedly towards his aim—the recapitulation. The entry of this he always prepared with especial care; emphasizing its significance in the structure of the movement as a whole. (It may be noted that Haydn often masks the entry of the recapitulation in his sonatas, evidently on purpose.)

None of these three sonatas has as a whole the perfection of the late sonatas of Haydn and Mozart. That in E flat, op. 7, is the first of Beethoven's that maintains the same high level from start to finish. This, taken as a whole, is his first masterpiece. It is the truest realization of the early Beethoven, and is throughout of the greatest charm of sentiment. The profusion of ideas is curbed with a light but powerful and unerring hand; each one is in its place; and the unity of the first movement is assured not only by the clearly perceptible connexion between the themes, but also by the 6/8 rhythm that takes almost complete command from the very first bar. The drop of a third at the beginning:

Riemann:

is as much a motive (*pace* Riemann!) as the throbbing quavers in the bass or the commencement of the phrase on the up-beat of bar 4. The first subject ends at bar 25, and the second is not reached until bar 68. All that takes place between them is a constant indication of what is coming. The syncopation towards the end of the exposition is of importance, for it converts the 6/8 time into 3/4 time. This is particularly effective in the short development section, in which the syncopation is carried on for sixteen bars, in preparation for the entry of the mysterious A minor passage. It is not only harmonically that we are now far away from the starting-point: yet another new theme appears, first in A minor and then in D minor, which, however, is merely hinted at in passing. The transition to the recapitulation is masterly: how short, after all, is the way back to E flat major! The coda, nearly fifty bars long, is richly elaborated.

There is little to say about the glorious Adagio. Two passages are of special beauty: first, shortly before the return of the first subject, where the principal theme makes a mysterious appearance in B flat, high up in the scale; and second, in the last few bars of the coda, where the bass falls by semitones with the theme making one more shadowy appearance above it. Here, again, note the similarity between the surprising *ff*'s and those in the slow movements of op. 2, nos. 2 and 3. Comparison with the last sonata of Haydn, also in E flat, which was probably composed about the same time and was published in 1798, is of great interest. Beethoven's movement is undoubtedly the more firmly and regularly constructed of the two.

The whole of the third movement is made up of the four-bar motive (bar 4 by itself, bar 4 together with the up-beat of the previous bar, or bars 1–2).

The very beautiful last movement is, up to the coda, the purest and most regularly constructed rondo that Beethoven ever wrote. The coda is, indeed, out of the common; the first subject breaks off with a pause before the end, with an imperfect cadence on B flat, as previously at the entry of the second episode. Again this rises to B, not, as before, with a crescendo leading to C, but with a sudden diminuendo. Actually the note is not B, but C flat. And now the first subject makes a shadowy reappearance in F flat major, *pp*. It disappears as it came, and with a sudden *ffp* we are back in E flat. There follows an epilogue, clearly reminiscent of the second episode (note the sforzati on the fourth quavers in each bar), which in its breadth and ease forms a fitting close to the whole sonata.

It is impossible within the scope of this book to examine all the sonatas in the same detail. Of those forming op. 10, no. 3 in D major is of particular importance, not only for its famous Largo, which in the closeness of its structure forms the climax of the whole work and, for once, serves to heighten and not to relax the tension. The first movement starts straight away in an entirely new style, with a powerful swooping and soaring figure in unison:

Finale

Never before has Beethoven shown us his fist as he does in these first twenty-two bars. That the first four notes are the germinal motive is already clear; this becomes still more manifest as the movement progresses. With the impassioned melody that follows, introduced by the three double octaves marked *ff*, the principal key is not yet quitted (actually it is in the relative minor). In due course, however, it modulates to the dominant, thus preparing the way, in a magnificent episode of thirty bars, with some expressive, rushing passage-work for the second subject. This, strangely enough, does not appear in its full form; instead the germinal motive is played with for a time, as if to allow for relaxation after the mighty soaring flight of the opening. This now reappears immediately in the development section, together with a new theme that is related to the first subject. The development section, *ff* throughout, is like a great single arch leading direct to the recapitulation. The extended coda, some fifty bars long, plays about again with the germinal motive, rising from the subdominant, as is often the case in the coda. The movement seems about to die away, but gathers strength again at the end and builds up a crescendo above a bass in which the germinal motive reappears in augmentation. With the possible exception of the last movement of this sonata, Beethoven wrote no others of the same construction.

The 'largo e mesto' is one of the few really sombre slow movements of Beethoven. He once said to Schindler that he wished to depict in it "the spiritual state of a melancholy man, with all the various nuances of light and shade that make up the picture of melancholy." The opening theme, with the key-note (D) repeated eight times in the first three bars and adjacent notes hovering round it, is indeed deeply melancholy; and this intensity of expression is maintained throughout the movement even where for a moment or two the mood lightens, e.g. at the modulation to C major, bars 13–16. What is new and individual here is the concentrated accumulation of ideas, which are thematically more closely related than is apparent at first sight. In particular the melody of bars 9–17 contains almost all the subsequent motives. Again, nothing like the change of mood that the melody of bars 30–35 undergoes had probably ever been heard before. The broadly figured cadenza leading to the return of the first theme, and particularly that in the coda, after the magnificent crescendo that begins with the theme in the bass, have an effect as of relaxation after subjection to almost intolerable tension. At the close of the movement the first theme, reduced to the dimensions of a motive, dies away, a contrivance that foreshadows the close of the Funeral March from the *Eroica* Symphony and of the *Coriolanus* Overture.

The bright-toned key (D major) of the third movement ('Menuetto, Allegro'), with its graceful, flowing melody, seems like sunshine after cloud.

The fourth movement, in full rondo form with certain characteristics of sonata form, begins like an improvisation, as if Beethoven had taken three notes with the intention of building up a subject on them. It is certainly not by chance that these three notes appear in the first subject of the first movement, where they form part of the germinal motive (notes 5–7). They dominate the Finale as that motive dominates the first movement; and it is only logical and consistent that the close of this movement also should be based upon them.

The *Sonata Pathétique*, op. 13, is one of the most famous of all, and rightly so—even though it is to be feared that its fame rests more on its title, and the mood indicated thereby, than on its actual content. And since the true worth of this content so often goes unrecognized, the work is rated lower, by those to whom it appears somewhat too typical of its age, than other and less 'pathetic' compositions. However this may be, the fact remains that with it Beethoven took an immense stride forward. Never before had he written so concentrated and yet so dynamic and expressive a whole as the first movement of this Sonata. The very introduction (Grave) was a bold stroke, conventional and slightly theatrical as its pathos may here seem to us. It is in reality not an introduction in the older sense of the word, and such as Beethoven himself only uses once again, but is bound up organically with the Allegro. (To some extent a model for this is to be found in the first movement of the late E flat Symphony of Haydn (the *Drum-roll*), in which the introduction not only reappears at the end, but is also touched upon thematically in the

Allegro.) This is only clear in the development section, where the opening motive of the introduction forces its way into the Allegro and is there combined with the principal theme. For the rest, it is mainly an inward and spiritual association that is as difficult to express in words as it is clear and obvious in the hearing. Seven times does this short motive strive to rise, only to fall back defeated. The fate of Sisyphus seems to overtake it in its constant frustrated efforts to attain the heights; and tremendous is the impetus with which the theme of the Allegro at last bursts its bonds and soars aloft unhindered. This upward impulse governs the whole Allegro; and when the conquered heights must be surrendered, this is done with headlong downward rushes, of which, as Engelsmann has rightly observed, the prototype is to be found in the introduction. That the second subject also opens in the minor is only in keeping with the atmosphere of the whole movement, though there is nothing unnatural in the modulation to E flat major, in which key, significantly enough, the stormy impetus of the whole never comes to rest, in spite even of the broad melodic line that dominates this passage. It was a magnificent inspiration that caused Beethoven to insert into the coda a few bars of the Grave, like a shade from the past, thus retarding the close of the movement, and then to finish it off with one last grand assault by the principal theme.

The well-known, but, alas, too often maltreated Adagio is, in spite of the two related subsidiary themes, more simply put together than any of the slow movements we have so far considered. The themes are finely constructed, and their song-like character, in particular that of the first, is maintained throughout the whole movement.

The Finale, too, is a more simple rondo than many other last movements of those days, even though here and there we find hints of sonata form. The likeness of the principal motive to the second subject of the first movement, which has often been remarked on, is of no importance. In spite of the passionate urgency of the movement, its truly rondo-like breadth is, in contrast with the dramatic points of concentration of the first movement, consistently maintained.

The fame of the *Pathétique* obscures other and more modest works of the same period, such as the charming little Sonatas of op. 14. The first of these, in E major, is as a whole of wonderfully light texture. The first movement of the second, in G major, is one of the loveliest and most perfect pieces that Beethoven had up to that time written. In style, moreover, it was quite new; the whole of the exposition, sixty-three bars in length, is a song that proceeds without interruption, full of incident but clear and logical in its articulation, from the gently agitated first bars of the principal theme onwards. Up to the fifth bar the rhythm is doubtful—only from the score is it possible to say exactly where the bar-lines come; and with the fixing of the beat at bar six the mood of the subject entirely changes. (It is known that it was in connexion with this Sonata that Beethoven spoke of the "two principles", (see p. 80) about which, through misconception of the significance of this work, people have often expressed surprise.) The astonishing thing is that the formal lay-out of the work in no way deprives it of its song-like character. Observe also, only to mention one of many fine points, how in the short coda (the last fourteen bars) the main motive is rhythmically clarified and brought into uniformity with the last section of the movement.

The next Sonata, op. 22, Beethoven himself called *Grosse Sonate*, and said of it "*sie hat sich gewaschen*".[9] In actual dimensions it hardly exceeds some of the earlier ones (e.g. op. 2, no. 3, and op. 7), though it certainly does in bigness of style. The energy and spaciousness of the beginning of op. 10, no. 3, is here maintained throughout the whole of the first movement; and the florid passage-work, such as we noted in op. 2, no. 3, is informed with a more individual expression. The development, based entirely on the germinal figure of the principal motive and the last new theme of the exposition, is impressive in the steady and forceful pursuit of its aim. If in spite of its brilliance the Sonata is less of a favourite than the others, this may be due to the Adagio, in which, apart from the beautiful middle section, Beethoven perhaps just fails to touch the high general level of his inspiration. This is the more noticeable if we compare the movement with the Adagio of the first String Quartet, the melodic line in each case being similar. The third movement is a true Minuet. The Finale begins like a rondo; but in the two episodes rondo form is almost entirely abandoned, for they are deprived of their independence in favour of a very significant transition passage, appearing for the first time at bars 18 et seq., which, particularly in the second episode, is worked in true first-movement style. The outstanding feature of the movement is the way it falls into the minor and gradually emerges again.

Beethoven now appears to be seeking a new form for the sonata. The first movements of op. 26 in A flat, and op. 27, no. 1 in E flat and no. 2 in C sharp minor, are not in sonata form. Both no. 1 and no. 2 of op. 27 he marks *quasi una Fantasia*. This argues a tendency towards looser construction, as if Beethoven were now willing to admit into his formal compositions the random inspiration of the moment, to which he gave full rein in his improvisations. That the form of these compositions as a whole in no degree sacrifices its significance thereby is obvious to all who know them. In this respect they even represent a substantial step forward. But in detail, too, almost every movement in them is as firmly knit as in the previous sonatas. As we all know, a first movement in variation form is to be found in Mozart's well-known Sonata in A major. This and Beethoven's op. 26 are in many respects comparable. The unusual form of their first movements seems to influence others: thus, in the Mozart, the Finale is 'Alla Turca', while in the Beethoven, in place of the slow movement, which Mozart transferred to the variations, we find a Funeral March. In each case the minor variation paves the way for the movement in question. It should be noted that in the Scherzo of op. 26, the tonic (A flat major) is not reached for several bars. This is similar to the opening of the later Sonata, op. 90 in E flat; but in the present case the reason is obviously that the ear may have relief after the almost continuous A flat of the first movement. Typical of Beethoven too, is the skill with which, in the middle section of the Scherzo, the harmony (the dominant minor ninth in F minor, C–E–G–B flat–D flat) is maintained for sixteen bars without the least relaxation of the restless energy of the movement. At the same time, the F that immediately follows, at the re-entry of the opening theme, is only an apparent tonic.

That Beethoven conceived the famous Funeral March under the influence of an opera by Paer, as is stated by Ries, is not impossible. In its somewhat decorative style, it may perhaps be said not to reach quite the high level of the other movements—even of the often underrated Finale. This, though it is kept concise, is in complete rondo form. It is full of life and expression, but must certainly not be rattled off like a Study.

This is the only sonata of Beethoven that has no movement in sonata form; and, significantly enough, it is the only one in which there is no true climax.

The first of the two 'Fantasia-Sonatas' of op. 27 begins with a movement in a form that, together with the Fantasia, op. 77, gives us an excellent idea of what Beethoven's free improvisations were like. With the opening theme we seem to see the composer sitting at the piano and dreamily allowing his fingers to strike what chords they will; and even when he collects his thoughts and gives shape to his ideas, as he does for the rest of the movement, all the thematic material and its development remain surprisingly simple. This development does not, indeed, amount to more than figuration and change of position; and the very beautiful middle section, in which a tender tune grows out of the opening chords, remains entirely detached. The composer seems to bear in mind only the bright-toned C major bars of this middle section when he interrupts his dreams with an energetically figured Allegro, out of which, however, no formal development takes place as it does in his other sonatas. The same applies to the Scherzo, which follows without a break, and which, if we regard the first bar as the up-beat, is really in 6/4 time. In spite of its firm and shapely form, this movement shows fewer traces of truly organic construction, such as we expect to find in Beethoven, than any other Scherzo in the whole of the sonatas. This is also the case in the Adagio. It is only in the Finale, which likewise follows without a break, that matters change. As if all that has passed has merely been an introduction, we now find a theme that from the very beginning gives promise of something different. This movement is frequently regarded as a rondo; but, although there is no double bar and repeat, it is important to realize that it is in genuine sonata form, and highly developed at that. The second subject is approached by means of a modulation to F major, the 'dominant of the dominant'; and here for the first time it is kept continuously within the region of that tonality, as if in preparation for the concluding theme, which at last definitely establishes the new tonic, B flat major. With the reappearance of the first subject, the development begins, and pursues its impetuous course to the recapitulation, even imparting its restlessness to the coda. Now the Adagio makes a brief reappearance, throwing, as it were, a noble bridge back to the past. It is the final Presto, however, which is based on a motive from the first subject of the Finale, that gives the movement still more weight and so assures its position as the peak of the whole sonata. Through what a variety of emotions has the composer led us, from those first dreaming chords, down to the Finale, with its sturdy, almost slap-stick humour!

The C sharp minor Sonata is similar in one respect to op. 27, no. 1: its true peak is the Finale. Here again, at the opening of the first movement, Beethoven seems to be improvising, lost in dreams; though in this case both form and emotional content are upon a different level to those of the previous sonata. Here is no embroidering of a simple thought, but a well-defined structure—tender though the hand may have been that shaped it—a melody that slowly rises from repose. Follow this melody through, and observe its transmutations, hardly perceptible at first, and the manner in which the key of C sharp minor extends its sway. The tremendous influence this movement has exercised, even on later music, is due to its complete unity of mood. There is no second subject; and where the middle section would normally come, the melody ceases, leaving the triplets to pursue an independent course. But observe, too, that the movement passes without a break into the Allegretto. To assert that this lovely little movement, so essential for contrast, destroys the unity of the Sonata is to argue one's judgement superficial.

The Finale is one of those famous 'stormy' movements of
Beethoven, the first being the rather naïve Finale of the first
sonata. Even this movement itself is in many respects naïve, especially in the conventional lay-out of the periods. But this is
also true of the thematic material, in particular the first theme of
the second subject, a passionate melody whose first note, D
sharp, is repeated in each bar. The movement is very regular in
form, even in the development section, which, however, lacks
the usual thematic elaboration. The first subject is pure passage-
work, which, though unusual, is in character with the superscription *Quasi una Fantasia*; for it is as if this were merely the
preparation for a true first subject—the passionate melody
already referred to. But this latter is in the dominant, and is
therefore the second subject. What is so fine about the movement is the breathless impetus of its forward rush. This even the
clarity and firmness of the construction never succeed in slowing
up; it is not until the end that the more subdued closing phrase
reins it in and so allows it to recover breath after its headlong
flight. An important point usually overlooked by performers is
that the greater part of the movement is explicitly marked *p*.
Only a few individual chords are marked *ff*, in particular the
very important chord that appears to be that of A major but is in
reality the Neapolitan sixth in G sharp minor.

In later days Beethoven is known to have been annoyed at the
popularity of this sonata, and to have remarked on one occasion
that that in F sharp (op. 78) was far better. Actually its popularity, like that of the *Pathétique*, is no proof of a true understanding of Beethoven's greatness. At the same time it would be
wrong, merely because we feel that this particular type of pathos
dates, to deny the mastery of these two sonatas.

And yet it must be admitted that a composition like the next
sonata, op. 28 in D major, is on a higher level. Again the contrast
between the two contemporary works amazes us. This contrast
is, indeed, one not only of mood but also of structure. So far as
style is concerned, there is nothing to indicate that the works
were composed almost at the same time. Beethoven had never
yet written anything more broadly developed or anything in

which he allowed his feelings freer play, than this first movement. In it melody takes first place: the first and second subjects are broadly flowing tunes, though these, it is true, are genuine 'sonata themes'. It is only the pulsing crotchets at the beginning of the movement that can be described as a 'motive'. The entry of the second subject is magnificent. It does not take place at once when, at bar 61, the key of E major (the dominant of the dominant) is arrived at; instead, a connecting passage is inserted modulating after fourteen bars to C sharp major—the dominant of F sharp minor, which here takes the place of A major. The step up from B sharp to C sharp is repeated, then again a semitone higher, and so after eight bars the harmony again points unmistakably to A major. The progression is now reversed (D to C sharp, at bars 90–91), at which moment it passes into a smoothly flowing tune—the second subject. It is important for the correct understanding and performance of the Sonata that this moment should be recognized. This tune has no true close; after a cadenza-like passage of six bars, the second subject reappears, this time a third higher; the same passage is now repeated and leads to the coda, forty-five bars after the entry of the second subject. It is of interest to note that each theme throughout the movement is repeated in its entirety, a token of the ease and breadth of the movement. The development, too, is unusual. It opens with the principal theme in full, repeats this with a florid accompaniment, takes the last four bars and repeats them three times, now takes the last two bars, which it repeats four times, and now the last bar but one, repeats it nine times, inverts it and so repeats it again and again, first in the treble and then in the bass, shortened to a motive consisting of a minim (or crotchet) and two quavers, treated contrapuntally, until at last nothing remains but the 3/4 rhythm, long after the harmony has come to rest, with a half close, in B minor (the relative minor of the principal key). As a result of all this play with motives the development section is the very antithesis of the exposition, with its broad growth. It shows evidence of deliberately planned contrast. But unity within the movement is not thereby destroyed, as might be thought possible; all this play with motives is firmly held together by ample and lucid harmonic development; and when the themes, in their old breadth, reappear in the recapitulation, they retain some of the motive-like quality that they acquired during the working-out.

The Andante, in D minor, which consists largely of florid, but quite straightforward variation of an unpretentious, romance-like tune, was for a long time Beethoven's favourite piece, and one that he himself was fond of playing. This is significant, for it is the first slow movement entirely devoid of pathos that we have so far encountered. The movement has a striking close: at the sixth bar from the end an entirely new and more serious note is struck, only to die away again immediately.

The downward octave leaps forming the principal motive of the Scherzo are reminiscent of those at the end of the first movement. This motive is made use of with extraordinary skill throughout the Scherzo. No less extraordinary is the Trio, in which an eight-bar theme consisting of two halves, *a* and *b*, similar but with different endings, is repeated four times in reversed order and with varied harmony. This arrangement (*a-b*, *a-b*, *b-a*, *b-a*), is very infrequent in Beethoven.

The final rondo opens with a jolly tune in the bass, like a bear-dance, with a 'folk tune' above it. The bear-dance motive reappears in the treble in the transition to the second episode. This episode suddenly strikes a new note, but the old mood soon returns. What art is concealed beneath this innocent artlessness!

The majority of the works we have considered up to this point bear traces of hard thinking about the problem of the sonata. Other works were composed during the same period—works that showed less evidence of mental struggle and were therefore perhaps in many respects more perfect, but at the same time less individual. Such were the two Violoncello Sonatas, op. 5, composed in haste for a virtuoso player. These are brilliant and charming pieces, laid out on the grand scale, but without the depth that had already shown itself in the piano sonatas. There is no doubt that Beethoven composed works of this kind with ease; but the road he was treading with them was not without danger. With the Trio, op. 11, he took a few steps further along it. It is odd how the banality of Weigl's theme, of variations upon which the last movement consists, seems to have infected the composition as a whole. It is as if Beethoven had purposely kept the rest of the work down to the low level of this theme.

The popularity of compositions of this kind gave him little satisfaction, as we know particularly in the case of the Septet, op. 20. He was fully conscious that every characteristic of a work of this kind—the glittering brilliance and perfection of external form, and the unaffected charm of the melodies—weighed light in comparison with all that he really had to say.

The five early Violin Sonatas, opp. 12, nos. 1–3, 23, and 24, call for more serious consideration. They are chamber music in the truest sense of the words, intimate and delicately built, often playful in their gay figuration, especially the third in E flat. They are perhaps not as profound as many of the early piano sonatas, but to make up for that they are more mature and finished. The movements are perfectly balanced. The Andante of the second already bears the stamp of the true Beethoven. Many would doubtless say that first place should be given to the fourth, in A minor, though the fifth, sometimes called the *Spring Sonata*, with its delicate, indescribable charm, runs it close. What mastery Beethoven already shows in the contrast between the two headlong minor movements—the first and the last—of the fourth!

But the most perfect works of Beethoven's early period are the six String Quartets of op. 18. In these we find no unsolved problems; all but no. 4 in C minor, which in part probably belongs to a considerably earlier period, show a consummate mastery, which however is admittedly founded upon that of his great predecessors. The perfection of Haydn's and Mozart's late Quartets influenced the younger man so powerfully that here more than in any other of his works his own personality receded into the background. This does not mean that either of the other two composers could have written these works; the only movement of which that might conceivably be said is the very Mozartian Finale of the third Quartet, in D major. But that part of them that is truly characteristic of Beethoven—the melodic and thematic material—is not of sufficient weight to assert itself against the 'style' he inherited from his predecessors. Only in certain individual movements is Beethoven entirely himself, particularly in the first and second of the F major Quartet. In the Allegro the short but highly significant principal motive is not only elaborated in its capacity as such, but is subjected to transformations so extensive and so expressive as to provide a foretaste of the significance of his later motives. And the Adagio, the breadth and pathos of whose themes are themselves evidence of an original mind, shows in the coda, at the point where the principal theme suddenly breaks off, a form of construction of which there is no example in the works of his predecessors.

Comparison of the fifth Quartet in A major with the well-known late Quartet of Mozart in the same key, is instructive. Beethoven undoubtedly took this as a pattern; and in this instance his work falls short of its model. In face of one such as this of Mozart's, we can well understand the modesty with which Beethoven, both then and for a long time afterwards, spoke of his great predecessors. The same applies to the delightful Quintet, op. 16, for piano, clarinet, oboe, bassoon, and horn, which is better known in Beethoven's own arrangement as a Piano Quartet. For this the model was a Mozart Quintet (1784) for piano and wind instruments—a work that Mozart himself considered the best he had at that time written. With all his wealth of invention and assurance of form, Beethoven has yet not quite succeeded in capturing the inspired ease and inevitability of growth of his great model.

In about 1802 Beethoven said to a friend, the violinist Krumpholz, that he was not satisfied with the works he had hitherto produced, and that he was anxious to strike out on a new path. Czerny believed that this was after completion of op. 28, and that the "new path" showed itself for the first time in the three Sonatas of op. 31, which were written in 1802.

Like the three Violin Sonatas of op. 30, dating from the same year, these are important works. But it is difficult to say in what respect there is anything fundamentally novel in them. Halm sees it in the recognition of greater harmonic possibilities, as shown, for example, in the exposition sections of the first movements of nos. 1 and 2, in which, respectively, passages in D major and F major, and A major and C major, are immediately adjacent. But this will not do, for fundamentally it is merely an extension of the normal tonality. In the first case the modulation to the dominant from the tonic is followed by the corresponding modulation to the subdominant from its own subdominant, from which point the return to the tonic is perfectly regular. Precisely the same thing happens later, at the beginning of the *Waldstein* Sonata, op. 53. In the second case, however, the two keys in question are simply the dominant of the principal key (D minor) and that of the relative major (F). Those who wish for evidence of a 'new path' in these works must look for it in their ever increasing simplicity and spaciousness. These are the only qualities that the three sonatas have in common; in every other respect they show marked differences.

The first, in G major, is full of delicious humour, which even dominates long passages of the remarkable 'adagio grazioso', and in the Rondo is enhanced and given greater depth by the splendid minor episode.

The second, in D minor, well-known as one of Beethoven's 'stormy' sonatas, opens with an arpeggio chord, like an improvisation, immediately after which it breaks into a tempestuous Allegro. But for a short check at bars 6–7, this pursues its strenuous course up to the close of the exposition, forming as it were a bold, single-spanned bridge. As in the Finale of op. 27, no. 1, the second subject is approached by way of the 'dominant of the dominant'. The entry of the recapitulation provides a much-discussed 'surprise': the broken chord with which the movement opens is expanded into a recitative passage—a welcome

i

occasion for programmatic commentary! Yet it should be borne
in mind that from the time of Bach's *Chromatic Fantasy*, instrumental recitative has by no means been infrequent, and it has
never been considered necessary to imagine words that are left
unspoken. Here the creative power of absolute music stands the
test with particular success. A form that originally only had
significance when allied with a text is gradually so permeated
with music that it no longer requires the support of words. The
notes now speak for themselves. True, this form is not appropriate to all cases; but nowhere is it more so than here, where the
opening improvisation returns and the composer slips back into
his dreams again for a few moments after the strenuous exertion
he has been through. The construction, hitherto strict, becomes
freer—though not for the rest of the movement, for agitated
chords and arpeggios lead back in a mighty crescendo to the
second subject, over a bass line (E sharp, F sharp, G, G sharp,
A) that is a shortened repetition of the passage leading to the
same point in the exposition. The recapitulation now proceeds
unaltered, and in it there remains not a trace of any loosening of
structure—in the hearer's mind there remains only a reminiscence of moments of relaxation. So it is a purely musical experience, and only those who are capable of apprehending it as
such will grasp the essence of this movement.

The Adagio, like the first movement, opens with an arpeggio
chord; in it, again, the subject only gradually takes definite
shape, and the opening arpeggio reappears during the course of
the movement. But here there is no agitation; a glorious sense of
peace rules throughout.

The last movement, however, is agitated enough, though here
this is neither manifested in violence and tension, nor interrupted by moments of relaxation. The movement rushes along
in uniform motion, with long passages dominated by a little
motive of four semiquavers. The second subject, which is related to that of the first movement, has an effect of syncopation,
which heightens the sense of unrest. It is easy in performance to
misrepresent the mood of this movement. All the "Allegretto"
here means is "Do not drive it to death!"; it is not intended to

deprive the movement of the profound passion that should speak from every bar.

The third Sonata, in E flat, also opens with a kind of improvisation, on the chord of the 'added sixth'. Thus we enter the tonic, as it were, by a side door. All is now bright and cheerful, almost tenderly emotional, and in spite of the key-signature—E flat has often been called Beethoven's 'heroic' key—there is not a heroic note in the whole work. It is in four movements; and in place of the slow movement, as later in the Eighth Symphony, there is a Minuet with a beautifully moulded melody. The Scherzo is unusual on account of its 2/4 beat and of the fact that it is in sonata form, in which the development section takes the place of the Trio. Pianistically, it is a highly original movement. Again the Sonata is rounded off with a Finale of restless impetuosity, which after a harmonically simple opening—in the first twenty bars we only find tonic and dominant—contains long passages of unrelaxed tension. Again the second subject (bar 34) hovers about the dominant of B flat major—this time for thirty bars, until at last the tonic of that key is reached (bar 64). To avoid the obvious danger of harmonic monotony, Beethoven modulates to G flat major in the recapitulation, only regaining the original tonic with the seventy-bar coda.

The three Violin Sonatas, op. 30, are no less important. It has been remarked that they are related by a similarity of motive consisting of what may be called a 'turning' figure:

Op. 30. 1   Op. 30. 2   Op. 30. 3

Except for this, however, they are all three entirely different. No. 1 in A major, and no. 3 in G major, are almost miniatures, much in the delicate style of the early violin sonatas, though they excel these in freedom, richness, and compactness. In no. 1, with its wonderfully tender Adagio, the last movement, composed later, is perhaps not altogether in keeping with the others.

It is known that the Finale of the *Kreutzer* was originally intended for this Sonata.

No. 3 is perfect from the first to the last note. There is delicious humour both in the 'bear-dance' of the Finale and in the easy, graceful middle movement, in which Beethoven seems to unbend, and to refrain from thematic development, a fact that gives it an almost Schubertian flavour. In the first movement both the bridge passage leading to the development section, and this section itself with the restless forward impulse that it has caught from the end of the exposition, are magnificent.

No. 2 in C minor strikes another note. Here is heroic pathos, in the grand style and bearing the true stamp of Beethoven's personality. This quality is to be found not only in the first and last movements, which are both in the minor, and are brought to a final climax in their magnificent codas, but also in the broadly flowing Adagio. The concise and somewhat short-breathed Scherzo, with its Trio in cross-grained canon, has its use as a contrast, but cannot be said to have the weight of the other movements. Schindler maintained that Beethoven, who is supposed to have considered cutting down many of his four-movement works to three movements, wanted later to do away with it.

From here it is only a step to the magnificent Sonata of the following year, which was written in great haste during the composition of the *Eroica*. This is the *Kreutzer*, op. 47, surely the crowning achievement in the sphere of sonata composition up to that time. Beethoven wrote on the original title page of the sonata the words *Scritto in uno stile molto concertante* (written in a specially brilliant style). He had composed it for a mulatto violinist, Bridgetower by name, with whom he played it in public in Vienna. It was only completed just before the concert, and there was no time to have it copied—the last movement alone had been copied for a long time, for it had formed part of op. 31, no. 1. The Sonata shows no sign whatever of the haste in which it was composed. It is mature in every respect—the fruit of hours of stress and strain, bathed in the light of the growing *Eroica*. It is the first really great sonata—no longer true chamber music in the old sense, but at home only in the concert hall, for there alone can music of this power and magnitude be heard in its true perspective. The peak of the work is undoubtedly the first movement, which in its turn—most unusually—has its climax in the towering last theme that dominates the development section. At the same time we should not underestimate the variations on the very beautiful theme that seems to bring peace after the tempestuous first movement; and in particular the florid passages must never be rattled off as if they were so much mechanical ornamentation. The last movement was originally composed for an earlier sonata (op. 30, no. 1), and it is remarkable that it is entirely suitable to its present setting. Probably when composing it, Beethoven had yet no inkling of the *Kreutzer*. He did not leave it in its place in the earlier sonata because its style was too brilliant to suit the remainder of that work. It was perhaps the first glimmering of the idea of a truly great sonata, which he was a year later to bring to such glorious fruition.

THE SPIRIT OF THE SYMPHONY

MAGNIFICENT as Beethoven's achievement with these seven sonatas seems to us to-day, and imperishable as is their vitality, yet it was not long before he himself grew dissatisfied with them. On the 21st of June, 1804, while working on *Fidelio*, he wrote in his sketch-book: "Make Finale simpler—all piano music, too—God knows why my piano music still seems so bad to me ..." Then and later it was only his other works that he took quite seriously, in particular one that he regarded as the real achievement of those years, the decisive step upon the 'new path'. This work was the *Eroica* Symphony.

The only major orchestral compositions that had preceded this were the first two Symphonies, op. 21 in C and op. 36 in D, and the first three Piano Concertos. What was said of the op. 18 Quartets may be said of these works, particularly the two symphonies. That is to say, for the time being the perfection of his predecessors, especially Haydn, impeded the free development of Beethoven's own personality. The widely held opinion that these works were still pure Haydn or Mozart, is mistaken; in particular it is idle to compare the principal theme of the first movement of the First Symphony with that of Mozart's *Jupiter* Symphony, for in the Mozart there is nothing of the forward drive inherent in Beethoven's theme.

Yet we must admit that, when it was a question of the architecture of his movements as a whole, Beethoven had not yet succeeded in shaking himself free of his predecessors' influence. And in this respect the contemporary statement that he was "a coarser Haydn" is not altogether wide of the mark in so far as Beethoven was impelled by the tension of his thematic

Mozart:

Beethoven:

etc.

material to strengthen the scaffolding that supported the form as a whole. The wonderful elegance and delicacy of articulation that characterize Haydn's and Mozart's symphonies were impossible here; hence the primitive lay-out, and hence also the exaggerated, somewhat superficial reinforcement of the close of the first movement of the C major Symphony. (It should be noted that the reason for the still more powerful close of the Finale of the Fifth Symphony is entirely different, for in this case it is inherent in the work.) What applies to the First Symphony applies equally to the Second, the Finale of which, as well as the first movement, is dominated by the same tension, while that of the First Symphony—the only movement of Beethoven of which this can be said—is kept entirely within the bounds of expression laid down by Haydn. All the rest is unmistakably the language of Beethoven, though we feel that, tied by the symphonic form handed down by his predecessors, his actions were never quite free. Hence it may be that, in spite of their many glorious passages—notably the Larghetto and the coda of the Finale of the Second—these two works to-day have a weaker effect than the last symphonies of his two predecessors;

and also that they are below the level not only of his own later symphonies but of other compositions of his.

Beethoven must have started work on his Third Symphony, the *Eroica*, op. 55 in E flat, immediately after he had completed the Second. And as this work was finished in about twelve months, it is clear that with it he took a greater stride forward than had ever been known in so short a time in the whole history of the arts. The chains were broken, and he was free. And this freedom had been gained not by transgressing existing laws, but because it was granted to him to discover, and at the same time to obey, a new law.

It has been said a thousand times that with the *Eroica* a new page in the history of music was opened; but hardly ever for reasons that touch the heart of the problem. Napoleon's connexion with the Symphony has always seemed to show us a royal road to the understanding of its special characteristics: it was not merely to be dedicated to Bonaparte, the First Consul, as the homage of a German musician who, like many other leading Germans of the day, regarded him as one of the greatest geniuses of history; it was actually to be entitled 'Bonaparte'. There is a well-known story that Beethoven, the passionate republican and partisan of the cause of liberty, on hearing that Bonaparte had made himself Emperor of the French, tore up the title page of the copy lying ready for despatch to Paris. That this anecdote has some truth in it may be concluded from the fact that on the title page of a copy corrected by Beethoven himself, are still to be read the words: *Sinfonia grande, intitolata Bonaparte*, though the last two words have been carefully erased. Beethoven wrote in pencil under those words: *Geschrieben auf Bonaparte* (composed upon the subject of Bonaparte). It was not for two years, when the parts appeared in print, that the work was called the *Sinfonia Eroica*. The title was then extended by the words *composta per festiggiare il sovvenire d'un grand'uomo* (composed in celebration of the memory of a great man). This sounds as if the great man were dead; and, indeed, for Beethoven the 'greatness' of Napoleon was a thing of the past once he had become Emperor. So much is known fact; all the rest is mere tradition. We know nothing about the commencement of the work or the gradual development of the general plan, or, especially, about Beethoven's object in inserting the Funeral March. When in 1821 he received news of Napoleon's death, he said he had already composed the proper music for this twenty years before.

Thus the commentators could give free rein to their imagination. In particular they saw in the first subject a character sketch of Napoleon. Paul Bekker sees in the opening an expression of the contradictions in his character—his "forceful and forward-pressing energy, and his plaintive and resigned reflectiveness." But this gets us no further. More to the point, perhaps, is Bekker's reference to the fact that the Finale is built up on a theme already used in the *Prometheus* ballet. Although Beethoven also made use of the theme for a simple little dance and for a set of Piano Variations, both composed before the *Eroica*, it is quite possible that in its Finale he may have had in mind this hero and the benefits he brought to mankind. The comparison between Napoleon and Prometheus accords entirely with the spirit of the age. Others, such as Hegel, saw in Napoleon the "*Weltgeist, der durch die Geschichte reitet*" (the eternal spirit of the world, riding through history).

But none of these things help us to understand the details of the Finale any better. What does help a great deal is a comparison with the earlier settings of the theme. In the *Contre-danse* we find merely the tune, without any elaboration. In the ballet the theme (which occurs in the Finale, the *Dances of the Men of Prometheus*) is repeated in an amplified form, with episodic passages. The Variations have an Introduction, in which only the bass of the theme appears, with gradually multiplying contrapuntal parts. In the Symphony, however, this bass becomes the real theme, the tune itself being associated with it only as the movement progresses. This, also, begins like a set of Variations; but instead of strict repetition of the thematic periods the form soon becomes freer, with fugatos and similar contrivances inserted. The *Prometheus* tune and its bass dominate the whole movement, there being no second subject. This, and the variegated rhythmic patterns and harmonic colours, are alien to symphonic style. Often as we may remember that the tune of the theme had its origin in the world of ballet, yet we cannot help admiring the art and skill that has raised it up and made it worthy of the higher level of the symphony. What we hear is no longer a mere juxtaposition of phrases of equal standing, but a truly symphonic range of climaxes, the last of which, where the theme strikes a solemn, hymn-like note, forms a monumental close to the whole movement. What depth of feeling, what wealth of humanity, does it comprise, and what contrasts are born of this one theme that seems to carry in itself a whole world!

And yet this world is revealed to us in the very first bars of the work. It is at once clear that with it a new epoch of classical music is indeed about to open. The first movement is one of the most complicated structures that Beethoven ever created. (A detailed analysis of it is given in the Appendix.) Everything in it, not only its huge dimensions, which frightened the first hearers, was entirely new, and much never appeared again even in Beethoven's own works. Never again, for instance, did he write a great symphonic movement without a full-grown main theme; and never did he place so many other ideas side by side with the principal motive, which in the truest sense of the word acts as the 'motive power' and, at the same time, as the brace that holds everything together. Most of these tunes are in themselves not particularly 'heroic'. And if in spite of this the movement as a whole is more heroic than any previous ones, that is due to the dynamic force that energizes it from beginning to end, even in the very broad cadential phrases. It is in truth 'heroic' music, and at the same time that Beethoven paid homage with it to Napoleon, he took his own place side by side with him, though as a 'hero' of a very different calibre—the creator of a more lasting empire.

The second movement also, which is expressly marked 'Marcia funebre', and which, notwithstanding the *tempo* indication 'adagio assai', Beethoven intended to be played at a solemn walking pace ($\flat = 80$), is heroic music of the most lofty

kind. A few years previously Beethoven had written a Funeral
March 'on the death of a hero', in the op. 26 Sonata. This was
an effective piece, but without depth, and not free from echoes
of contemporary operatic music, though it was more suitable
than most others for the accompaniment of a funeral procession.
The opening of the Funeral March from the *Eroica*, it is true,
is also suitable for marching to; but when, soon after the return
of the first theme, the magnificent fugato starts, which has
rightly been compared to a tragedy of Aeschylus, it loses its
march-like characteristics. The image that up to now has been
present to the hearer's mind—that of a procession of mourners
seeking consolation from serene memories of the great dead—
vanishes in the flood of light shed upon it at the return to true
symphonic style. The process is the same as in the Finale, where
the melody that had its birth in the humbler sphere of mime and
ballet is raised by the creative hands of the composer to the
symphonic level. It is the third section of the movement, the
reprise, with its inexhaustible wealth of invention both in the
creation of new ideas and the variations of old ones, that shows
a mastery hitherto undreamt of.

After the emotional tension of the first and second movements, the Scherzo, with its restless movement and the 'romantic' horn passages of the Trio, comes as a welcome relief. It
serves also to prepare the hearer for the rich and many-coloured
world of the Finale. Its melodic material no doubt lacks the
weight and importance of the first two movements. But as we
follow it through and see how the lively, almost frivolous principal theme is tossed playfully about on rippling waves of harmony until at last, after nearly a hundred bars, it settles down
on the tonic, we can appreciate the true symphonic compass of
the movement. And though perhaps at the beginning of the
Trio, the horns sound a somewhat programmatic note, yet the
passage at the end leading to the re-entry of the Scherzo, is
again of truly symphonic proportions, worthy of the remainder
of the work. The dark note of warning in the striking little
progression D flat–D–E flat in the coda should not be overlooked.

The intrinsic merits of the Fourth Symphony, op. 60 in B flat, were long unrecognized, for it was overshadowed by the *Eroica* and the C minor. Compared with its two neighbours it is, to be sure, full of an untroubled happiness that does not fit in well with the long-ruling conception of an unhappy, daemonic Beethoven; for which reason it was often regarded as a playful but inspired work, with which a genius sought relief from his burdens. But to-day its secrets have been laid bare, and we know that its consummate harmony is founded in darkness. Evidence of this appears as early as in the Introduction, which is probably more beautiful, and laid out on a bigger scale, than any that had until then been written. In the truest sense of the word it 'introduces' the work. In it all is preparation, expectation, tension; it is full of dim, crepuscular light; its mood hovers between major and minor; and its modulations, in which enharmonics have their place, are rich and bold. The only things that are unambiguous are the very clear and simple lay-out, which is characteristic of the whole movement, and the rhythmically striking motive of the abrupt, tramping crotchets that heralds the principal theme. "Take what comes to you in earnest; all is not play and high spirits!"—so the whole Introduction seems to warn the hearer; and this is emphasized once again at the magnificent moment in which those fortissimo chords of the dominant seventh prepare us for the plunge into the Allegro.

In style, this Allegro is without doubt as far removed as possible from the *Eroica*: from the very beginning the principal theme stands out clearly as a complete entity. It consists of broken chords, as in the *Eroica*, but in this case they embrace all three primary triads, and are followed by a soft legato passage. Here the principal theme dominates a far greater part of the movement than in the *Eroica*, accounting for 270 out of 460 bars of the Allegro, as against 186 out of 691; and even the rest of the movement does not actually form a contrast, in the deeper sense of the word, to the principal theme, but rather carries on and maintains its restless impetus. A wonderful effect is achieved towards the close of the working-out, when, with an apparent change of key to C flat major (not F sharp, be it noted), the brightness of day yields for a time to the half-light of the Introduction.

The Adagio opens with one of the most deeply felt and beautifully constructed melodies that Beethoven ever wrote; and the breadth and grandeur of this noble archway of sound remains the standard for the rest of the movement. The accompanying figure begins like a pulsing heart-beat and often reappears as a motive; and why, when it is given to the bassoons, it should be "humorous", as Schumann strangely enough felt it, it is a little difficult to understand; nor is it clear in what way "humour" may be said (San Galli) to be predominant in the movement as a whole. The sudden darkening of tone by the hint at the minor mode early in the course of the theme, which however immediately gives way again to the brighter major, conveys a sense of loftiness. It is like a warning reminder of the dark substratum beneath the cheerful serenity of the music, and at the same time an affirmation of the 'grand style' of the whole work.

The Scherzo opens finely with a syncopated theme. This is at once answered by a progression of mysterious broken chords of the minor ninth, which have an effect as of spectral disembodiment. The syncopated theme is tossed playfully to and fro during the movement; and the manner in which the Trio is fitted in at each appearance is simple to the point of artlessness —a trait in which we recognize the breadth and spaciousness of the first two movements. Yet in spite of all this playfulness and simplicity, the movement is in the same 'grand style' as its predecessors.

The Finale is often regarded as below the level of the other movements, or even as a makeshift and not as a true *dénouement*. The reason for this is probably that in performance the 'allegro ma non troppo' is mistaken for 'presto', and the movement is rattled off like a *Perpetuum mobile*. Played in this manner, it certainly suffers a loss of weight and dignity. Beethoven showed quite clearly by his marking that he wished the figuration of the movement to be given due weight. And if it is correctly played, if all the little surprises of accentuation and the magnificently prepared outbursts are given their due prominence, then we cannot fail to hear the menacing rumblings that come from the depths—even if it pleased Beethoven to allow them on this occasion to speak in a voice of blustering humour.

The Fifth Symphony, op. 67 in C minor, is one of the—superficially—best known works of Beethoven. Countless people will maintain that they know "every note" of it; and they are right to the extent that no performance holds anything in the nature of a surprise for them—except possibly that which some-times results from the conductor's 'interpretation' of the familiar strains.

Yet there are certain important points in the first movement that are essential to an understanding of it and yet are hardly ever realized. For example: the principal motive of the move-ment—which incidentally leaves the key indefinite, for until the end of the sixth bar it might be E flat major—is generally under-stood to be the first four notes. That this motive consists not of those four notes, but of bars 1–5, was first established by Hein-rich Schenker. And yet the whole movement depends upon this; it is only the realization of the fact that the step E flat–F in the second and third bars forms a motive of its own, that en-ables us to understand correctly certain specially important passages of the movement, not only in the development section, in which this step is isolated and given the utmost harmonic sig-nificance, but also in the great coda, in which, first in its original form and then in diminution, it becomes the basis of entirely new formations.

It is not until we are clear as to the structure of the principal motive that we can understand the 'conciseness' of the move-ment, to which reference is so often made, and which, to be sure, far surpasses anything in symphonic music either before or after that time. We can see better from the autograph score, which has fortunately been preserved, than from the sketch-books, how well Beethoven knew what he was about; for this shows, among other things, that the coda was originally much longer, and that it was a long time before he succeeded in com-pressing it into its final compact form. Yet as it is, it contains much that is novel. Even when he was scoring the symphony its final shape evidently gave him plenty to think of.

This compactness indicates a new and dimly foreseen concentration both of the thematic material and its evolution (only some of the early sonatas, such as op. 2, no. 1, and op. 10, no. 1, contain any such augury); here besides the principal motive there is only the second subject (compare the wealth of ideas in the first movement of the *Eroica*), and even this only occurs in the exposition and the recapitulation, and not in either the development section or the coda. Evolution proceeds unremittingly; each bar is filled with expression; no freedom, not a moment's breathing space, is allowed. Hence the tremendous effect of the short phrase given to the oboe, which starts at the pause early in the recapitulation. One detail may be referred to here: the transition from the first to the second subject is compressed into seven bars, 56–62. Hitherto it has never been clearly recognized, but only dimly felt, that the immediately following second subject is, as it were, only a tender echo of the transition:

The spaciousness of the periods is no less than, say, in the first movements of the Third or Fourth Symphonies. This point is easily overlooked, particularly under the influence of the throbbing rhythm of the principal motive, which, it may safely be said, those who fail to grasp the work correctly always single out for attention. It is Schenker who first pointed out (in *Der Tonwille*, Nos. 1, 5, and 6) the great curves in which the movement grows. Even though this throbbing rhythm accompanies the song-like second subject, its function is simply to ensure that the momentum shall not slow down; so far therefore from impeding the flow of the musical periods, it helps to hold them together. Never has better disciplined music been written; never has violent and stormy impetus been guided by a firmer hand.

Romain Rolland has said that this movement is nothing but "Muscle and Sinew"—an opinion also widespread in Germany; but it is something more: it is full-blooded life, a fact that should not be overlooked even if in many performances we are shown not the living organism but merely the framework.

The variations upon the principal theme of the second movement ('Andante con moto', A flat) consist of figuration, and to this extent, it is true, the movement is perfectly simple and straightforward. But apart from this, as we know from the sketches, it was only after long experimenting that it became the admirable but unusual symphonic structure that we know. The melody of the opening theme itself is not so self-contained, so simple and song-like, as is generally thought. Its peaceful, flowing course is the result of a concentration of motive and rhythm that we only perceive when we observe that the whole is dominated by one germinal motive—the up-beat followed by the crotchet or quaver, the rhythm of which however is varied in bars 4–6.

Similarly it is to be observed that the phrase that now follows and is repeated (bars 10 et seq.) is merely a melodic extension and reaffirmation of the close of the principal theme, which appears first in bare octaves (bars 7–8) and then fully harmonized (bars 9–10). And now the close of this phrase is in its turn twice repeated, still clearly in A flat, with no hint of modulation to the dominant. And so, firmly fixed in the tonic, the new theme opens. Not only is this related to the previous one through the 'up-beat' motive, but it also develops as a new motive the three quaver-beats of the last bar. Four more bars, and we come to the first modulation, through a chord of the diminished seventh, which culminates in a radiant C major. The modulation seems to give promise of something new; but this promise is unfulfilled, for what follows is simply a repetition, clothed though it be in resplendent colours, of the foregoing phrase. This time, however, it has no definite close, but leads back to the opening A flat, as before through a diminished seventh, but this time followed by a mysterious chromatic progression.

The first variation opens in the same key. Thus, in spite of all its external brilliance, and although it was introduced by means of a perfect cadence, the C major was in fact not a true harmonic development, but merely a passing phase. And thus, too, the forty-eight bars of the theme form a self-contained symphonic unit that maintains its entity, though in ever new forms, throughout the movement. In his symphonic movements in variation form Beethoven never merely strung, as it were, a series of variations next to each other, but, as in this case, used all his skill and art to group them and connect one with the other by bridge passages. The A flat tonality is never abandoned; and in the coda, from the 'piu moto' onwards, it is affirmed emphatically again and again.

Beethoven originally planned the movement on entirely different lines: the second section of the theme was to have formed the Trio of a 'quasi Menuetto', repeated with a close in C minor (or major?), while the second part of the Trio was to have consisted of the same section in C major, this time closing in A flat and likewise repeated. How primitive and unsymphonic that would have been!

The Allegro (which, be it noted, is not marked Scherzo) also originally had a different appearance. The passage connecting it with the Finale was a later invention, and the movement in its first form ended, like the present close before the major section, with the downward skips C–G–C, piano. Then, when the link with the Finale was decided upon, in the inspired guise of an abbreviated repetition of the first theme in a shadowy pianissimo, the usual form was nevertheless preserved by the fact that the first part of the movement had previously been repeated, and followed by a repeat of the C major section (the Trio). As in the Fourth Symphony, therefore, it was a Scherzo with a double

k

reprise, the first part being abbreviated at its second repeat. It was in this form that the movement was played at the first performance in 1808. Not for some years did Beethoven cut out this double repeat; but he allowed the link with the Finale to stand, so that in its present form the first part only makes a shadowy reappearance after the C major section. This deprives the movement of much of its independence; it is now no longer properly balanced, like an ordinary scherzo or minuet, for not only does the Trio die away to a pianissimo, but the rest of the movement loses weight steadily as it approaches its end. It may be remarked here that the Trio is supposed to have ended originally with a definite close, forte.

The result of all this is that the Allegro is not a self-contained movement, which is attached to the Finale by a bridge passage, but merely a kind of broad introduction to the last movement—an introduction organically bound up with the latter and intended not only as a contrast to it, but as a preparation for it by the creation in the hearer of a feeling of suspense. To this the form of the movement is appropriate; it is throughout of very loose construction (Schenker speaks of "whims and fancies"); both the first part and the Trio lack the usual clear articulation of a minuet or scherzo; and definite closes are avoided. Appropriate also are the famous coda, fifty bars long—the uncanny and exciting preparation for the Finale, and the reappearance of the movement in the Finale towards the end of the development section. Such a reappearance occurs in one of Haydn's early symphonies (B major of 1772, no. 46 in the Collected Edition); but what is there only a sudden and surprising caprice here serves higher ends. As regards the Finale, it is true, the 'height' of these ends has often been contested; Beethoven, we are told, had "badly forgotten himself"; the "ordinary, not to say banal" themes were incapable of artistic development; "they are nothing but shouts and shrieks; they are not even gestures, still less do they express anything" (Krug). This nonsense is shown in its true perspective by the deep impression that even Krug admits is made, now as much as a century ago, by the last movement as the crown of the whole work.

Nor is it only on the simple-minded, and those who have no understanding of art, that this impression is made, but also on all but the few for whose oversensitive natures this music is too robust. It has, indeed, its effect on the least musically educated; for it is truly 'popular' music, and that not because of tunes adapted from folk songs or the like, but because its themes are perfectly simple and perfectly intelligible. There is a story of an old soldier who, at a performance of the Symphony in 1828 in Paris, jumped up at the beginning of the Finale and cried "*C'est l'empereur!*"; and this, like the story told by Schumann of the child who said as he heard the transition to the Finale "I'm frightened!" is proof of the elemental working of this music on the minds of those who have no knowledge of art. Such stories are, of course, only an indication of its power of expression, and cannot be regarded as proof of its merits as symphonic music. The latter lies in the structure of the work; and it is certainly difficult to understand how anybody can fail to recognize its greatness, or the mastery with which the forces of expression are held in check—all those things, in short, that make of this music a symphonic movement and not, let us say, a Triumphal March or a Hymn of Joy. Although here, in contrast to the first movement, the lay-out of the thematic material is spacious, yet the concentration of form, and the compactness and significance of the phrases, are no less marked. To take but one example, how great is the wealth of invention in the exposition, and how neatly and closely do all the parts dovetail into one another! Each motive, each little fraction of a theme, is as it were a carefully hewn ashlar, perfectly regular in shape; but it is only through the skill with which they are piled one on the other that the edifice achieves its true structural perfection.

Beethoven's constructional principle, which first came clearly to light in the first movement of the *Eroica*, that each individual section of the structure, significant as it might be, should at once lead into the following one, here celebrates its greatest triumph. Only upon this principle would it be possible to make of the first thirty-four bars of the Finale, with their sheer C major and their unremitting *ff*, a well articulated musical struc-

ture full of life and incident; and only so, after a few modulating
bars based on the last C major phrase, would it be possible to
proceed straight into the second subject without any sign of a
'join'. This subject is at first only given out shortly; but later it
forms the material for the whole of the working-out down to
the re-introduction of the passage from the third movement.
The short motive for trombones, which asserts itself more and
more strongly during the working-out, is not new, but merely a
reiteration of the upward steps in the bass of the second subject.
For forty bars the rhythm—monotonous in itself—here remains
unchanged; and yet something new is always happening. But
what is so amazing is the way Beethoven succeeded, after this
brilliant triumphal progress, in bringing the movement up to an
even higher climax in the very long coda, which begins sixty-
eight bars before the Presto. He achieves this by consistently
avoiding a full close in C major until the entry of the Presto, for
the *ff* entry of the bassoons with the second C major motive abbreviated is not to be understood as a full close but as a broken
6/4 chord on G. All this time he remains within the ambit of C
major, subject to which limitation the motives and harmonies
are fully and vivaciously expounded; and it is only when, at the
Presto, the full close is reached, that the C major proper is released. This continues for sixty-eight bars, in a passage that is
by no means shapeless, for it is restrained by the clear lay-out
and the dynamic marking—sixteen bars piano, and only then
crescendo. It is, to be sure, a close of such breadth that it cannot
be regarded merely as the tail-end of the Finale; every listener
who has truly felt the work as an adventure of the spirit will see
in this Stretto not only the end of the Finale, but the culmina-
tion of the whole Symphony.

The tremendous energy of the last movement ensures the
unity of the work. Needless to say, it had to be different to the
first movement; not only is its brilliant major opposed to the
more sombre minor, but its close-packed breadth contrasts
with the almost excessive tension and compactness of the other
movement. It was just this compactness that called for a *dénouement* of this kind after the two middle movements, which them-

selves had to be different—and different in this very way—to the first and the last.

The Andante with its sense of relaxation, is the only slow movement that would be tolerable after the opening movement. The third, with its almost spectral groping, points to a *dénouement* that could not well be other than it is. The fact that it runs into the last movement without a break shows quite clearly the close inward relationship of the two; and this relationship is re-affirmed by the much discussed re-introduction of the theme in the Finale. The resulting contrast certainly has a striking effect, and it enabled the composer to avoid the risk of the jubilant tone of the Finale becoming monotonous. But if there were no other relationship, the exciting effect of this re-introduction would be incomprehensible. Actually it has an effect of inevitability: the gloom and the ghostly visitants have not been finally exorcized by the radiance of the Finale. When the strains of the third movement are heard again, the full depth of the abyss from which triumph has emerged is brought clearly home to us. The similarity of the motives in different movements, which is so often referred to, is not in itself proof of the unity of the work as a whole. That the three throbbing beats of the first motive re-appear in the third movement is obvious, and they may be heard here and there even in the Finale. And in the C major passage of the Andante, which has no formal close, we can hear in anticipation the triumphant strains of the Finale. Beethoven would perhaps not have permitted himself this musical anacoluthon had he not intended its logical fulfilment in the last movement. The latter was originally planned on entirely different lines, i.e., as a passionate minor movement; this passage in the Andante was then intended to have a definite close.

No amount of critical research into the respective styles of the Fifth and Sixth Symphonies could ever have revealed that they were composed at the same time. Yet that this is so is proved by sketches that have been preserved. (The first performance of the two Symphonies took place on the 22nd of December, 1808, at an *Akademie* organized by Beethoven, at which other new works of his, the G major Piano Concerto, of which he played the solo part, the Fantasia for pianoforte, orchestra, and chorus, and two numbers from the C major Mass, were also performed.) The Fifth was probably begun earlier than the Sixth, but for at least a year work on both proceeded simultaneously. The almost superhuman concentration demanded of Beethoven by the C minor evidently compelled him to relax by composing a work that was its very antithesis. Actually, just as he never wrote more intense and concentrated music than that of the Fifth Symphony, so none was freer of any sign of stress and strain than the Sixth (the *Pastoral*), op. 68 in F. A good example of this is afforded by the working-out of the first movement, of which seventy-two bars consist solely of repetitions of a figure taken from the second bar of the principal theme, and based on a scheme of harmonies not functionally related to each other but having purely a 'colour effect'. B flat major is followed by D major, and then, after a short interruption by another motive, G major is followed by E major. It will be seen that the step is not the same in each case. It is simply that delight in the common chord and the eternal repetition of the same figure, that was characteristic of the musical romanticism of the day, particularly Schubert's. Beethoven never again came into such close contact with it. This approach to the romantic is, however, confined to this one passage, and does not affect the style of the work as a whole. For all its freedom from tension, this is true Beethoven, and, with its lucidity and symphonic finish of form, is truly in the classical tradition. The work, to be sure, stands out from all Beethoven's orchestral music as something individual, not to say unique, and shows us an unfamiliar side of him. This we should feel even if we did not know that it was the *Pastoral* Symphony—true programme music, and not merely music of a very individual kind, like the *Eroica*. The headings that Beethoven himself gave to each movement are familiar. These are capable of further interpretation in detail, such as that provided by Hans Pfitzner in his masterly analysis of the Symphony (Vol. II of his collected writings, Appendix to the Pamphlet *Die neue Aesthetik der musikalischen Impotenz*). This analysis reconciles the poetic content of the symphony with its musical

form, but at the same time shows that the music is not only, as
Beethoven himself wrote, "expressive of feeling," but also
"painting." But the decisive point is that nowhere is the music
prompted by the poetic motive alone, but that it has, like all the
rest of Beethoven's music, its roots in itself—in the logic of its
organic development. Thus, the passages in the second movement, in which the nightingale, the cuckoo, and the quail are
heard, are as much 'pure' music as a recitative, which, though it
interrupts the course of the music for a moment, does not divert
it. Or when, at the end of the 'storm', the rain, thunder, and
lightning cease and the clouds clear away, so that we "smell the
good air" (Pfitzner), the whole movement is given unity by the
calm progression of minims in C major, which is merely an
augmentation of the quaver figure that ushers in the 'storm'.

Storm.   Beginning   End

etc.

Even without the headings, the music is in itself expressive and
fraught with meaning; and, apart altogether from the bird-
calls, the storm, and the shepherd's song, it would mean essentially the same to us that it does now that we know the descriptive headings. That of the first movement is *Joyous sensations
aroused by arrival in the country;* and the 'joyousness' is so entirely individual that no other cheerful movement ever written,
whether by Beethoven or by any other composer, says anything
like it. It is of an almost transcendent harmony and wealth of
expression, a radiant and unclouded happiness, such as are only
to be found in Nature itself. Music of this kind occurs nowhere
but in compositions that set out to reproduce the moods of
Nature, such as the pastoral music in Bach's *Christmas Oratorio*,
or landscapes such as Galatea's E flat aria from Handel's *Acis
and Galatea*, or again, in Beethoven's own time, Haydn's late
Oratorios.

But all these works are different in two respects from Beethoven's. First, except for the first subject of the last movement of

the *Pastoral*, which is developed from a typical *Ranz des vaches*, he almost entirely avoids conventional 'rustic' or 'bucolic' tunes; he invents his own themes, inspired by the task that he has set himself. The extraordinarily significant first theme, which really establishes the mood of the whole work, and which, as Pfitzner has shown, contains the germ of the whole first movement except the second subject, seems to be a true 'inspiration'—an unusual phenomenon in Beethoven—for in the very first rough sketch it appears in its final and complete shape. Second, and of more importance, is the fact that this thematic material is used for the building up of a great and truly symphonic form; though it might indeed be thought that this form, of its very nature, was hardly apt for such a task. When we hear a Pastorale like that of Bach, or a number from Haydn's *Seasons*, we ourselves seem to feel the divine peace of Nature itself stealing over us. Here is no conflict of dissimilar forces, but only dissimilar emotions in peaceable apposition. But it is just this conflict that is the essence of the symphony or the sonata in its final form as Beethoven left it. Even some of his more peaceful movements, such as the first of op. 28, which has quite unnecessarily been dubbed the 'Pastoral Sonata', here and there contain points of concentration—stretto-like passages in which motives and portions of the various themes are heaped one on the other. Of these there is not a trace in the *Pastoral* Symphony, although there is no less thematic development here than elsewhere. It is remarkable how consistently Beethoven avoids all possibility of 'conflict', and how in spite of this, obedient to the laws of sonata form, he builds up every movement with the most intensive thematic development, keeping before the mind's eye in each bar the image of Nature as he saw it in his devoutness. In his diary for 1815 he wrote: "Allmächtiger im Walde! Ich bin selig, glücklich im Wald: jeder Baum spricht durch dich"; and "O Gott! welche Herrlichkeit! In einer solchen Waldgegend, in den Höhen ist Ruhe, Ruhe, ihm zu dienen." ("Almighty God in the forest! I am blessed and happy in the forest. Every tree speaks through Thee." "O God, what splendour! In such a forest, on the heights, is peace—peace to serve Him.")

Like the Fifth and Sixth, the Seventh and Eighth Symphonies are 'twins'. So far as we can gather from the sketch-books, Beethoven took the Eighth in hand immediately after completion of the Seventh (May 1812), and finished it in October of the same year. This was at Linz, while he was carrying on troublesome negotiations concerning the marriage of his brother Johann. The sketches date from the time of his association with Goethe at Teplitz. They show that the work made very quick progress; the final form of the themes and even of large parts of their development was quickly found, whereas in the case of the Seventh this cost him much time and trouble. (Whether work on the latter began before 1812 cannot now be ascertained.) We may take it that the Sixth, also, took less time to complete, and caused Beethoven less hard thinking, than the Fifth, which, again, accords with the character of the two Symphonies. At the same time, the later works do not perhaps form such an apparently irreconcilable contrast as the earlier ones: the Seventh and Eighth, after all, are alike in that each is a joyous profession of faith in all that the words 'Life' and 'Strength' connote— strength, be it noted, that is not called upon to fight and conquer a hostile power, as might be said in the case of the C minor.

And yet the Seventh, op. 92 in A, is also a monument commemorative of victory, though in this we shall find no programme. It is the victory of the Symphony over the tyranny of Rhythm. Never before or afterwards did Beethoven write music so dominated by rhythm of the highest significance as this first movement. Five sixths or so of the Vivace are in the same rhythm, long passages, particularly the hundred bars of the development section, being in its original form:

$$\text{♪.♫ ♪.♫,}$$

and not $$\text{♩. ♪.♫ .}$$

In only one place is it abandoned for any length of time, viz. in the magnificent passage in the coda in which a two-bar 'basso ostinato', repeated eleven times, prepares the way for the final cadence. The sketches provide irrefutable evidence that for Beethoven this rhythm was the central idea of the movement, the starting-point from which he set out in its composition. At first both the tunes and the harmonies were only roughly sketched in; and it was only gradually that the former began to be permeated by the rhythm, and the whole to be bound together by the harmonic growth of the movement. But with its completion, balance was attained, and the 'symphonic' idea saved. It is impossible to understand how any one can speak, in connection with this work, of a "retrograde step from the Symphony to the Suite", which, though the result is successful up to a point, leaves to some extent a mere "damaged torso" (Krug); or how it can be considered that "creative power, and the entirely neglected harmonic element, are of less importance" than the primitive force of rhythm (Mersmann). The power and skill with which Beethoven controls his resources are enormous; and it should not be overlooked that he employs this very element of harmonic colour to prevent the rhythm becoming monotonous. See, for example, the beginning of the working-out and that of the coda; or, for a case of sudden and surprising contrast, the Neapolitan sixth (A–C–F) that twice appears, pianissimo, in the fortissimo passages towards the end of the exposition (bars 94 and 100).

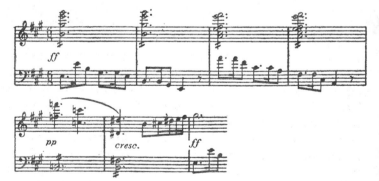

The transition to the second subject (bars 47–56) is also harmonized with exceptional richness, and the subject itself is introduced with consummate art (note its preparation in bar

53). How little this music depends for its effect on the com-
pelling motive power of the rhythm alone is clearly shown in
the working-out. Apart from the obstinacy of the rhythm, which
is only suspended for one single bar, this section is so perfect in
its harmonic construction and so abounding in melody, that the
rhythmic element might be eliminated altogether; that is to say,
there might be substituted another and less significant rhythm,
or a less monotonous one, which would still serve, in one way or
another, to bring out the full value of the melodic line. Yet even
if this were done, the music would remain not only logical and
organic, but brimful of life. Beethoven wrote no more purely
'symphonic' music; and never was he so self-disciplined as here,
where he had ostensibly surrendered himself to the domination
of rhythm. The same applies equally to the Finale, this "absolute
acme of shapelessness" (Mersmann), this "absurd," this "utterly untamed" music, this "delirium, in which there is no trace of
melody or harmony, no single sound to fall gratefully on the
ear" (Krug). Yet, surely, it is here in particular that Beethoven's
power of controlling his resources triumphantly stood the test!
At the opening of the movement, with the incessant repetition
of the principal motive, it certainly seems as if all bounds were
to be broken down in a scene of frantic turmoil; and it would
indeed be intolerable if this were to continue—that is, if the
structure of the whole were determined, as in the first movement, by this opening. Such however is not the case, for the
Finale, in contrast to the first movement, is distinguished by
great variety of rhythm; that of all the themes except the principal one is, in fact, in marked contrast to the rhythm of the
latter. This, though it is the principal theme, plays a compara-
tively small role in its original shape; but that part of it that may
be called the 'rolling' figure plays a very important part indeed,
and its impetus is strengthened by broad harmonic developments. This is evidenced by the way this figure now adapts itself to, and fits in with, the swinging, swaying musical phrases,
whereas at the opening of the movement it is fastened down no
less than twenty-eight times by vicious hammer-blows on its
highest note, which falls on the weak beat of each bar. In spite of

this, the movement as a whole gives the impression of being rhythmically homogeneous and of carrying everything before it; and the reasons for this are twofold: first, the insistent 'One-Two, One-Two' of the 2/4 time, the monotony of which is only broken by the displaced accent of the principal theme; and, second, the character of the various themes, all of which, as in the first movement, are in perpetual restless motion. This frenzied principal theme, turning and twisting as in a corybantic dance, is by no means typical of the whole movement, which only really gets under way with the developments that follow the principal theme. The scope of these developments is magnificent; and they attain their peak in the coda, in which for fifty-six bars the 'rolling' figure is heard again and again over a bass that first descends by semitones in a series of 'turns' and then settles down on a moving pedal (E and D sharp). Magnificent, too, is the manner in which the working-out aims at and prepares for the recapitulation. The movement is in sonata form, but the return of the principal theme, in C major, soon after the beginning of the working-out, almost makes it a Rondo. All these developments bear witness to the greatest mastery, and to equally great caution and discipline; it is like a gallop along the brink of an abyss on a fiery but firmly controlled racehorse. It is true that the impression the movement makes in performance depends entirely on whether the conductor is possessed of an equal controlling power—and whether or not he keeps in mind the Symphony as a 'whole'. Here as much as ever, the 'whole' is greater than the part—the one movement; inwardly the Finale is closely related to what has gone before—more so, probably, than in the case of any previous symphony but the C minor.

Since Wagner's dictum, it has been fashionable to refer to the Seventh Symphony as "the apotheosis of the dance." One evening during his last stay at the Palazzo Vendramini in Venice, Wagner actually 'danced' the Symphony to Liszt's accompaniment on the piano! As a counterblast to all this, Arnold Schmitz has recently emphasized the 'heroic' character of the work; and it is probable that it was this, rather than its dance-like attributes, that most struck the hearers at the first performance, when it was in the same programme as the *Battle of Vittoria*.

One thing is certain: in no other work are all the movements so dominated by rhythm; and, in particular, there is no other slow movement of its kind in which the lively dance rhythms of the first movement are transformed into a grave and ceremonious measure. Even in other works by Beethoven there is nothing to compare with this movement. From the very beginning it was the delight of the audiences, and even at the first performance it had to be repeated. Its form is simplicity itself, and yet of the greatest originality. A theme, consisting at the outset only of a gently tripping rhythm and certain harmonic developments, gradually acquires a sedately stepping melody. This is played four times without variation of any importance, except that from the second time onwards an expressive tune is grafted on to it, and is heard twice in the middle voices. At the last repeat, however, this tune pushes its way up and appears *ff* in the treble. The movement can hardly be called a set of variations, unless of the most primitive kind, for as the music proceeds only subsidiary parts in florid counterpoint are added, the thematic and melodic material remaining essentially unchanged. A middle section follows without any transition, and without modulation except that it is in the tonic major. The song-like melody of this section is accompanied by a triplet figure; but beneath it we hear the perpetual throbbing rhythm of the first part, with its two quavers. Towards the end of the section there is a modulation to C major, whose only purpose however is to lead back to the original A minor. The first section is now repeated, complete with its two-fold theme. There follows a fugato based on the first theme, which however very soon gives way to an impressive re-entry of that theme, but without the added tune. Once again comes the major theme, still in A, so that the whole movement diverges from the tonic even less than the Andante of the C minor. This time the A major theme is abbreviated, and connects immediately with the opening theme, which now makes its appearance, in its simplest form, in different octaves.

Here more than anywhere else does Beethoven prepare the

road that Schubert was later to follow in movements of this kind; though indeed it was only during Schubert's greatest period, towards the end of his life (particularly in the E flat Trio and the great C major Symphony), that he really attained a like assurance in the composition of such music—that is to say, of music whose sole function is apparently the depiction of 'moods'.

The function of a scherzo is as a rule primarily rhythmic. The rhythm of this movement, however, with its galloping crotchets, is freer and less significant than that of the first two. But in the Trio the solemnity of the Allegretto returns, this time with a hymn-like tune, in which the rhythm at last seems to come to rest, or at least to be marking time.

But we must not forget the Introduction to the first movement. This is the longest, and the richest in independent ideas, that Beethoven ever wrote. It has greater significance than even that of the Fourth Symphony. Thus it is something more than the indispensable preparation for what we are to hear in the first movement proper; for in its breadth and dignity it not only 'introduces' to us the following Vivace, but illumines the whole work. For some reason Schumann took it to have been intended ironically!

The Eighth Symphony, op. 93 in F, the shortest that Beethoven wrote, is considered by competent judges to be the finest of all. Yet for a long time general opinion rated it lower than others of his maturity; the 'pathos' and 'profundity' that were—and to some extent still are—regarded as characteristic of Beethoven, were lacking. How could this "good-humoured" symphony, as Krug so pertinently calls it, stand beside the other works of this Titan who was always either sunk in melancholy or else emerging victorious from a struggle with Fate? Its hearers even saw in it a return to an earlier style, and one that was more limited and more naïve. This shows a complete lack of understanding. From the first bar to the last, the work is the truest expression of Beethoven at the summit of his maturity. The same applies even to the Minuet, though this is not a real 'symphonic' scherzo, for which there would have been no place between the 'allegretto scherzando' and the Finale. Here the Minuet plays the same part in the sequence of movements as that of the E flat Sonata, op. 31, no. 3, in which, after a scherzando, a Minuet takes the place of a cantabile movement. In each case the agitated motion that characterizes the work as a whole is moderated to some extent in the Minuet only—a fact, by the way, that indicates the tempo at which it should be played.

It is true that Beethoven composed few works that are throughout so "good-humoured" as the Eighth Symphony. But how splendid are the thoughts that come to him in his "good humour", which surely is the joviality of the gods. From the opening theme of the first movement to the end of the Finale every bar has what may be called the same 'specific gravity'. That nothing was further from Beethoven's mind than graceful and cheerful trifling may be assumed from the fact that twice in the first movement he prescribes a *fff*. So far as I am aware he does this hardly anywhere else, not even at the great climaxes of the Ninth Symphony, where, indeed, it was not necessary expressly to indicate it. In the Eighth, however, this dynamic marking is required to make his intentions quite clear. But a second and still more obvious indication of the weight that Beethoven wanted here is given by those much discussed passages in the Finale starting with the sudden appearance of C sharp (really D flat), and culminating in the uncanny, daemonic key-change, whereby the principal theme is urged up into F sharp minor (really G flat minor). It is a striking example of those sudden and surprising contrasts of his, which seem to tear open a gaping chasm beneath the hearer's feet, but which illumine the whole movement—the whole symphony—and are prepared with the greatest mastery and form part of the living organism. As Oscar Kaul shows in Vol. V of the *Beethoven-Jahrbuch*, the very long Finale is in form a cross between 'first movement' and rondo. It has two development sections and two recapitulations, in addition to which there is an extended coda, beginning after the only pause in the movement.

The first movement also has a very important coda. Originally, and probably even at the first performance, this was shorter by thirty-four bars; that is to say, it lacked the last repetition of the principal theme, which forms a climax culminating in a *fff*. The working-out of this consummate movement is especially noteworthy. It is based almost entirely on the principal motive —in the earlier part the first two bars, and then, twenty-seven bars before the recapitulation, the first bar only. The re-entry of the principal theme, in its eight-bar form, is tremendously effective; for after we have been kept in suspense thoughout the development, we at last hear the theme again in its full and perfect shape. The stress and strain under which it has laboured are now relaxed, and, urged by the energy it has acquired, it now forges ahead instead of dying away to a *p* as at its first appearance. This return of the theme at the opening of the recapitulation shows very clearly that the essence of sonata form is growth —full and eventful evolution—and that "a theme will change its mood between its first appearance and its return".

CONCERTOS

Not only does most of the orchestral music that Beethoven composed during the decade 1803–1812, apart from the six tremendous Symphonies, take equal rank with them, but it, too, is imbued with the 'Spirit of the Symphony', whose influence extends far beyond the actual confines of its own sphere. This is especially so in the case of the Concertos. Beethoven had indeed already composed three Piano Concertos; but it was not until the Fourth, op. 58 in G, at the time when he was engaged on the Fourth Symphony and preliminary work for the Fifth, that he quite found himself. Like the *Eroica*, this Concerto ushers in a new epoch; and it bears the same relation to the *Eroica* that Mozart's magnificent late Concertos bear to his Symphonies. In both cases the symphonic structure is less rigid. In Mozart it gives way to vital and inspired figuration, which adds to the edifice a wealth of ornament; while in Beethoven the orchestra joins in mutual play with a solo part that gives the impression almost of free improvisation. At the very beginning of the G major Concerto we may note an effect of remarkable beauty: the manner in which the orchestra picks up the piano's pensive opening phrase, and extends and refashions it in such a way that it seems to evolve of itself with perfect freedom; and more wonderful still, if possible, is the way in which, in the second movement, soloist and orchestra go their different ways and seem to call to each other from separate worlds.

The Fifth Concerto, op. 73 in E flat, composed in the following year, is of a very different type. In the first and last movements its bearing is truly heroic. The whole work is a magnificent demonstration of the splendour of which tonality is capable. The rushing mighty arpeggio chords with which it opens seem like the entrance to the magic edifice of tonal harmony.

The glorious Violin Concerto, op. 61 in D, is charged with that sense of happiness that seems to flow from the unclouded major harmonies. In the first movement, however, this is several times interrupted in a manner that to many people, and particularly the Latin races, is incomprehensible, viz., by a pulsing D sharp that is unrelated to the surrounding harmony. It is one of those cases of 'open form' that points as it were from out a closed circle to a world of contrast. It is significant that this D sharp always occurs in conjunction with the same purely rhythmic motive, with which the movement opens and which appears again and again—some seventy times in all—and acts as a tie that holds together the whole movement. As in the case of the two Piano Concertos, the originality of form of the slow movement is especially noticeable. The lofty feeling of these slow movements is so entirely bound up with one feature that is characteristic of both—the antithesis of solo instrument and orchestra—that any arrangement that does not reproduce this feature, such as that for piano duet, deprives the music of its meaning, or at least substantially alters its nature.

With these three works Beethoven created a new form, that of the 'Symphonic Concerto'—a form later employed by Schumann and Brahms. These Concertos bear only a superficial likeness to Haydn's and Mozart's *Symphonies concertantes*. In the latter, certain individual instruments of the orchestra are

l

brought into prominence by being given parts of more brilliance and technical difficulty than the remainder; whereas with Beethoven the solo instrument is at once the *raison d'être* and the centre of gravity of the work, and as such determines the musical thought most appropriate to its own nature. (Beethoven's own attempt to arrange the Violin Concerto as a piano concerto shows plainly how indissolubly the music is bound up with the solo instrument.) At the same time its virtuoso quality, now far greater than in the case of Haydn and Mozart, is always merged in the symphonic organism.

OVERTURES

In the case of the Overtures the advance that Beethoven at this period made beyond the point at which his predecessors had left off was if anything still greater, and this in spite of the amazing genius and originality of Mozart's Overtures to *Don Giovanni*, *Figaro*, and *The Magic Flute*. Again Beethoven created something new, this time the 'Symphonic Overture', which sprang complete and fully fashioned from his brain. This by no means implies that he severed all connection with the theatre or with dramatic action—that is, with influences outside the domain of 'absolute' music; in the case of the *Leonora* Overtures 2 and 3, indeed, he actually drew the bonds still tighter. No one after him, not even Wagner, has ventured to introduce into an overture, note for note, and without any thematic connexion, such a passage as the trumpet-call, whose only *raison d'être* is to be found in the action of the drama. Yet Beethoven's skill as a symphonist never stood the test so brilliantly as in this very instance.

The two Overtures are unique also in another way: for this is the only case in which Beethoven took up again a completed work of any importance and not merely altered minor details of it, but entirely remodelled it. It is improbable that his only reason for doing so was that at the rehearsals certain passages proved too difficult. But however that may be, a new work was born, in its whole nature fundamentally different from the previous one. It was not an extension, for no. 3 is no 'bigger' than no.

2; it is only a difference of form. In no. 2 the centre of gravity is in the working-out, which is long and full of very dramatic points of concentration, and culminates in the Fanfare. All that follows is a reminiscence of Florestan's aria and, immediately after that, the triumphant close. Form is therefore here determined by dramatic action, every detail being filled with the prevailing excitement. In no. 3 the working-out is not merely reduced in length, but entirely re-written; the work has none of those dramatic points of concentration, but is worked up to a pitch of tension that, as at the beginning of the Allegro, is only equalled in the Fifth Symphony; and the composer's eye is kept throughout on the culminating point, viz. the Fanfare. Then follows a genuine recapitulation, also rewritten, which in its turn leads to the newly extended stretto at the close. The whole Overture has true symphonic balance, which Beethoven evidently thought the former setting lacked. Organic structure was to him more important than close connexion with dramatic action, of which we are now reminded by the Fanfare alone. Yet when we hear the work performed in a concert hall, we do not feel this flourish, whose sole *raison d'être* lies in the action of the opera, as an irruption, and we are in no way disturbed by it. This is proof that the form of the work—the symphonic conception—overcomes all logical considerations.

The *Coriolanus* Overture is of a very different type. It was written for a play of which we now know nothing but the name, by H. J. von Collin, a contemporary of Beethoven. Here the conception is purely symphonic; it was inspired not by details of the action but by an abstract notion—that of Tragedy—which is here cast in such compact mould as is to be found nowhere else but in the Fifth Symphony. There is something crabbed about the Overture (witness the perpetual syncopation)—an uncanny gloom that is only lightened for a moment here and there by the major mode. Yet in the midst of this gloom we can discern an equal stubbornness and self-assertion, that lasts almost up to the moment of collapse at the end. The Overture might also serve for Shakespeare's *Coriolanus*, or for that matter any other of his tragedies—supposing, indeed, that music of any kind is appropriate to those plays. But it is no less suitable for performance in the concert hall.

The *Egmont* Overture is oftener heard in the concert hall than in its original setting, viz. as the introduction to Goethe's drama, although it is more closely bound up with the drama than in the case of the other Overtures by the incidental music to the play. It is on the whole undoubtedly more operatic and less symphonic than any of Beethoven's other overtures. The triumphant conclusion, after the magnificent and genuinely symphonic evolution of the work, is called for by the exigencies of the drama, which at this point itself becomes operatic. It may be noted that this triumphant music reappears at the end of the play, and it is only with this that the *Egmont* music as a whole can be said to be properly rounded off. This is the reason why concert performances of the Overture are never quite satisfactory unless they are in celebration of some special occasion, and not merely a number in a programme.

PIANO SONATAS

Evidence of the influence that the 'Spirit of the Symphony' wielded over Beethoven during these years is provided by the growth in the dimensions of his piano music and a new tension that is to be found in it. This is first seen in the *Kreutzer* Sonata, which was contemporary with the *Eroica*; and it reaches its peak in the two Piano Sonatas, op. 53 and op. 57. Just as the *Kreutzer* could hardly be regarded as chamber music in the older sense of the words, so these two, more than any other of the sonatas, are most at home in the concert hall. They are simpler than the earlier sonatas—a fact that calls to mind the memorandum (see p. 134) in which Beethoven impressed upon himself the need of simplifying his piano music—but more spacious and magnificent than anything he had up to that time written for the piano. Without being virtuoso pieces in the narrower sense, they provide opportunities for a display of brilliant technique. Even in op. 53, dedicated to Count Waldstein, Beethoven's friend and patron of his Bonn days, the exuberance of his figuration is entirely in accordance with the spirit of the work. With the exception of the two episodes of the Rondo, which for variety's sake are in the minor, this is throughout in bright-toned major keys. Once again he sets sonata form against rondo form in such a way as to show clearly their different attributes, though it is true that to the latter he here adds a broad coda, which, in its power and brilliance, forms a worthy conclusion to the whole work. For the usual slow movement is substituted the glorious introduction to the Rondo. This introduction strikes a deeper note than might be expected; but it is to be taken as a warning both to the player and the listener not to allow the brilliance of the first and last movements to blind them to the serious side of the work as a whole. Beethoven is known to have composed this introduction later than the rest of the Sonata, to take the place of a broad Andante in F. This subsequently appeared alone under the name of 'Andante Favori', without opus number, a charming but somewhat superficial piece that no one unaware of this fact would connect with this magnificent sonata. It is to be hoped that no attempt will ever be made to reinsert it. Beethoven knew very well what he was about.

The F minor Sonata, op. 57, long known—though not to Beethoven!—as the *Appassionata*, is one of his most famous compositions. This is rightly so; and in this respect it compares only with the C minor Symphony, though in almost all others the two works are entirely different. Here Beethoven gives full vent to his passion. The tempest rages over the land, furious and insatiable. It is a phantasmagoria in which all the contending powers of nature are let loose. A large measure of cool-headedness is required to perceive, even here, the restraining hand— the hand that still retains control of the turbulent figuration and the broad, sweeping melodies. This is the last of Beethoven's works that begin in the minor and end with a minor chord; the only other examples are op. 2, no. 1, opp. 13 and 23, op. 30, no. 2, and op. 31, no. 2, but it is only in this case that he seems so to luxuriate in the minor. With the single exception of a subsidiary theme in the first, all the themes of the first and last movements are in this mode, and even that quits the major after a few bars. This theme he inserted late, when work on the Sonata was already far advanced, in order perhaps to let fall a hint that there

was also a 'major' side to the world. All the more striking, therefore, is the effect of the D flat major of the almost religious-
sounding Andante, whose Variations show how inspired sheer
figuration can be.

Here we find a case in which one motive holds together the
whole work:

This motive consists of the note-sequence C-D-C in the third
bar of the first movement. It returns again and again in various
shapes, and is the germ of themes in the second and third
movements. A very unusual point is that the first and third
movements are to a certain extent similar in design, for in both
cases the climax comes at the end, its peak point being reached
through a tremendous stretto. (No performer will do justice to
the work unless he holds in reserve sufficient strength for these
concluding passages.) Apart from this the ends of the two movements are, in accordance with their contrasting nature, of entirely different structure. In the first, which is full of conflict and
contrast, the stretto is preceded by a broad passage in which the
music pauses to take breath, and the movement finally dies
away to a pianissimo. In the last, which is almost entirely devoid
of contrast, the stretto works up in a simple and straightforward
climax, the peak being reached at the very end.

But this tendency towards a more brilliant 'concertante'
style was only temporary, and after the two Sonatas just discussed, Beethoven felt the need of again using the piano to speak
to us more intimately. In the next sonatas he returned to true

chamber music style. Of that in F sharp, op. 78, he himself had a very high opinion. In it there is no pathos; it is simply a glorious song, and in the first movement even the delicate figuration is infected by its glowing animation. In the second movement, 'Allegro vivace', this gives way to restless, playful activity.

The E flat Sonata, op. 81a, is the only one Beethoven wrote with a true 'programme'. This programme originally provided the title of the work, and refers to the departure and return of the Archduke Rudolf; and though it should not perhaps be taken too seriously, yet it is not unreasonable to see in the first movement (built up on a motive—'*Lebewohl*'—that dominates the whole movement in genuine sonata fashion) a 'farewell', and in the last movement a 'reunion'. Between them comes a monologue, in which the one who remains behind laments his loneliness. This is clearly differentiated in form from the two other movements, which are dialogues. It should be noted that these are between a higher and a lower voice. As in the case of the *Pastoral* Symphony, so here the individuality of the musical language is unmistakable—a second warning to those who scent a hidden programme in the other sonatas. Where shall we find another coda like the long one of the first movement, which, after the conciseness of all that has gone before, seems even longer than it is, and which, with its repeated cries of '*Lebewohl!*', brings the scene before our eyes with almost pictorial clarity?

The E minor Sonata, op. 90, is almost the only serious work of the barren years 1813 and 1814. Like its two immediate predecessors, it is remarkable for its lightness of touch and its ease and directness of expression. The first movement is full of life, and is made up of numerous contrasting themes and backgrounds that return again and again. It is quite simple in form; the recapitulation repeats the exposition unaltered except in key. The second (and last) movement is a tender and song-like Rondo, whose principal motive is related thematically to the close of the first movement. The themes return unchanged, as if eager to show off their beauty, until at last, in the coda, the principal theme after all undergoes a change; it is extended, and here and there bars are repeated, only to die away like a breath of wind, in a series of delicate figures.

CHAMBER MUSIC

No type of musical composition seems to be so little open to the influence of the 'Spirit of the Symphony' as the string quartet. A symphony may at a pinch be arranged for the piano, but any attempt to arrange one for a string quartet would be foredoomed to failure. In the case of no other kind of music are the bounds of dynamic expression so narrow; none is so intimate, none so entirely suited to performance in a room or small hall. Against this is to be set the greater range of expression and polyphony that is granted to the four equal partners—partners who are equal both in kind and, in spite of the first violin's leadership, in their rights and their importance.

It was not until six years after the completion of op. 18 that Beethoven again turned to the composition of string quartets. It was as if he had wanted to wait until he had shaken off the domination that his great predecessors, in their perfection, had exerted over him. And now, with op. 59, there came into being three works so personal in expression, of such unprecedented individuality, that no other compositions of the same kind will bear comparison with them. Not only that, but they stand alone even among the remainder of Beethoven's own works. So at least his contemporaries felt, however familiar they may have been with the rest of his music. To-day it is indeed difficult to realize that these very compositions were at their first appearance not only misunderstood, but even derided. A tune like that of the opening theme of the first movement of the F major Quartet was not regarded as music—this tune that gradually rises from the bass to the treble, four times repeating the same four-bar phrase, with no harmonic developments but the alternation of tonic and dominant.

The opening motive of the second movement—a rhythmic, pulsing beat for the cello on a single note—gave rise to nothing but laughter on the part of both players and audience. Clearly these musicians, professional and amateur alike, only heard the work piecemeal, and were thus incapable of feeling the terrific tension inherent in these opening phrases, or of awaiting the due development of the movement, upon which alone everything here depends. Beethoven constructed these movements with the greatest possible synthetical ability, building them up from true 'quartet-ideas' with a breadth and grandeur that is, we may after all decide, deeply imbued with the 'Spirit of the Symphony'. This is at once clearly apparent in the first and second movements of the F major Quartet. The former, one of Beethoven's longest Allegros, unites in an amazing manner intimacy of expression and softness of contour on the one hand, with a truly symphonic breadth of development and organic closeness of weave on the other. The principal theme seems to stroll calmly and quietly along, and this unflurried gait sets the tone for almost the whole of the movement. The second subject, beautifully introduced at bar 60, is not a contrast to the first; it even—very unusually—contains an echo of the first subject in the quaver figure in bars 71–77, which at the end of the working-out (bar 253), and in the coda (bars 367–369 and 391–393) attains a considerable degree of importance. On the harmonic side, long passages are almost rudimentary; everything is subordinated to clear definition of the melodic line. A contrast to this is provided by passages (bars 85–90, 144–149, and 332–337) in which the melody is for the moment silent, and a series of chords seem, with their apparently disconnected harmonies, to be following an ever-receding goal. The working-out is a marvel of lucidity and is fully charged with musical expression. It consists only of the principal theme, which is elaborately worked, and an expressive counter subject in the splendid Fugato, which is itself derived from the principal theme. At the beginning of the coda (bar 348) comes the one violent explosion of sound, but it lasts only for a few bars. The movement fades away, without a cadence in which the subdominant side of the key is clearly expressed. In the very striking bass line, F–D–C (bars 394–398):

End of
move-
ment

may be seen a reminiscence of the important thematic figure in
bars 3–4:

Bars 1–4

It is not sufficient for a complete understanding of the second
movement—the most extensive that Beethoven ever wrote of
the scherzo type—merely to note that all the various 'answers'
to the throbbing motive with which the movement opens (bars
4, 39, 72, etc.) are similar in structure. It should also be noted
that the movement is in true sonata form. Only in two places is

Cello   2nd Violin

Opening of recapitulation

1st Violin

2nd Violin   Viola

Bar 39   Bar 72

etc.

it allowed any latitude. The exposition is not repeated in its original form: at the first statement (bars 1–67), the second subject (bars 39 et seq.) is in D minor instead of in the usual dominant (F), and is merely a rhythmic and melodic modification of the first subject. At the second statement (bars 68–153), the first subject is altered in its 'answering' phrase (bar 72 et seq.), and a new and broader second theme is added, this time in F minor (bar 115).

After a very full working-out, the recapitulation starts at bar 239, not, as usual, in the principal key, but in G flat. The main theme is repeated note for note, now divided between the two violins and the viola, and accompanied by a fresh counter-theme. After thirty bars the principal key is again reached, and the rest of the movement, except for deviations from the normal modulations, is in accordance with the rules. The coda, which incidentally has the same number of bars as the development section, starts at bar 392.

The movement has no less 'depth' than the Adagios of this and the second Quartet. To realize this we need to be capable of hearing the diversity of expression, and the grace, the high spirits, and the often pensive seriousness that not only consecutively, but simultaneously, dominate the movement. Here no less than in the Adagio, for instance, whose deep melancholy is again and again lightened by moments of solace, of triumph almost, are the 'strata' clearly visible. No music is less susceptible than this to verbal exposition: none reveals itself more exclusively to those of us who are capable of hearing it 'absolutely'. And though throughout our lives we return time after time to these works, always we shall find in them some new perfection, some new manifestation of their magnificent organic growth.

As a compliment to Count Razoumoffsky, to whom the quartets are dedicated, Beethoven, as is well known, included a *thème russe* in each of the first and second Quartets. In the first it forms the principal motive of the Finale. Since this tune is not strictly in F, but in the Aeolian Mode (which corresponds to the modern A minor with G natural—here, however, transposed to D minor) he accompanies it, when it appears in its complete form, with a series of trills instead of harmonizing it; otherwise he brings it into line with the character of the movement as a whole by remodelling it.

The other *thème russe* is in the Trio of the Scherzo of the E minor Quartet, no. 2. This is the old Russian National Anthem, which is also heard in the coronation scene of Moussorgsky's *Boris Godounoff*.

In the C major Quartet, no. 3, there is no actual *thème russe*, but instead Beethoven wrote the slow movement (A minor) in the 'Russian' style. In the passive melancholy of the continuous quaver motion, and in the use of the harmonic minor scale (with the augmented second, G sharp–F), this movement is unique among all Beethoven's music. On hearing it, we are tempted to think of a piece like the *Ruined Castle*, from Moussorgsky's *Pictures from an Exhibition*, to which it is very similar in mood. Beethoven's authorship of this Andante, however, is betrayed not only by the perfection of its form, but also by the moving C major episode, although this appears only to vanish again immediately. The first and last movements of this Quartet are in C major, the brightness of which contrasts vividly with the remote and somewhat crepuscular harmonies of the Introduction to the first movement and the transition from the Minuet to the Finale. The inward brilliance and the vital energy of the Finale, which, though partly fugal, is no more a fully developed fugue than the Finale of Mozart's *Jupiter* Symphony, are incomparable.

The Finale of the E minor Quartet also, curiously enough, opens in C major, which, though it shortly modulates to E minor, returns again and again to C. Not until bar 53 does the principal key come into its own. To understand the first movement of this Quartet properly it is essential to realize that the treble notes of the opening chords (E–B) form an intrinsic part of the thematic material, and to connect them with the succeeding melodic figure:

Three years later Beethoven composed his famous op. 74, in

E flat, commonly known as the *Harp Quartet*. With the exception of the impetuous Scherzo, in C minor, it is light and easy-going music, free of all tension. The most beautiful movement is the first, the peak point of which comes in the magnificent coda. The manner in which, over the first violin's rustling arpeggios, the principal subject, which hitherto has been soft and tender, is worked up in a tremendous climax to a triumphant close, is admirable, if not unparalleled. The short Finale seems almost like an epilogue after the long and important Scherzo; the Variations of which it is composed are mostly serene and cheerful, and yet Arnold Schering has disclosed to an astonished world that this movement was intended to depict the death scene from *Romeo and Juliet!*

The following year Beethoven composed another Quartet, op. 95 (F minor), this time of an unusual, not to say curious, kind. He called it *Quartetto serioso*, and marked the third, scherzo-like movement, "Allegro assai vivace, ma serioso."

The first movement is described by Thayer (Riemann's Edition) as "the most splenetic piece of music Beethoven ever wrote"; and indeed traces of this quality, which is hardly to be found anywhere else in Beethoven, appear throughout the Quartet. It has been ascribed to his refusal by a lady to whom he had recently proposed marriage; if this is so, it is probably the only case in which he allowed one of his compositions to be affected by his personal experiences. The music, particularly that of the first movement, undoubtedly gives an impression of irritability, even of ill-temper, for it is violent and entirely devoid of humour; but it would not be true Beethoven if it did not also strike a deeper note—a note of sweetness and tender yearning. Here, too, the 'strata' are to be seen, more clearly even than in any but the latest works; and here we find, in particular, a unity that rises superior to mere facile contrast. The same applies to the harmonic scheme. The apparently arbitrary and far-fetched D major and A major scales are, in fact, properly within the ambit of the principal key. It is just the 'splenetic' main motive, which again and again drowns the more tender passages, that gives the first movement its structural stability.

Notwithstanding its brighter key—D major—the colour of the second movement is no less dark; again and again it encroaches upon the minor mode, while the theme of the Fugato, with its perpetual gyrations, is like a melancholy counterpart of the violent turmoil in the first movement. In the Scherzo, the gentle, almost devout Trio seems strangely amorphous; and even the plaintive, song-like melody with which the Finale opens is never allowed fully to unfold itself. After no more than seven bars, the 'Allegretto agitato' sets in with nervous haste until suddenly, towards the end, all the burdens under which the music has suffered are lifted. This corresponds in no way to the triumphal close of the *Egmont* Overture, as Krug appears to think, but is merely an awakening from a nightmare. Suddenly the tone lightens; but here it is as if the music itself had longed for this relief. Nor do we need any programme to understand the conclusion of this work—or indeed any work of this nature—but simply a clear apprehension of the meaning of 'open form'.

In addition to the String Quartets, Beethoven wrote during this period five chamber music works with piano, every note of which bears witness to deep inward happiness.

The Cello Sonata, op. 69—the first since the two of op. 5, which are among the most brilliant, if not the most profound, of Beethoven's early works—contains, like these, a great deal of broad figuration. At the same time it is full of tender and intimate song-like passages, whose long-drawn lines are settled at the very opening by the principal theme. This twice undergoes a striking change to the minor: first soon after the opening, where the music seems about to assume a heroic mood; and second, at the broad, almost passionate cantilena of the working-out. The Scherzo also, at the opening of which Beethoven wanted the piano part *ff*, has a song-like Trio, though no harmonic developments take place. The hearer who, at the opening of the very beautiful introduction to the Finale, expects a full Adagio movement, will suffer disappointment. Such a movement is no more than hinted at; and, indeed, to do more would have resulted in almost too great an extension of a work already packed with melody, particularly since in the Finale itself there are many more song-like tunes to come. These, in accordance with the character of the last movement, stream forth freer and more spontaneous than ever. The codas of the first and last movements are especially beautiful. On a presentation copy of the Sonata Beethoven, strangely enough, wrote: "*Inter lacrymas et luctus*" (amid tears and sorrow).

As is so often the case with Beethoven, the two works composing op. 70, the Piano Trios, are entirely different in style. The first movement of no. 1, in D—sometimes known as the *Geistertrio* on account of its gloomy, 'spookish' Largo, though there is little enough in either the first or the last movements to justify the title—is unusually concise, even for Beethoven. The first subject bounds merrily and vigorously along, and closes surprisingly on F natural; this is followed, with no more transition than a chord (a bare fifth on B flat) held for one bar, by an equally concise cantabile theme, which, though related to the principal theme, is diametrically opposed to it in feeling. What wealth and breadth is in these first few bars!

The working-out also is a miracle of concentration: the sprightly principal theme, only now clearly in 3/4 rhythm, and the cantabile second theme, contrast with each other in their manifold transformations. Not until it reaches the broad coda does the movement pause for breath. The Largo is in striking contrast to the first movement, owing to the breadth of its growth and development rather than to its dark and gloomy colour. The music does not, like the wind, blow "where it listeth," for each bar is held under firm control. The Finale, on the other hand, takes the bit between its teeth and dashes ahead without restraint from start to finish. It is without the points of concentration of the first movement, to which it is in many respects thematically related.

The second of these Trios is throughout of an entirely different type. From the Introduction it emerges slowly into the Allegro, whose second subject is unfolded almost after the manner of a Schubert song. Similarly in the second and third movements we find a foretaste of Schubert in their changing harmonic colour and the simplicity of their thematic material. This is not elaborated but merely embellished with figures. In the first movement the reappearance of the theme of the Introduction in the transition of the Allegro is genuine Beethoven, though later this procedure was followed by Schubert; typical also is the Finale, which here again forms the peak point of the whole work, and which is magnificent in its climaxes and in the fullness of its development section. With what care and skill does he prepare the second subject, in the unusual key of G, and how unexpected is the opening of the recapitulation, pp, so high up in the scale!

The Finales of both these Trios are in sonata form.

And now Beethoven crowns the edifice of his pianoforte chamber music with the great B flat Trio, op. 97. This is one of his best-known works, and has given its hearers more pleasure, perhaps, than any other. Yet it is seldom properly understood. The first movement is unusually loose-knit, in particular at the transition to the second subject, which, contrary to custom, is in G, and which seems to show less of the skill in modulation that is so admirable in the Finale of op. 70, no. 2. The whole movement is bathed in a glow of feeling. But comparison with the principal theme of Schubert's last Sonata, in B flat, which is similar in feeling to this, will prove how complete and self-contained Beethoven's structure is. How much happens to that theme in the working-out, and how tremendous is the tension under which the recapitulation is reached! The Scherzo, which like that of the Ninth Symphony takes the unusual place of second movement, is broader than is customary, and at the same time is given greater significance by the Variations to which the principal theme is subjected, and by a Trio that seems like an abyss into whose gloomy depths a ray from the triumphant sun suddenly strikes.

The theme of the lofty Andante is one of the finest upon which Beethoven ever wrote Variations. These for some time consist only of figuration—though needless to say this figuration is highly significant. The earlier Variations simply resolve, as it were, the cantabile line of the theme into pure movement; they only attain their full depth towards the end, when the theme reappears in an extended form and raised to E major. The coda is one of Beethoven's sublimest inspirations; the manner in which fragments of motives from the theme are gathered up and developed into a new melody of profound and tender feeling, is truly magnificent. And then, when the Finale suddenly breaks in, with its rough and sturdy humour, comes one of the boldest and most vivid contrasts that Beethoven ever ventured upon. No one with an ear to hear and to realize the full growth of this Finale could ever say that with it Beethoven had "left the rails", or that he had "lowered himself" by composing it; the movement is far too significant for that, far too rich in contrasts that carry it into the domain of genuine passion. Here again, how much happens in the coda, the Presto! Take it for all in all, it is hard to imagine this Trio with a different Finale.

The B flat Trio approaches very closely to the domain of the symphony; the Violin Sonata in G, op. 96, on the other hand, which was composed at the same time and is the tenth and last of a series of works that are almost all first rate, is music of the most intimate kind. At the same time it is exacting both from the technical and from the musical aspect. The first movement is one of Beethoven's most delicate structures, elaborated with the utmost skill from the short opening motive; it seems almost like a free improvisation, but in reality it has strict organic unity. The Adagio and Scherzo are played without a break, but are in the sharpest possible contrast. The Finale consists of Variations

m

on one of those 'popular' tunes that Beethoven, particularly in later life, was so fond of; it is cheerful and full of humour, but has gentler and more serious passages interspersed. The work is nearest of all to the threshold of that mystic realm, Beethoven's 'last style'.

BEETHOVEN IN 1823
(Portrait in oils by Waldmüller. In the posses-
sion of Messrs Breitkopf and Härtel, Leipzig.)

THE VOCAL WORKS

THAT Beethoven wrote hardly any but instrumental music during his first ten years in Vienna—during the period, that is, in which his personality was still in process of formation—is a matter of the greatest significance. It is doubtless to be ascribed to a deep-rooted propensity, for it happened in spite of the fact that public interest was at that time almost entirely concentrated upon vocal music, whether in church, theatre, or concert hall. Later, indeed, after *Fidelio* and in spite of the disappointments that this opera brought him, his mind was very much occupied with vocal music. He wrote songs, planned operas, composed the D Major Mass—his "greatest and finest work", as he himself called it—and even crowned his last Symphony with a stupendous choral movement. Further choral works that he had planned never saw the light; his return to absolute music, with his last Quartets, was final.

SONGS FOR SOLO VOICE

From the sketch-books it is clear that in the composition of songs Beethoven's main difficulty was to find the right melodies for them. It is difficult for us to realize the trouble he had with a tune such as that of the opening song of the cycle *An die ferne Geliebte*, which charms us just because it sounds so 'natural'. This seems on the face of it to argue lack of skill, and indeed his contemporaries took it as such. When Cherubini heard *Fidelio* in its original form, he ascribed its failure to Beethoven's lack of experience in writing for the voice, and presented him with a

French treatise on vocal composition. That even in his later years Beethoven did not feel quite sure of himself in this *genre* is shown by a sketch for the D major Mass, on which he had noted down a few phrases from *Don Giovanni*, evidently seeking a stimulus in Mozart's masterly treatment of his text. This awkwardness in writing for the voice is deeply rooted in the very nature of Beethoven's musical language. The organic growth of a tune, which is only determined from within, in accordance with the laws of absolute music, was to him of such importance that he never felt himself free when the music was influenced from without, i.e. by the words. Since at the same time he always wished to give each word its full due, a hard struggle ensued. The result of this, however, was as a rule conciliation, and not the victory of one side over the other.

He set Goethe's *Wonne der Wehmut:*

> "Trocknet nicht, trocknet nicht,
> Tränen der ewigen Liebe!
> Ach, nur dem halbgetrockneten Auge
> Wie öde, wie tot die Welt ihm erscheint!
> Trocknet nicht, trocknet nicht,
> Tränen unglücklicher Liebe!"

(Cease not, tears of eternal love! Ah, how bleak and desolate does the world seem to him whose eyes are but half-dried! Cease not, tears of ill-starred love!)

The free rhythm of this heart-felt cry gives the composer little help in setting it metrically; but the slight alteration in the first two lines when they are repeated gives it something of simple song-form (*a-b-a*). Beethoven made use of the repetition to build up a climax corresponding with the poetic idea—the substitution of "ill-starred" for "eternal". But apart from this, the melody interprets faithfully each spiritual and rhythmic impulse, and sensitively reproduces the declamatory effect, inherent in the words of the poem. To the half-spoken words *Trocknet nicht*, the piano replies with a figure that clearly shows us the flowing tears, and with the middle section piano and voice are combined in a melodic phrase of great perfection of form and closeness of texture. And so the poem, in the truest sense of the words, 'is made music'—music, it is true, that is inseparable from the voice, for it would be impossible to replace this by an instrument, but whose meaning is to be found in itself alone. Thus we can understand it and respond to it in spirit even if we do not understand or listen to the words. Through some mysterious process song entered the domain of absolute music, and therewith the *Lied*—the 'Art-song'—came into being, to be developed, first by Schubert and Schumann and later by Brahms and Pfitzner, to full and glorious perfection.

Goethe, as is well known, took no interest in either Beethoven's or Schubert's songs; the only settings of his poems that he considered satisfactory were those of Zelter and his associates. This has often been regarded as proof that Goethe was not musical, or that he was dependent on Zelter's often limited judgement. Actually the reason why he did not approve of Beethoven's and Schubert's settings lies deeper: he could not endure his poems being 'translated' into music. He demanded of music little less than complete subordination to his words, so that not only their spiritual essence but also their form should be unimpaired, and that they should thus retain their full dominance. Looking at matters from a poet's point of view, it cannot be said that he was altogether wrong. As we know only too well, the words of a poem are often overshadowed by the music, with the result that the more the hearer cares for music the less attention he pays to the words and the less impression they make on him. For this reason, too, song-composers as a rule prefer poems in which it is not so much the actual words that count as the 'mood' of the poem. (Hugo Wolf is, characteristically enough, an exception to this rule, for he more than any other composer was content to give each word of the poem its full value by imparting to his songs a declamatory quality that was often raised to the highest pitch of dramatic clarity.)

All the songs of Beethoven to which the above applies were works of his maturity. Few of his youthful songs, some of which were published later with high opus numbers, are of any importance, except the delicious *Mailied*. The very beautiful *Adelaide*, the melody of which is instrumental rather than

vocal and takes little account of the words of the poem, is more
a concert aria or a solo cantata than a *Lied* proper. Also the well
known Sacred Songs, to words by Gellert, in which Beethoven
already showed considerable individuality, are more like sacred
arias, though the music of them was undoubtedly born of the
words. There are true *Lieder* among other settings of Goethe's
poems (1809–1811) besides *Wonne der Wehmut*, such as
Herz mein Herz, with its inspired and fervid melody, and
Mephistos Flohlied (The Song of the Flea) from *Faust*, with
its grotesque and humorous characterization. The four slightly
earlier settings of *Nur wer die Sehnsucht kennt* are good examples of Beethoven's search for exactly the right tune. It was
not until the fourth setting that he decided, in order to give
prominence to the words "es schwindelt mir", to avoid strophic
form. It is interesting also to compare the two settings of
Tiedge's *An die Hoffnung* (1804 and 1815). The broad curve
of the melody in the former is extended in the latter; strophic
form is abandoned, and in its place there are magnificent contrasting sections. The fact that the first verse is repeated at the
end, and that the whole is introduced by a stirring recitative,
gives the song the aspect of a solo cantata. At the same time, the
shape of the melody makes the second version less singable
than the first. The tune of *An die Geliebte* (1811) has a lovely
and very simple line. But Beethoven achieved the greatest perfection in the cycle *An die ferne Geliebte*, which was the first
of its kind. Side by side with this stands his last song, *Resigna-
tion* (1817), in which he succeeded in doing a remarkable
thing: a song in which the words are declaimed almost as if it
were a recitative, and in which every changing emotion is truly
reflected, is as strict in form as any piece of pure music.

Lisch aus, lisch aus, mein Licht! was dir ge-bricht, das ist nun

fort,   an   die - sem Ort kannst dus nicht wie - der   fin - den

CHORAL WORKS

Among the choral works there are, it is true, a number that
arc second rate, especially those commissioned for festivities
such as the Congress of Vienna. It is not uninteresting to observe Beethoven's reactions when his 'inspiration' came not
from heaven but from temporal powers. His work was no less
careful; but he seems to have been unable to turn out any but
dullish compositions, even given an exotic subject. A case in
point is the *Ruins of Athens*, though in this he clearly enjoyed
writing the brilliant *Chorus of Dervishes*. Moreover he had recourse to unusual prodigality: an aria of the High Priest is accompanied by four obbligato horns and two bassoons, thus
handsomely beating Leonora's aria. Yet even here we can trace
the hand of the master. But that the mature Beethoven could
come to grief in this class of composition is proved both by his
first attempt at an oratorio (the *Mount of Olives*), the first big
choral work since the cantatas of his Bonn days, and by that
strange composition the Choral Fantasy, op. 80, in which no
justification is even attempted for the introduction of a chorus
into an instrumental work—such, at any rate, as is essential for
the true understanding of the Finale of the Ninth Symphony. It
is to be found, perhaps, in a purely external incentive, viz., the
desire to write a composition for some occasion or other in
which piano, orchestra, and chorus shall just make music together. The work consists of a long Introduction for the piano,
of the nature of an extempore prelude; a short middle movement for orchestra of no particular importance; and a choral
movement, the tune of which, composed in Beethoven's Bonn
. days, lacks the necessary inner weight. The result of this is that
the choral movement has the effect of a long-drawn-out cadenza.
It is impossible to tell from internal evidence that this work was
written in the same year as the Fifth and Sixth Symphonies and
other magnificent works.

The *Elegischer Gesang*, and especially *Meeresstille und glück-
liche Fahrt*, are more worthy of our regard, the latter for its fine
depiction of the Calm of the Sea, which is disturbed by the
mystic cry of the chorus at the word 'Weite'. It is clearly owing

to the shortness of the work that it is hardly ever performed; being so short, it is presumably held not to justify the engagement of orchestra and chorus, a fate that it shares with many other short choral works of great and permanent value.

FIDELIO

The painful history of *Fidelio* is familiar. The failure of 1805 was its salvation. It was not only the alterations that Beethoven was then forced to make in it, but also the 1814 revision, that gave it the shape in which, for a hundred and twenty years now, it has gripped its hearers. It is one of the most German of all operas. Nowhere is it apparent that the story is of French origin or even that the words of most of the songs are a translation of those of Bouilly's revolutionary opera *Léonore, ou l'amour conjugal.* What is surprising is that Beethoven should have been influenced by the music, the composer of which was the singer Gaveaux. (In Gaveaux' opera, Marcelline's aria is in the minor, with a major middle section; the duet between Jaquino and Marcelline finishes with a stretto; Rocco's B flat aria has a somewhat similar theme in each setting; the duet between Leonora and Marcelline, which Beethoven later omitted, is in 12/8 time; Leonora's aria has a horn obbligato; and at the beginning of the Finale the voices enter *pp*, one by one. Towards the end of the Overture there are in both cases string passages that work up to a climax. On the other hand, there are only slight points of similarity with Paer's earlier Italian opera on the same libretto. In both cases Leonora's aria is introduced by the great recitative and in the Larghetto has an obbligato for wind instruments; there is also some similarity with the coloratura of Beethoven's first setting.)

But to what glorious heights did Beethoven raise these models! Never has music of greater fervour and tenderness been written, never did Beethoven reveal his soul as here, moved as he was to the depths of his being by the emotional content of the drama. The soul of the work is elemental in its intensity and freedom, a freedom that surpasses that of Mozart, but was the source of Weber's and Wagner's romantic and dramatic melodies, and is often almost overpowering. Yet nowhere does true sentiment degenerate into sentimentality, nowhere is passion torn to tatters; everything is entirely natural, and of a "chastity" that, according to Berlioz, hindered the success of the music in France. For here as elsewhere Beethoven's power of control, his symphonic genius, and his determination to achieve perfection of form, triumphantly stood the test. The very fact that this form was so highly developed, and that some of the individual numbers are therefore longer than was usual, has been cited as proof that, compared with Mozart and Weber, Beethoven had no dramatic gifts. From the point of view of external effect, this may perhaps be so; but it does not do justice to the inner dramatic vitality of his music. Surely even the canon in the quartet of the first act, *Mir ist so wunderbar*, for which Beethoven has so often been criticized, has a truly stirring effect, inappropriate as the static form of the canon (which here to be sure is somewhat naïvely employed) is to operatic conventions. The music is coloured by the mood of the simple and beautiful words of the dialogue: "*Meinst du, ich könnte dir nicht ins Herz sehen?*" (Thinkest thou that I cannot see into thy heart?); it has caught the tenseness of the action, and gives to both full scope for display. The tone of the first two numbers (the duet between Marcelline and Jaquino, and Marcelline's aria), which is more that of the German 'Singspiel', here gives way to something deeper and more serious, which, except for the next aria, that of Rocco, remains in force for the rest of the opera. This aria was cut after the first performance, but was later reinstated to satisfy a singer who demanded one of his own. Beautiful as it is, it gives us a feeling of slight discomfort; it is the only passage, in which anything remained of the first setting, that is not entirely worthy of the human and dramatic dignity of the opera in its final form. At all events, little is lost by its omission; whereas to make any other cuts, or to change the order of the numbers, at once affects the substance of the opera. Everything is in its right place and is indispensable; whereas in, say, the *Magic Flute* cuts are undesirable only because they rob us of an aesthetic pleasure—our delight in the beauty of individual numbers, while to change their order makes no essential difference to the work as a whole. This is a proof of the closeness of texture of *Fidelio*, consisting though it does of separate numbers with spoken dialogue.

The failure of the first performance turned out a blessing in disguise. Never otherwise would Beethoven have been induced to make the alterations that gave the opera its peculiar perfection. Doubtless much beautiful music was sacrificed; but doubtless also many a *longueur* was avoided, to say nothing of the rather absurd duet between Leonora and Marcelline on the subject of marital life, which actually followed that between Pizarro and Rocco. But new glories were added: Leonora's great Recitative; the end of the first Finale, which replaced Pizarro's highly coloured aria with chorus of Guards; and the greater part of Florestan's aria, with his "vision" of the "Angel Leonora", which replaced a beautiful but somewhat ineffective 'lament'. A stirring 'melodrama' follows, the music of which, as was seldom the case except in a few passages of the *Egmont* music, is emotion without form. It is not certain whether this was in the first setting. We know that Treitschke, the librettist, had a considerable share in the revising of the opera. He consulted with Beethoven on all points of detail, and showed that he was sensitive to musical effects. We also have him to thank for the simple but often very beautiful dialogue of the libretto in its final form. The alteration he made in it towards the end of the Prison Scene was nothing less than inspired: Florestan's and Leonora's very beautiful recitative, originally following Pizarro's exit, was cut, and in its place was inserted a short but affecting dialogue. The idea of a change of scene, also, before the Finale of the second act, which originally played in the prison, and was given its present magnificent form, was a substantial improvement, for now the Prison Scene as a whole stands out clearly from the rest of the opera and is seen to be one of the greatest musico-dramatic conceptions of all time. Wagner's adverse criticism of the libretto will hardly be accepted: "What is the dramatic action . . . but a tiresome and feeble version of the drama we have lived through in the Overture, like a tedious commentary by Gervinus on a scene from Shakespeare?" Another question is whether the tremendous symphonic tension of the two great Leonora Overtures nos. 2 and 3 does not overwhelm the music of the opera itself. As we all know, this question is to-day generally answered in the affirmative; but since audiences will not be denied the pleasure of hearing the magnificent no. 3, another place has to be found for it. It is therefore played between the two acts, or immediately after the Prison Scene. The first solution of the difficulty merely gives rise to another, for it destroys the connexion between the first and second acts; the second would be satisfactory as a sort of retrospective glance at the drama at the moment of its highest tension, if it did not spoil the brilliant effect of the Finale, with its broad C major opening. The question is really insoluble; the best thing to do would be to follow Beethoven's original intention and leave it where it belongs, overlooking the sharp contrast between it and the first duet. If this is done, we at least know from the outset to what heights of grandeur the whole work will ascend as it runs its course; a glimmer of light falls from these heights on the somewhat naïve music of the first two numbers; and we have been prepared for the jubilant final chorus, as it unfolds itself in all its symphonic breadth. Thus we feel that the opera has returned to the sphere whence it came.

THE MASS IN D, op. 123

This, the *Missa Solemnis*, has up to now been disregarded by the commentators. In no single dissertation has its musical essence been penetrated to any depth. Even Schenker has written nothing about it. It is indeed Beethoven's least approachable work; perhaps it never will receive a fully adequate performance. Even the best performance leaves something unsolved. This is due not only to the technical difficulties, especially those with which the chorus is faced, but also to the connexion of the work with the Roman Catholic form of worship. Its 'catholicism' has often been called in question; the Mass has, indeed, often been taken as proof that Beethoven was not a believer in revealed religion. This is untrue. Though as a Catholic he was not, like Haydn and later Bruckner, strict in his religious faith and observances, he had at least been in close touch with the Catholic world from his youth upwards. He was not, as some people think, a Deist, but a true Christian. And when he decided of his own free will to write a mass in celebration of the enthronement of his patron and pupil, the Archduke Rudolf, as Archbishop of Olmütz, it was the Church and nothing else that was in his mind. It is true that the Mass was not finished in time for this ceremony, and when it was, it had grown to such dimensions that it seemed to be only in the most exceptional cases that it could be used for religious services. It is, however, sometimes sung in Austria at High Mass on the most important ceremonial occasions; and only recently, in fact, its suitability for this purpose was expressly confirmed by the Roman Catholic authorities. And, indeed, the first chords of the *Kyrie*, as they echo through some great cathedral, raise us to the sublime and mystic world of the divine office. In contrast to Bach's B minor Mass, which does not suffer from the atmosphere and garish light of the concert hall, the *Missa Solemnis* is never quite at home there. In a church, on the other hand, where the divine office is of prime importance, full justice can never be done to its music. Thus, in common with many other great works of art, it has grown up in a realm that lies beyond the bounds of practical possibilities.

Ten years earlier Beethoven had composed for one of his patrons a Mass in C, op. 86. This is a fine but not very individual work; but from it we can see clearly that at the time other things —the Fifth and Sixth Symphonies—occupied his mind. It is obvious that when writing his second Mass he gave no thought to the first, but tackled the problem as if it were new to him. He had the text translated word for word into German, and again buried himself in old church music. He often said that only Palestrina's style was suitable for ecclesiastical music, though this does not mean that he was a mere imitator of another man's style. All he wished to do was to steep himself in the spirit from which this grew, in order to produce a work that in every note should be himself at his truest and boldest.

Wagner is only partly right when he says that the Mass in D was "a purely symphonic work bearing the true stamp of Beethoven's mind", in which the text "serves only as material for the vocal parts," and "does not disturb our musical sensibilities simply because it excites in our minds no ideas of reason . . . but only moves us by the impression of familiar and symbolic religious formulae." For Beethoven the text was something more than "material for the vocal parts"; he gave full significance to the religious and human content of every word. But when he turned the word into music, it must be admitted that he was then the symphonist; and in doing so he accomplished something that is almost unique even among his own works. If yet another proof were needed that the problem of the symphony was the central point of his creative work, it could be found in the manner in which he acquitted himself of this task, of which the most important parts are diametrically opposed to the 'Spirit of the Symphony'. None of the great men who had composed masses before him had ever attempted anything of the sort. The greatest setting of the liturgy before Beethoven, Bach's B minor Mass, juxtaposes section against section, each one stupendous in itself but not welded into larger movements. The second *Kyrie* has even no connexion with the first. Mozart's magnificent unfinished C minor Mass follows Bach's example. In it the *Gloria* is divided into sections, some of them of splendid breadth of development; but they have no inner continuity or even homogeneity of style. Where, in the 'short' masses of Haydn and Mozart, the *Gloria* and the *Credo* are treated as separate entities, they consist of individual sections, without anything in the way of thematic development, in which the text is set straight through and often without much heed to the significance of individual words, or at most with a return of the motive of the *Credo* in the style rather of a *Leitmotif*. The *Leitmotif* in this sense already occurs in Palestrina and his predecessors, but without any grouping of separate numbers in larger movements. In Beethoven's C major Mass it is much the same, though here the dimensions are considerably greater. It is not until we come to the *Missa Solemnis* that we find the individual parts, now much extended, treated not only externally but also internally as symphonic units, to which each word, now as never before interpreted in its full spiritual depth, must adapt itself. To prove this in more detail would require a special article; here a few examples must suffice.

"*Von Herzen—möge es zu Herzen gehen!*" (From the heart may it go to the heart!) Beethoven wrote over the *Kyrie*. And in truth nothing more fervent and devout has ever been written than this cry for mercy, nor anything simpler than the whole movement, the melodic and harmonic proportions of which are throughout firmly held and of truly cosmic breadth. It has not yet been noticed that bars 4–7:

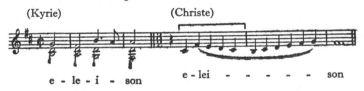

already contain a germinal motive of the greatest fertility. From the treble line (F sharp-B-A-G-F sharp) both forms of the *eleison* are developed:

(G-F sharp-B-A in the *Kyrie*, C sharp- F sharp- E-D-C sharp in the *Christe*). Palestrina's famous *Missa Papae Marcelli* has an almost identical *Leitmotif* (G-C-B-A-G):

Later on in the Mass this same germinal motive reappears

several times in various shapes. The middle section, the *Christe eleison*, is related to the *Kyrie* not only by the *eleison* phrase, but also by that given to the word *Christe*. Into both this breathes a spirit of humanity. A genuine symphonic touch is given to the return of the *Kyrie*, when everything reappears slightly altered, in part abbreviated and compressed; and again, particularly, at the magnificent passage in which, at bars 170–183, the *eleison* makes a ninefold entry, as in a stretto, which is immediately followed (bars 184–223) by an extended cadence that gradually dies away, though still full of melody, to the end.

The *Gloria in excelsis Deo:*

Glo - ri - a   in ex - cel - sis   De - - o

is a cry sent out by the heavenly hosts into the universe, and as such it is at first rudimentary, almost shapeless, as if it had grown out of the primal elements of music. But as the movement progresses it is curbed and subjected to manifold transmutation; and so form is achieved, and contrasts are firmly bound and held. As in the *Kyrie*, so here, at the moment the name of God the Son is heard this motive changes its mood to one of human tenderness and devoutness (bars 190–209):

Do - mi - ne   fi - li   u - ni   ge - ni - ti

How skilful are these transitions!—first at the soft entry of the *Gratias*, and then again in the broad middle section of the *Qui tollis*, that second cry for mercy after the *eleison*, which is this time intensified to the most passionate remorse. The final Fugue, whose subject is related to the germinal motive, contains points of concentration of an intensity until then unheard of, which however is urged up to still greater heights by the repeated shouts of "Gloria" at the Presto towards the end.

in glo - - - - - ri-a de-i Pa - tris

Though the skill with which, in the *Gloria*, the various contrasts of mood are held together in true symphonic style calls for our highest admiration, it is almost inconceivable that Beethoven should have been able to achieve the same in the case of the different 'articles of faith' in the *Credo*. Here too, as in the *Gloria*, there is a germinal motive that holds together a tremendous edifice. But this time it is a confession of faith, and not a shout from the heavenly hosts, and Beethoven accordingly built the edifice of square-hewn blocks of stone. (At the beginning of the *Credo* he wrote: "*Gott über alles—Gott hat mich nie verlassen*" (God above all—God has never deserted me). In one of his conversation-books of the year 1825 we find the theme of the *Credo* as a canon, with the words "*Gott ist eine feste Burg*" (God is our stronghold). The articles of faith are not simply set one against the other as equals; the more important ones are given prominence, others, particularly those referring to the Holy Ghost and the Church, are kept in the background. But in the principal articles there is not a word whose full depth he does not plumb. The symphonic skill with which he connects the different sections is amazing—as for instance the transition from the first part, dedicated to the majesty of God the Father, to the moving *Qui propter nos homines*, describing how Christ was "made man", and from there to the word *descendit*, which he depicts as impressively as later he depicts the word *ascendit*. To see in this, or in the hammer-blows of the *Crucifixus*, a form of naturalism is quite wrong; it is the highest expression of the true inner sense of the words. Never did the *et incarnatus est* sound more mystic than here, where for a moment Beethoven abandons tonality and approaches the style of Palestrina, and where he symbolizes the Holy Ghost by a soaring passage for the flute—a passage that might equally be regarded as 'naturalistic'. In the immediately following *et homo factus est* the contrast afforded by the resolute return to tonality has an effect of great nobility; both here and in the *Gloria* the boldness of Beethoven's contrasts attains its zenith. Often it is a word or a short phrase that occasions the contrast, but this contrast is always an integral part of the general growth. The movement climbs to ever higher peaks: after the Resurrection comes the announcement of the Last Judgement, with the word *judicare*. The next few articles are less fully dealt with; but here, by way as it were of a recapitulation, Beethoven repeats the principal motive of the *Credo* again and again, piling climax on climax, and so attains the heights from which the final Fugue announces the Life Everlasting. These two Fugues of the *Gloria* and the *Credo* are conclusive evidence of Beethoven's contrapuntal skill. And here too is to be seen with particular clarity in what respect they differ from Bach's fugues. The rules are observed as strictly by Beethoven; but his are no longer static, as those of Bach were, but magnificently dynamic; no longer merely the unfolding of something already complete though not yet manifest, but a ceaseless growing and developing towards new aims. The Fugue of the *Gloria* is one of the mightiest that ever Beethoven wrote; that of the *Credo*, for all its tremendous climaxes, is the furthest removed from worldly things.

In his C major Mass, already, Beethoven had connected the *Sanctus* with the *Benedictus*, a treatment that was contrary to ecclesiastical use, in accordance with which there was generally no music during the consecration, the most mystic and sacred part of the service. But the soft playing of the organ during the consecration is expressly authorized, and in the *Missa Solemnis* Beethoven avails himself of this sanction to write a movement in a magnificent and quite individual form. The *Sanctus* is usually set as a solemn and majestic cry of adoration, working up to a pitch of great brilliance. Here Beethoven causes it to be sung *piano*, as if in awe, by the lower voices. The orchestral part also is given to the lower instruments; the violins are silent, and the violas and cellos are divided; while the trombones utter pianissimo interjections. The section dies away without any formal

n

close, and is followed by the jubilant *Osanna*, in two short fugued passages; this, strangely enough, in spite of the exuberance of the orchestra, is given to the solo voices. These two sections also have no definite close; but the *Osanna* is followed without interruption by the orchestral *Preludium* for lower strings and wood-wind only, played during the consecration. In this the germinal motive appears and reappears in various shapes, steeped in mystery, reassuming and giving still further profundity to the mood of the *Sanctus:*

It prepares us for a piece of truly celestial music: the *Benedictus*, in which the solo violin joins with its ethereal voice, as if from the other world. Here for the first time in the whole work the music expands in complete and undisturbed peace, as though there were nothing else on earth. And the closing *Osanna in excelsis*, the motive of which is taken from the interlude for wind instruments, is enwrapped in this same peace. Yet the music is in no way romantic or 'melting'; it is throughout of the greatest concentration of form and closeness of texture. Some remarks on the individuality of the melodic material of this section will be made in the last chapter.

The first part of the *Agnus Dei* is no less broad and spacious. Here for the first time a complete movement is dominated by the darker colour of the minor mode. It is like a procession of sin-laden humanity to the gentle and compassionate Lamb of God. (The *Kyrie* and the *Gloria* were cries for mercy; this is the third, and the most despairing.) How simple the harmony and the melodic line, and how full and broad the development! Thrice does the *Agnus Dei* enter, first as a bass solo, second as a duet for tenor and alto, and third sung by the four solo voices, in tones of the deepest penitence; and each time it is answered by

the *Miserere!* of the chorus. The whole is an Adagio almost a
hundred bars long, and it seems to be spanned by a great three-
arched bridge. The last twenty-five bars are simply a prolonged
passage in B minor, which delays the close and into which towards the end D sharp suddenly shines like a first ray of hope.
The transition is of the tenderest beauty and simplicity. After
two chords the cry of *Agnus Dei*, as yet faint-hearted, comes from
the chorus as from a people from whom a burden has been lifted,
or who can descry in the distance signs of redemption and peace.
And when the first *Dona nobis pacem* descends in unison:

it seems that the fulfilment of the "Prayer for inward and outward peace", as Beethoven wrote over this section, could not be
far off. But it is not yet at hand. From the beginning, it is true,
the melody has reflected the image of peace in a series of lovely
and tender, but tremendously impressive phrases. Yet clearly
it is still far away—of this no doubt is left by the inner agitation
of the music, a 6/8 'allegretto vivace', richly embroidered in the
orchestra with semiquaver figures. Assuredly this last movement is the least approachable of all and, in spite of the simple
devoutness of the music, the most enigmatic. The first part
already, sixty-eight bars down to the opening of the 'allegro
assai', in B flat, is unusual, if not unique, in its wealth of ideas
and sudden change of mood. The melodic phrase of the first
Dona is taken up by the orchestra and invested with the quality
of gentle pathos. The chorus enters with a new and still more
devout phrase, and works it as a short double fugato (bars 12–27)

which runs into four unaccompanied bars for the chorus:

do - - - na no - bis pa - cem

in which the spirit of devoutness and humility is still more
strongly marked. With these four bars, which reappear later
and form the close of the whole Mass, the movement comes to
rest, as it were, at the peak point of a climax. It is as though all
humanity were kneeling in prayer for peace. Again a fugato
seems to be about to grow out of the first bar of this prayer, only
to give way after four bars to a vision of peace. The same thing
happens with a new fugato:

etc.

do - na do - na

which is closely related to the germinal motive, but which, after
an expressive extension of the melody, runs into a broad and
surprisingly energetic cadential phrase.

do - - - - na pa - - cem

And now follows the section that offended, and still offends,
so many people and which, according to Krug, was Beethoven's
"worst error of judgement." This is the trumpet fanfare which,
after the hollow drum beats and the uneasy sixths for the strings,
smacks of 'war'. It is interrupted by a dramatic recitative, which,
significantly enough, is a cry not for peace but for mercy. Haydn
thirty years before did the same thing in his *Missa in tempore
belli*; but the D major Mass was composed in times of peace.
These trumpet calls, then, mean something else, something
more general; it is not war as against peace, but the hurly-burly
of life on earth—worldly affairs, that is, as the root of all sin—
as against inward as well as outward peace. Hence the first cry

is not for peace but for mercy. It is only the third cry that is for
peace—and the spectre has vanished! This is followed by the
first working-out, musically speaking, of the thematic material
stated at the opening of the movement, which leads, here also,
to a cry for peace in which all the voices join. This time, however,
it is followed at once by a fugue:

do - - - na no - - bis pa -

which is carried on for at least twenty-five bars and finally leads
to the same cadential phrase as that which closed the first section. Now at last we come to the real riddle: an orchestral
fugato, presto,

in which the subject of the first fugato is joined by a very
energetic counter-subject (bars 12 et seq.). The section is
extremely animated, and as it progresses it is dominated more
and more by the wood-wind, playing in thirds. What is the
meaning of this second interruption of the vision of peace?
Certainly not war, this time. Rather is it the confusion of the
world in general, or at least a second 'contrast' that Beethoven
thought necessary in order to set clearly before us the chaos
from which our longing for peace springs. And out of this chaos
are heard the passionate cries of the chorus for the last hope of
mankind—the Lamb of God. Again the storm subsides beneath the cries for peace that now usher in the second working-
out. This is shorter than the first, and leads back very soon to
what is apparently the final cadence; but to this a wonderful
coda succeeds, in which, interrupted by the distant thunder of
the drums, the united cry for peace is twice heard, at the close of

which, with its repeated '*Pacem, Pacem!*', we again hear the
germinal motive of the work:

One thing is certain: any solution based on 'psychological
naturalism' and so forth is entirely false, or at least entirely
superficial. Beethoven's aim in this movement was assuredly to
do something more than conjure up in the hearer's mind a scene
in which war and terrified mankind were to play their part.
Only one thing is true: having pictured in music, in the *Kyrie*
and especially in the *Benedictus*, the self-existent majesty of
God and the eternal peace of heaven, Beethoven was concerned,
in the prayer of mankind for peace, with something quite
different. The unrest of human existence was at this moment
by no means absent from his thoughts; it was, indeed, very
much present. Or, bearing in mind his creative work as a whole,
we may say that the deepest meaning of his contrasts, this exploration of the 'world-background' behind a foreground of
whatever shape or kind, is here manifested in his own highly
individual manner. It is Beethoven's boldest case of 'open form':
he dared to allow the confusion of the world outside to invade
the sacred domain of church music. Only to him—to his
creative genius—was it given to bring this bold venture to a
successful conclusion: only he had at his command this music,
behind whose exalted piety all the confusion of the world disappears like a fleeting vision.[10]

NINTH SYMPHONY IN D MINOR, OP. 125

NEVER has one single composition of a great master provoked so much controversy as Beethoven's Choral Symphony, not only among his contemporaries, but even to-day, more than a hundred years after it was written. And just as his contemporaries' attitude varied from ecstatic admiration to antagonism, or at least reserve, so to-day in the musical world there is a diversity of opinion as to its merits, both from the emotional and from the intellectual standpoint. Nor is there unanimity as to its 'meaning', apart from its 'value' in relation to the rest of the composer's creative work. Probably no one to-day accepts Wagner's view that with the choral movement Beethoven had sealed the doom of instrumental music. But we are still given to passionate disputation upon the question whether this work is to be regarded as an isolated phenomenon, and must continue to be so regarded, or whether with it Beethoven created a new type of symphony; whether in fact the composers of the numerous 'choral symphonies' written during the last hundred years are Beethoven's legitimate followers on the path leading to a new art form, or whether their products are imitations, doomed to failure, of an inimitable work of a genius.

One thing it is important to realize: the Ninth Symphony as it exists to-day did not come into being according to a plan that was complete from the very beginning. For a long time Beethoven had been busy with the sketches for the first three movements, and still he had not made up his mind whether to give the Symphony a choral or a purely instrumental Finale. In sketches for the latter, dating from the summer of 1823, is a

theme that he later used for the Finale of the A minor Quartet.
That he had previously had it in mind to write a genuine Choral
Symphony is shown by a note made in 1818: "... religious songs
in the old modes in a symphony ... voices to enter in last movement or even in the Adagio ... text of Adagio from Greek
mythology Cantique eclesiastique—in the Allegro Festival of
Bacchus." On the other hand, he had long intended to set
Schiller's *Ode to Joy*. After much hesitation, and even after the
great theme was in its final and complete form, he decided to
use Schiller's Ode as the basis of his Finale. We do not know
what in the end turned the scales in its favour; possibly the fact
that the first three movements had during composition grown
to greater and greater dimensions caused him to consider
'weighting' the last movement with a chorus. It will be remembered that he had recently had experience, in the D major Mass,
of the tremendous things that can be expressed by means of a
choir. The story that after completion of the Symphony Beethoven saw the "error of his ways" and decided to write a new
and purely orchestral Finale to it, was circulated only by
Czerny; but it has been proved in other cases that Czerny was
not a reliable authority, and in any event he disapproved of the
choral Finale. It is desirable that all this should be clearly
understood, because it precludes the idea, which is the principal
basis of Wagner's interpretation, that with this work Beethoven
was from the very beginning carrying out a definite design.
In actual fact the Symphony only gradually assumed the shape
in which for over a hundred years now it has been a living force.
And in spite of all the adverse criticism levelled against it at the
beginning, and even now at times, this force is as great, and
above all as durable, as only that of a work can be that owes its
existence not to man's arbitrary will but to some mysterious
inner law.

The first movement is equalled in length only by that of the
Eroica (547 bars in the 'allegro ma non troppo', as against 691
in the 'allegro con brio'). But the 'length' of the former is
of a different quality to that of the latter. In the *Eroica* we have
at the opening no means of foreseeing the dimensions that, by

reason of the growing tension under which the thematic material
develops, the movement will attain as it runs its course; whereas
in the Ninth the dimensions of the whole movement are established once for all at the first statement of the main theme. For
this, indeed, the famous first sixteen bars really suffice—those
bars in which, above the bare fifth on the dominant (A–E), the
principal theme is developed from the 'germinal motive', and so
gives us a foretaste of the wonders to come. (That the fifth
should have been on the dominant and not on the tonic (D–A) is
generally accounted for by the far greater effect thus made by
the entry of the principal theme in the tonic, D minor. This is no
doubt correct; but there is also another reason, viz., that when a
bare fifth is held for some time the vibrations set up harmonics
that include the major third, and this gives the effect of a major
chord.)

These wonders appear already in their full glory at the first
statement of the principal motive. In the first two bars, this is
nothing more nor less than a broken common chord, though its
headlong flight down two octaves gives it a more powerful effect
than it would otherwise have. The most important bars of this
motive are the third and fourth, which later appear again and
again in the development section and the coda. These bars are
joined, by a wide-spanned bridge containing many new motives,
to a figure that runs down in demisemiquavers to the bare fifth,
this time D–A. These last eight bars never appear again either in
the same or in any other form; are we, in spite of this, to agree
with Schenker that the whole passage as far as this point is the
'principal theme' of the movement? However that may be, the
close of this phrase forms an important caesura; and it is essential that we should feel the phrase as a unit. Not until the movement reaches this point is the key of D minor definitely acknowledged as the tonic. Now we have heard enough of the minor for
the bare fifth D–A to be completed with the minor third. The
principal motive returns, apparently in B flat major, which here
represents G minor—the subdominant of the principal key. The
latter is thus still in force; broadly speaking the harmonies have
up to now been: dominant (bars 1–14), leading via tonic (bars

15–49) with the broadest harmonic expansion within the
tonality, to subdominant (bars 49–62), which is soon succeeded by the dominant again (thirteen bars after the second entry of
the principal motive, or sixty-three from the beginning). The
'ben marcato' quaver phrase that follows is hardly a new motive,
as Schenker calls it; it merely refers back to the tenth bar of the
principal theme. This is the starting-point for the wonderfully
concise and expressive transition—a melodic phrase six bars
long—to the second subject:

Transition   2nd Subject

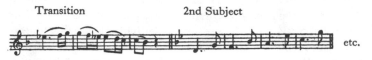

The second subject enters at bar 80, where the key-signature
is altered to two flats. The phrase that forms the melodic contrast with the first theme is only eight bars long; but it is followed immediately by broad harmonic developments, the semiquaver motion of which is charged with expression. Here it is
that we are faced with undeniable difficulties in the way of an
understanding of the movement as a whole. This passage, with
its great variety, its broad development, is indeed difficult to
hear in its totality, for it seems now and then to be 'short-
breathed', and contains marked contrasts of mood—though
this is primarily a matter for the conductor. Nor is it easy to
realize the intimate connexion between this development and
the closing phrase. It is essential to understand that the short
cadential phrase in bars 94–95 corresponds to the longer one in
bars 102–105, and, more important still, that the apparent B
major of the next eight bars is really C flat, i.e. the Neapolitan
sixth in B flat.[11]

But it is no less essential to note the connexion between the
chords of the sixth in bars 132–137 (with the passages for the
violins in demisemiquavers) and the immediately following bars,
138–145, which contain the melody of the actual closing phrase.
In the first case it is a sequence of chords of the sixth, the bass line of
which is C–D–E flat–F–G–A; in the second, the sequence, at two-

bar instead of one-bar intervals, has in the bass D–E flat–F–G.

Bars 132–137   138–145

This, together with the following cadential phrase, brings us at last, at bar 150, to the full close we have been expecting ever since bar 106, after which the key of B flat is affirmed in a rhythmic figure nine bars long.

These can at best be no more than indications of points to which the reader may care to give his attention. We cannot unfortunately examine in detail here all the tremendous points of concentration that dominate the latter part of the movement. (Those who wish to go more deeply into the subject are referred to Schenker's book on the Ninth Symphony.) Never for a moment does this concentration slacken—this passion for clamping the motives together or for causing one to engage the other like the cogs in a piece of machinery. But neither are breadth and spaciousness forgotten. When in the development section the principal theme is split up into its constituent bars and these are worked one after the other with an inexhaustible wealth of synthetical imagination, the form of the movement as a whole in no way suffers. On the contrary, the hundred and twenty-one bars of the actual working-out (bars 160–179 are the transition) form a bridge consisting of only four great spans (bars 180–197, 198–217, 218–274, and 275–300). Only in twelve bars (275–286) are we reminded of the second subject, the whole of the rest of the section being based on the principal theme. The finest part of it is the fugal working, in the third span, of the third and fourth bars of the theme, in which the intervals of the fourth bar play an increasingly important part. What variety of expression is obtained from the semiquaver figure of the third bar! From it is derived not only the fluttering wood-wind chords (bars 267 et seq.) but also the emphatic downward-rushing figure leading to the recapitulation.

The famous opening bars of this section form one of the

most stupendous passages in all music. Here Beethoven's
synthetical skill is unexampled. The recapitulation does not
open with the principal motive itself, but with the introductory
passage. This time, however, it is not the bare fifth that supports
it, for that would be out of place at this dynamic climax, but a
chord of the major sixth, which assures close connexion with the
foregoing passage, and from which, after a fleeting glimpse of G
minor, the looked-for D minor is reached with great skill. The
next passage is magnificent: the extension of the principal
theme, in which bars 5–10 of the theme are subjected more and
more to imitation and which calms down gradually until the
second subject is reached. (From the beginning of the recapitulation to the second subject there are only forty-four bars, as
against seventy-nine in the exposition.)

The long coda also has many surprises in store. First, the
principal motive is subjected to a second working-out, this time
with special attention to the third bar. Then follows a passage
consisting of a number of repetitions of the cadential phrase
that closed the second subject, in which the A is more and more
strongly emphasized as the dominant, both in the bass and in the
treble, until at last the third and fourth bars of the principal
motive, surprisingly changed to the major, blossom forth from
them. The forty-three bars that now follow, down to the entry of
a new closing phrase that sounds like a funeral march, are a
magnificent demonstration of Beethoven's synthetical power.
Still more new things are to come out of the principal motive,
though this at last points definitely to the close of the movement.
This close is very unusual. Not only is it introduced by a new
phrase heard over a curiously rigid two-bar basso ostinato, repeated seven times, but—and this is still more unusual—at the
very end the principal motive itself makes one more impressive
appearance, in its most significant form, this time with its
second bar stretched almost to breaking point—as though everything were still as it had been in the beginning. The close of the
movement is entirely 'static', almost as in a pre-classical Prelude; but for all its power, it cannot obliterate from our memory
all that has taken place in between.[12]

As in the first movement, the dimensions of the Scherzo are greater than is customary; but here again this is not due to mere repetition, but to a heightening of tension that finds expression in the thematic material. Doubtless the movement is 'easier to listen to' than the first, although contrary to custom it is in sonata form, complete with second subject and a full and skilful working-out. (So far as I know, there are only two other examples of this in Beethoven: the Scherzo, also unusual in its 2/4 time, of the E flat Piano Sonata, op. 31, no. 3, and, in rather freer form, the long Allegretto of the String Quartet, op. 59, no. 1. But neither of these has a Trio, whereas in the Ninth there is a full-length Trio of profound significance.) The second subject is related to the first by the rhythmic germinal motive that is in evidence almost throughout the movement. This subject is given more prominence than Beethoven intended by the horns that Wagner added for the purpose of enhancing its clarity and expressiveness. It is extraordinary that throughout its sixteen bars it should keep to the tonic, C major. What now follows seems already about to lead back into the principal motive; but now comes the only passage that is not immediately comprehensible. The rhythm of the principal motive, which hitherto has been strongly in evidence, is not heard for ten bars. It has given way to an expressive legato melody, which, though clearly recognizable as a drawn-out echo of the second subject, gives the impression of having dropped from another world. It is one of those sudden contrasts whereby Beethoven conjures up before our eyes remote and unsuspected things. A second contrast of this kind is heard at the end of the Scherzo, where the 3/4 rhythm changes to 'alla breve' (two minims in the bar) as in the Scherzo of the *Eroica*. Here it comes at the short transition to the Trio. For a long time, owing to a misprint in Beethoven's metronome mark, the character of the Trio was entirely misunderstood. Beethoven's intention was that a half-bar, and not a whole bar, should be taken as fast as a bar of the Scherzo.[13] Played at the double speed, the Trio would still not be meaningless, for these twenty-three repetitions of its four-bar phrase would suggest say a frenzied Bacchic dance, such as savage

races, and also certain civilized peoples, indulge in to the accompaniment of music. (Beethoven's note "Festival of Bacchus" would in this case be appropriate.) But clearly he intended something quite different. What he had in mind was nature
in a peaceful mood—a bucolic idyll, perhaps—as he indicated
by his dynamic markings, viz., piano rather than forte, with not
a single *ff* after the one opening blast from the trombone. In
either interpretation the contrast with the Scherzo is much the
same from the purely artistic point of view: to the urgent and
genuinely symphonic growth of the Scherzo is opposed a state
of 'timelessness', whether this is due to Bacchanalian revelry or
to peaceful dreaming. In the Seventh Symphony the Trio, with
the quiet solemnity of both its melody and its harmony, is similarly opposed to the Scherzo. The Trio of the Ninth, whose
melodic material derives from 'natural' music, is 'closer to
nature', and therefore more 'mystic'; but it must not be imagined that this is purchased at the price of Art, for even this music is
shapely to a degree. The melodic line of the counterpoint that
accompanies the theme throughout, now above and now below
it, is magnificent. Later the counterpoint breaks free of the
theme, and acquires melodic importance in its own right at the
entry of the oboe with its legato tune. Remarkable, too, is the
way in which the theme gradually fades out in the coda, with the
forty-bar pedal on D, after this D had already dominated a great
part of the Trio.

Thanks to the clarity and impressive breadth of its melody,
the third movement, 'adagio molto e cantabile', is also 'easy to
listen to', in spite of its emotional depth and grandeur. Where
else shall we find an adagio theme of such perfection of growth
and such sublime, unruffled development? Like all else in this
Symphony, its dimensions are greater than usual. The unwonted length of the first subject—no less than twenty-one bars—is
accounted for largely by the echo-like interjections of the wind
instruments—by an expedient, that is, that might well have an
effect of superficiality were it not for the skill with which these
echoes are merged into the general growth of the theme, so that
their function is in effect to heighten the tension. Note also the

two mysterious introductory bars, whose connexion with the
theme itself is not revealed until later. As Schenker has observed, they foreshadow bar 9, which is repeated in bars 14 and
15, and is given prominence both in the theme itself and in its
subsequent working-out.

Beethoven originally intended the movement to be in
straightforward variation form, and it seems that he did not until
considerably later make up his mind to introduce a second subject or episode. This he had already composed for a different
movement in quicker time. (A sketch of it is marked 'tempo di
Menuetto'. Later, however, Beethoven decided simply upon a
slight speeding up of the tempo of the Adagio ($\downarrow = 63$ against
$\downarrow = 60$.) This episode is interposed between the first subject and
the first variation, and again between the latter and the second
variation. Thus it gives the movement greater depth and variety
of significance, and allows a glimpse of the 'background'. The
transition from the first subject to the episode is as short and
simple as possible; neither has a definite close, and the two arcs
meet, so to speak, in mid-air. The variations consist mainly of
florid embroidery of the theme, though the figuration is more
fully charged with spirit and vitality than in any but Beethoven's
later works.

Nor in the rest of the movement do the variations follow one
another without an interruption. The second appearance of the
episode is succeeded, not by the second variation, but by a
bridge passage of sixteen bars, which is based on the opening
bars of the first subject. Remote harmonies are touched upon in
this passage, in a carefully prepared modulation to C flat apparently culminating in the famous scale passage in that key for
the horn; but after these harmonic adventures a return is after
all made to the principal key, B flat. These sixteen bars also
contain a skilfully managed change of rhythm, which takes place
almost unnoticed: from the second variation onwards the movement is dominated more and more, at first in the accompaniment only, by triplet rhythm, to which, as it were, official recognition is soon given by the alteration of the time signature to
12/8.

Immediately following the second variation is a tremendous coda, which not only serves to bring the movement to an end, but also shows us at last its full depth. It begins after the second variation, at the point where we expect the full close; but in place of this there comes a surprising change to the subdominant, with a few bars like a fanfare, apparently in E flat. What now follows consists of harmonic developments, enlivened by a melodic phrase derived from the principal theme. These developments progress purposefully to the end, but are interrupted by the first perfect cadence nineteen bars before the close of the movement. The theme is immediately resumed, and in particular the two bars that were foreshadowed in the introductory bars are worked. The whole movement shows the consummate perfection of Beethoven's synthetical skill.

As regards the last movement, the crucial question is: how could it have been possible so to combine a choral Finale with the other movements that the whole should create an impression of genuine organic growth and not of chance or arbitrary will? That the former impression has for long been present to hearers' minds is indisputable; nor is the argument affected by the fact that many people are critical of the Finale because they fail to realize its inner justification. What is of more importance is that it is just the unbiased listener, and indeed the most musically educated, who surrenders himself unreservedly to this impression, whereas for the majority of such people a similar surrender to say Mahler's Second Symphony would be out of the question however much their emotions might be stirred by the contralto solo *O Röslein rot*, and the *Resurrection Chorus*.

Little is known of the history of the Finale, but what we do know is highly significant. Beethoven appears originally to have intended the chorus to enter without any preliminaries, as in the Choral Fantasy, but to use the main theme of the chorus —the *Theme of Joy*—also as that of a set of variations for the orchestra. While working on the movement he hit upon the idea of starting it with a recitative, to begin: "*Heute ist ein feierlicher Tag . . . dieser sei gefeiert mit Gesang . . .*" (To-day is a day of solemn celebration . . . let us celebrate it with song . . .);

then of passing in review the principal themes of the first three movements; and finally of greeting the first hint of the *Theme of Joy* with the words: "*Ha, dieses ist es! Es ist nun gefunden, Freude . . .*" (Ha, this is it! It is found, Joy . . .) (The notes of this introductory passage are almost the same as those of the recitatives for double basses.) In a later version of this passage we find: "*Lasst uns das Lied des unsterblichen Schillers singen!*" (Let us sing the song of the immortal Schiller!). It is clear therefore that Beethoven felt the need of justifying the inclusion of a chorus by reference to some kind of festal occasion. This was open to no logical objection so long as it did not give rise to any clash between chorus and orchestra. Anxious at all costs to avoid this pitfall, he hit upon the final solution, in which, however, what Schenker calls a "logical lapse" was inevitable.

Now, in its final form, the movement opens with an orchestral Introduction, in which a shapeless, blustering passage for full orchestra minus strings is followed by a recitative for double basses, which, on the authority of the sketches, rejects the first three movements, but finally proclaims the *Theme of Joy* as the long-sought-for tune. This is now given out as the principal theme of the movement, and followed by three orchestral variations. We expect still more to follow, but instead we again hear the opening bars of the movement. This time the cacophony is appalling. Again the recitative follows, now sung by bass solo to the familiar but very simple and beautiful words: "*O Freunde, nicht diese Töne, sondern lasst uns angenehmere anstimmen und freudenvollere!*" (O Friends, not these sounds! Let us sing pleasanter and more joyful ones!) This is, to be sure, illogical, for we have already heard in full, several times over, these "pleasanter and more joyful sounds"; and what is now rejected in words has already been faithfully dealt with by the double basses in their recitatives. But with this "lapse" something of infinite importance was gained, viz., the unity of the whole movement, the organic connexion between the vocal and orchestral sections. Schenker is quite right when he says that the key to a true understanding of the Finale is to be found simply and solely in the orchestral Introduction. But this is a

o

piece of purely symphonic music. An introductory recitative was no novelty, for Haydn employed it; though here its dimensions are vastly greater, as of course is only appropriate to the character of the work. The re-introduction of themes from previous movements, also, is to be found elsewhere, notably in Beethoven's own Piano Sonata, op. 101. And the great theme of the variations is a genuine instrumental tune, and as such is one of the noblest conceptions of all music. As Wagner finely said, "Never has Art produced anything more artistically simple than this tune, whose childlike innocence inspires us with sacred awe."

We are in the midst of a noble and freely constructed set of variations when suddenly the Introduction reappears. A symphonic Finale in variation form is nothing new, for it occurs in the *Eroica*; nor is the reappearance of an Introduction a novelty, though here, much to our surprise, it returns with the addition of a vocal part, which is soon joined by the whole choir. The variations now proceed on their way, to be replaced after a time by a new theme that subsequently turns out to be an episode. The interruption of a series of variations by an episode we have already seen in the slow movement of this same Symphony. The point to be observed is that by the time the voices enter, the form and thematic material of the movement have already been firmly established, and its organic development is well under way. Thus the voices are, as it were, a new means of expression, introduced during the course of the movement's growth to heighten its intensity.

The deep emotions aroused in the hearer by this passage are not to be fully explained by the increased expression due to the entry of the voices. Voices, after all, are not simply new instruments added to the orchestra, but something essentially different. Here their entry means the association of *words* with the music, though their significance is in this case not the same as in ordinary choral works, cantatas for instance, whose structure throughout depends on the text.

What then is the function of the words here? Wagner was in no doubt as to the answer to this question. According to him it is summed up in the word 'Elucidation'. It is like an "awakening from a dream." This interpretation is coloured too much by the outlook and mentality of its author to be quite acceptable; for, curiously enough, the musical genius of the Poet-Composer was only fertilized by the 'word', and the dramatic word at that. Beethoven could be lucid without the help of words. The decisive point is not that "a human voice, with the clarity and confidence of speech, makes itself heard above the uproar of the orchestra" (Wagner); but that it is Man himself who appears, no longer as one of the many whose only function at the moment is to play a musical instrument, but as a human being, endued with all his spiritual attributes, and that it is not to the orchestra but to the assembled people that he cries: "O Friends, not these sounds!" With this, it is true, the bounds that hedge the domain of absolute music are abolished, not, however, for the sake of something more 'lucid', in which the word is all-supreme, but for the sake of a co-partnership in which the hearer, who hitherto had merely listened passively to the music, now has his share. Wagner, too, had this in mind when he wrote: "It is not the thoughts expressed by Schiller's words that henceforth occupy us, but the familiar strains of choral song, in which we feel that we are invited to join so that we may take part, like a congregation in church, in an ideal service, as was actually done in the case of the Chorales in Bach's great Passions." It is perfectly true that it was not Schiller's Ode itself that mattered to Beethoven. This indeed is proved by his treatment of it, for of its twenty-four verses he set only nine, arranging them arbitrarily to fit the requirements of the music, with the result that the association of ideas is often sensibly affected. (The order in which Beethoven set them is: 1, 2, 4, 5, 7, 8, 12, 3, 9.) He took little account of the poem itself, still less of any philosophical meaning that might underlie the words; that is to say, he found in it no hidden programme. It was simply and solely the 'idea' of the work, as fertilized by individual thoughts from the poem, in which he was interested. This idea has nothing to do with the congregation of a church; it is a community of a very different kind that we are admitted to. The moment the voices enter, a barrier is broken down—not that absolute music thereby transgresses the bounds that separate it from the domain of lingual 'lucidity' and thus of human existence in general; on the contrary, the hearer, who up to now has stood listening, timid and reverent, before the threshold, now enters the mysterious realm of absolute music and takes part in the miracle of its making. He is drawn into the solemn train of "ever-changing, ever-growing forms" that previously, enraptured and stirred to the depths of his being, he had watched as it passed him by. Thus, and not by the significance of the work alone, or by the thoughts expressed by Schiller's words, is to be explained the rapt attention of the audience at any worthy performance of this Symphony in particular. It is almost as though the words with which Beethoven had originally intended to open the Finale were hovering inaudible in the air: "To-day is a day of solemn celebration!" And the "celebration" is of a very special kind—that of the *unio mystica* of Man and Symphony.

The marvellous edifice of the classical symphony is not destroyed by this choral Finale. On the contrary, it is made still more perfect. Any one who disputes this shows that he has failed to understand the noble and truly symphonic structure of the movement as absolute music. Upon this subject all that is essential has been said by Schenker in his masterly and detailed description of the Symphony. Here there is space for an account of only a few fundamental points.

The musical substance of the first ninety-one bars—the Introduction—is only properly comprehensible if we look for the gist of it not in the quotations from the first three movements but in the recitatives for double basses. These are thematic developments of the two blustering fanfare-like passages for the orchestra, and the speed at which they are to be played should therefore, as Beethoven himself prescribed, approximate as nearly as possible to that of those passages. The quotations are merely *revenants*. With the last recitative, in which the full close occurs, the Introduction comes to a magnificent end. The movement now plunges direct into the 'theme and variations'. In the earlier variations the theme is unchanged; it mounts gradually from the obscurity of the bass up to the regions of light, there to hover without any firm harmonic support. So far, it has been varied only by the addition of contrapuntal parts, as in Haydn's *Emperor* Quartet. Not until the third variation, the first that sounds a note of triumph, does the harmonic foundation become firmer. It is followed by a coda based on the last bar of the theme, which works up to a pitch of intensity that warns us that something of unusual interest is about to happen. This now duly comes with the return of the first blustering orchestral passage, followed by a much shorter version of the recitative, now given to baritone solo, consisting of the opening bars of the first recitative and the cadential finish of the last one, welded into a homogeneous whole. (That this recitative does not, like the one in the Introduction, end with the traditional full close—dominant-tonic— is important. Had it done so here, where the recitative only recapitulates shortly something that has already been heard, the result would have been a too marked interruption of the flow of the music.)

The variations are now resumed, as if, from the purely musical point of view, nothing had happened. After the sixth variation—the first in which the theme itself is altered—the coda that now follows each variation is again extended ("*Und der Cherub steht vor Gott*") as after the third. This, too, leads us to expect something new, which likewise duly happens, and with tremendous effect, viz., the immediate juxtaposition of the chords of A major and F major—an anticipation of 'romantic' effects. (Harmonically there is more in it than this. It is a sequential bass (E-A-F-B flat), whereby arrival at the objective, B flat major, is delayed.)

Now with the seventh variation (B flat, 6/8, "*Froh, wie seine Sonnen fliegen*") the aspect of things undergoes a complete change. The theme has not only been transposed to B flat, but much altered both rhythmically and melodically. It is clothed, too, in strange colours: it is 'Turkish' music, in which the percussion plays a prominent part and gives the variation the air of a

military march, though at first this sounds almost incorporeal,
as if it came from another world. (Here, where Beethoven had in
his mind's eye the "*fliegende Sonnen*"—the suns in their courses
—Schering sees "a crowd of people so fuddled with wine that
they can neither walk straight nor sing the tune properly. All
they can produce is an incoherent babble—hence the *pp* that so
surprisingly holds the field for more than forty bars.") The verse
is followed by an energetic and stimulating fugato, in 6/8 time,
based on the theme, in which the counterpoint gives new life to
the rhythm of the variation. The *Theme of Joy* still holds sway,
though since its first appearance much has happened, and much
is yet to happen, to it. Just as the Variations in the Finale of the
Eroica are interrupted by fugato episodes, so here, the dimensions of the movement have long outgrown those of an ordinary
set of variations. At last, however, the fugato comes to a close,
in D major. It is followed by a variation with the theme in its
original form, for the first time in the full splendour of the
chorus, over a racing triplet bass in which the rhythm of the
fugato is still felt. The coda breaks off suddenly in the second
bar on the chord of the subdominant, G. What now? Without
warning a new and entirely different theme is heard, to Schiller's
words, "*Seid umschlungen, Millionen, diesen Kuss der ganzen
Welt*":

Seid umschlun-gen

D major: tonic   subdomt.   subdomt.   tonic
                                                        G major: tonic domt.

The difference lies not only in key (G major), time (3/2), and
speed ('andante maestoso'), but in its relation to tonal harmony.
The passage for male voices in unison, without any harmonized
accompaniment, sounds like plain-song; and even when, with
the entry of the full chorus, the melody is harmonized, though
the harmony is strictly speaking tonal, its effect is very close to
that of pre-tonal music such as Palestrina's. This is felt especially at the magnificent passage "*Ahnest Du den Schöpfer, Welt?*

Such ihn überm Sternenzelt! Ueber Sternen muss er wohnen," in which seven triads in root position follow one another without a single chord of the sixth. A return to tonality is made by way of a mysterious and ambiguous diminished seventh, which seems to fade away into the infinite ("*Ueber Sternen muss er wohnen*"). This section ends as it began, without warning; and again without warning the 'allegro energico' (the main tempo of the Finale) returns, now in a form that promises a climax, i.e. as a double fugue, in which the theme of "*Seid umschlungen*" is combined with one based on the first two bars of the *Theme of Joy*, but varied rhythmically by its time, 6/4. Though use is here made of material that has previously been used, this passage is by no means a mere retrospective glance; it is something entirely new, and it fulfils its promise. Seventy-five bars of strict and closely worked fugue, and again a sudden stop, followed without any transition by a reminiscence of "*Ihr stürzt nieder.*" The words of this are sung in unison as before, but this time a new tune enters, towards the end, with the words "*muss ein lieber Vater wohnen.*" Here the movement seems to pause to take breath; but the passage is in A major, the dominant of the principal key, and is therefore not the end, but merely a preparation for what is to come: the tremendous closing passage, a hundred and seventy-eight bars long. This, though it repeats parts of the text, is full of new musical ideas, all 'cadential' in character. Again and again the principal key is emphasized by a succession of perfectly simple chords; yet with consummate skill Beethoven not only avoids wearisome repetition but builds up climax after climax even where, as in the two elaborate cadenzas, first for chorus and then for soli ("*Wo dein sanfter Flügel weilt*") the movement seems to slow up. In the second of these two cadenzas, the ecstasy of the music urges the singers up into B major, with an incomparable effect. This is followed immediately by the Prestissimo, which surely only the most superficial listener could call a "primitive succession of cadences." Actually this section is most skilfully articulated, and in its intensity of expression it certainly far excels everything that either music in general or this Symphony in particular can show. The *Theme of Joy* does not appear again in its original shape, but is hidden in the orchestral counterpoint. When with the last cry of *"Götterfunken!"*, and in the last two bars, chorus and orchestra respectively leap down the fifth from A to D, the whole work at once seems to be spanned by a great arch stretching from the first note to the last. For this leap of a fifth answers that of the fourth, D to A, with which the principal motive of the first movement started its headlong downward rush.

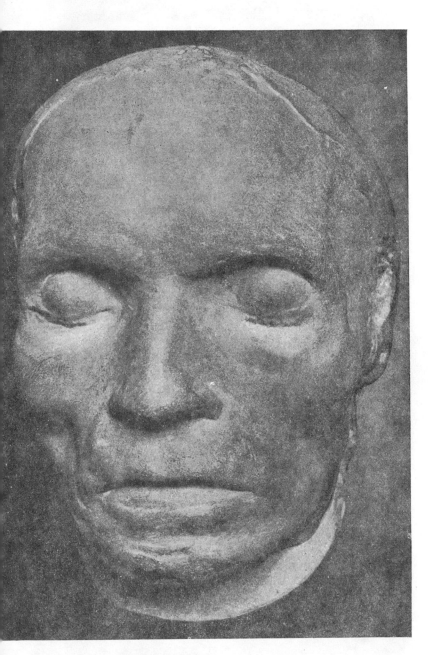

BEETHOVEN'S DEATH MASK
(In the Krieg Collection. Photo by Hürlimann.)

THE LAST STYLE

WHAT a great man has to say at the end of his life, whether this has been long or short, has in most cases certain special characteristics. Moreover the late works of all creative artists—whatever the art and whatever the epoch—have something in common: they resemble each other like old trees of different species, in which characteristics of the particular species are obliterated or at least hidden by the common quality of old age. The second *Oedipus* of Sophocles and Goethe's *Faust*, Part II, entirely different as they are in externals, have kindred sounds that meet across the millennia. And that it is not merely the octogenarian mind that thus expresses itself is shown by a last work such as Shakespeare's *Tempest*, Michelangelo's *Descent from the Cross*, his *Pietà* in the Palazzo Rondanini, and the Capella Paolina frescoes; Titian's *Crown of Thorns* in Munich; and Rembrandt's last paintings—the *Prodigal Son* and the Brunswick group: all seem to have had their origin in the same world. Nor will those capable of recognizing the existence of a general law governing all the means of expression of the various arts fail to see that even Bach's late works—the *Art of Fugue*, the *Musical Offering*, and the last Choral Prelude—belong to this same world. It is not only that the 'style' of every great artist ceases gradually to develop: as he approaches the end of his life, so the individuality —the uniqueness—of his genius becomes less clearly defined, and so all that points to 'eternity' in his works shines out the brighter. Only to the greatest, whose gaze has always been fixed on the eternal, is it granted to draw nearer and nearer to this distant aim. The ultimate depths have from the very beginning been closed to all that lack the power, even in old age, and though the spring then flow less freely, to say something new—unless perhaps, as in the case of Schumann, exhaustion is the outcome of disease.

In the case of Beethoven as in that of all other composers, no hard and fast line can be drawn between the last period and the preceding one. Nevertheless a broad division is plain enough: it occurs during the 'barren' years, when it was thought that his creative power was exhausted; the years, that is to say, following the completion of the Seventh and Eighth Symphonies and the op. 97 Trio. The great works that he subsequently wrote—the Ninth Symphony, the D major Mass, and the last Sonatas and Quartets—show us Beethoven on "new paths". Not that he broke with the past or denied his old aims: it was merely that his means and methods of expression were gradually changing. And when, with his last Quartets, he had run his earthly course, his 'last style' had achieved its perfect development. Looking back from this stage we can clearly perceive in some of his earlier works the first indications of that style.

Unlike Goethe, Michelangelo, and Titian, Beethoven, it is true, did not live to over eighty; he did not even glimpse from afar the threshold of the age when the passions relax their hold: in certain of his later works, indeed, there are movements, such as the first of the op. 111 Piano Sonata and the Finale of the C sharp minor Quartet, in which there is deep and genuine passion. And the most impassioned of all Adagio tunes, the second F sharp minor theme of op. 106, is to be found in one of his last Sonatas. Nor had he lost his humour: it happens, even, that the last movement he wrote, shortly before his death, is one of the most humorous—the second Finale that he composed for the op. 130 Quartet. The last Quartet, op. 135, which he had written shortly before this, is full of light-winged humour; and since the time of Hans von Bülow it is generally agreed that his inspired Rondo, *Anger at the loss of a penny* (published posthumously as op. 129) which is one of the most exuberant pieces he ever wrote, dates from his last period. It can by no means be said that in general these last works lack the passionate outbursts to be found in his earlier ones, any more than it can be said that they no longer contain the contrasts that are so typical of him—on the contrary these contrasts are bolder and more imposing than ever. Nor, generally speaking, did his thematic material become more complicated or less easily comprehensible, for even in his last Quartets we still find any number of themes and melodies of the greatest and most truly 'popular' simplicity. Examples of this are the *Danza tedesca* of the B flat Quartet, and the two themes of the Scherzo of the C sharp minor, in which moreover the formality and (apparent) artlessness of his periods are very striking.

Wherein then consist the peculiar features of his late works, which cannot escape the notice of any Beethoven student, or indeed of any musically sensitive person? If we look for the answer in the big works we shall find that the earlier ones lack the weight and fullness, the spaciousness of form, and the synthetic power of the later ones. Beethoven's control over the greatest forms of all was, in his last period, no less than stupendous, and the fertility of his invention never waned, as is proved by the Ninth Symphony, the great Mass, and the last Sonatas and Quartets. If we examine these latter for indications of his new style we shall discover a refinement and sensitiveness in the part-writing, and a feeling for the depth and significance of the smallest detail, such as is to be found in none of his earlier works. His anxiety to attain the highest perfection in part-writing became immeasurably greater. In a sketch-book he wrote out the last four bars of the variations of the C sharp minor Quartet twelve times in all, leaving the first violin part unaltered and making hardly any changes in the bass, merely because he was not entirely satisfied with the writing of the middle parts. And this was at a time when, owing to his deafness, he was popularly supposed to be indifferent to the sound of his music! There are innumerable passages in his last Sonatas and Quartets in which in a few bars of music he opens up a whole world of feeling. Among his earlier works there are indeed short movements, pieces in the smaller forms; but never before did he take them as seriously as he did in the composition of the Bagatelles, op. 126. These were composed at the same time as the Ninth Symphony, and on them he expended the utmost care. Nor is it often that we find among his earlier works short movements such as occur in the last Quartets—movements that say so much in so few bars, and that of such moment. On the strength of these, we might well imagine that Beethoven had become a master of the small form, which he filled with music of the deepest significance.

And if we examine his late works for the individuality of their musical language—of their melodic and thematic material—the result is no more definite and the extent of the possibilities is as great. Nowhere are the firmness and significance of his musical structures greater or more immediately comprehensible than, say, in the principal theme of the first movement of the Ninth Symphony, the theme of the last movement, or the subject of the Fugue in the *Gloria* of the D major Mass. These and many other themes of a similar kind show that his power not only of invention but also of shaping and moulding his material, had become still greater with age. The same applies to the melodies of his Adagio movements, such as that of the Ninth Symphony or the last movement of op. 109: the spiritual depth that permeates them is combined with a perfection of form and a structural firmness that assigns to every note its foreordained place in the harmonic scheme. But when we find an Adagio melody like that of the Ninth Symphony, firm and solid in its construction, avoiding the broadly prepared perfect cadence, and exactly the same thing happening immediately afterwards in the episode that follows, we see something that is characteristic of Beethoven's 'last style'. The same is to be seen still more clearly in melodies such as that of the *Benedictus* of the Mass. The beginning of this, indeed, has a well defined harmonic foundation; as it proceeds, however, it becomes more and more irresolute, until, at the point where we expect the perfect cadence, the melody comes to an end with the far less decisive plagal cadence. (During the whole of the very long movement, in fact, the hearer is again and again intentionally put off in his expectation of the per-

fect cadence, until the entry of the *Osanna*, which again ends
with the indecisive plagal cadence.) We find similar cases in
many of Beethoven's later tunes, such as the principal theme of
the slow movement of op. 106, the theme of the variations of op.
127, and the Cavatina of op. 130. It is this last that Beethoven
considered the finest tune he had ever written; as he once said:
"even the memory of it brings a tear to the eye." The harmonic
construction is always either looser, or else disguised by the bass
of the middle voices; or, as in the Arietta of op. 111, the elemen-
tary harmonization precludes any possibility of expression—
only in the variations does this emerge.

In 1818 Beethoven made notes for a 'Symphony in the ancient Modes', which it was his intention to compose simultaneously with the one that was to become the Ninth. This fact is of
the greatest importance to our understanding of Beethoven's
last style. Since 1810 he had had experience in writing music in
another system than that of the present-day major and minor.
He had undertaken the arrangement of some English, Welsh,
and Scottish folk songs for an English publisher, and had
seriously devoted himself to this work. His efforts were not directed to modernizing the harmonies of these ancient songs,
most of which were in one or other of the old modes, but, on the
contrary, to harmonizing them so as to emphasize as strongly as
possible their exotic flavour. He wrote to his publisher: "There
are any number of harmonies to choose from, but only one that
suits the particular character of the tune." Bach's method of
treatment, when he copied a mass of Palestrina, was the direct
opposite, for he altered much of the harmony in order to make
the music more 'tonal'. Beethoven, on the contrary, not only
allowed these unfamiliar harmonies to stand as the accompaniment to melodies not of his composition, but in his later years
even introduced them into his own works. This it is that gives
special significance to the famous 'Thanksgiving of a Convalescent to the Divinity, in the Lydian Mode', from the A minor
Quartet, op. 132. This mode corresponds to the modern key of
F, but with B natural instead of B flat, so that the whole sphere
of the subdominant, and thus one of the 'dimensions' of the

music, is lacking. The result is that the key perpetually fluctuates between C major and F major; and this is most strongly felt towards the end of the movement, where the apparent C major asserts itself more and more, only to give way at the end to F major. Never since Palestrina has such incorporeal, freely-floating music been written.[14] True, it is only an episode in the whole work, and Beethoven immediately ensures the return to tonality by means of the D major episode that follows: 'Feeling new Strength'. The effect of this return is very striking, giving as it does the impression of a descent to solid ground; though at the same time the florid figuration veils the robust clarity, so to speak, of the tonal harmonies. In the *Credo* of the Mass the same effect is created by the *Et homo factus est*, coming after the modal *Et incarnatus*. Similar effects are also to be found elsewhere in the Mass—vacillating tonality, or the juxtaposition of triads whose relation to any definite tonality is uncertain, e.g. the *In gloria dei* in the *Gloria*, the last sixteen bars of the movement, and the *Et resurrexit* in the *Credo*. In the Ninth Symphony, at the passage in the Finale "*Brüder überm Sternenzelt . . .*" the F major-C major harmony is obscured by the unaccompanied, freely floating melodic line, so that no tonal basis is apparent. Similarly at the words "*Ahnest du den Schöpfer . . . wohnen*", though we may perhaps hear the series of triads as if they were in the key of G minor; yet the real effect of the passage is created by these unattached triads, which more than anywhere in Beethoven remind us of Palestrina, the man he held in such high esteem.

Beethoven, to be sure, never wrote his modal Symphony; 'tonality' was to the last his true domain. But it must not be overlooked that in his later years he often felt the need of departing from this domain, not indeed for the sake of contrast or new colour effects, as was later the case with Brahms and others, but in the effort to free himself even now from the remains of those 'rational' bonds with which the tonal system fettered him. Almost infinite as are the possibilities of expression that this system brought to music, its resources do not extend to the realization of the full 'transcendence' of modal Church music.

Thus it was always the precincts of religion that Beethoven approached in the passages concerned, just as his modal Symphony was to be religious in character. (See note made by him in 1818, quoted on p. 200.) But he had already written Church music without making use of these means/ It was not until his last period that he felt the need of this ultimate degree of 'spiritualization'; and this is by no means confined to his modal passages. It is the principle that governs all his late compositions, and all the new means of expression that we can discover in these works serve the cause of this spiritualization. Only by a detailed analysis would it be possible to show this convincingly, and in particular to show that even at the moments of its greatest power and weight of expression this music is leavened with spiritualizing elements. One of the commonest and most important cases in which this happens is that of the perfect cadences, whose function as the pillars supporting the edifice was always specially emphasized in his earlier, monumental style, but which are now very often disguised. One example, from the first movement of the Ninth Symphony, will serve for many: at the first statement of the principal theme, although its close is prepared in a broad and resolute cadential phrase, when the decisive moment comes the 6/4 chord on A is followed, not by the expected dominant, but by the tonic of D minor, which is still further disguised by the downward-rushing figure for violins. Thus even this powerful musical phrase is left, so to speak, hanging in the air. We see much the same thing in Michelangelo's Capella Paolina frescoes, in which we should expect the figures, overflowing as they are with strength and vigour, to be standing with their feet firmly planted on the ground. Yet so far from any such firm stance being emphasized, it is altogether absent, with the result that the figures seem to be floating in mid-air. The same applies to those in Rembrandt's *Prodigal Son*, and to the "cliffs" in the last scene of Goethe's *Faust*, Part II, which "lean upon the billowing forest."

The first indications of Beethoven's last style are to be found in certain of his earlier works, in particular the last Violin Sonata (1812) and the op. 90 Piano Sonata (1813). They are clearer still in the two Cello Sonatas, op. 102, the only important works of 1815. These sonatas cannot be called favourites, for they are considered ungrateful for the instrument and problematic in construction. They are, indeed, difficult fully to realize in performance, the curiously cross-grained Fugue in the second being well-nigh unplayable. His contemporaries considered this Fugue a poor one, and saw in it a proof that Beethoven was incapable of writing fugues. It was his first attempt at a fugue of a new kind, a kind from which before long very different things were to materialize. The first movement of this Sonata is magnificent—short and splendidly compact, with many emotional contrasts in the short exposition. Tension is maintained almost thoughout the movement; it is not until towards the end that it is relaxed in a few pianissimo bars, in which the harmonies roam at will—and in which we are again shown a glimpse of 'the other side of the world'. The first Sonata, in C, is as a whole more out of the ordinary than the second. The two Allegros are introduced by slow movements that are almost as free in form as improvisations; and the last movement is related to the first Allegro, which is in A minor, by the reappearance of the first introduction. In the Adagio a short and very lovely tune makes a sudden appearance.

The Piano Sonata in A, op. 101, is the first of those much-discussed works, the last five sonatas. The first movement is nearer in style to that of the Romantics, particularly Schumann, than any other work of Beethoven's. (Schenker's detailed analysis of these last sonatas, with the exception of op. 106, gives us a deeper insight into their true content than we have into any of Beethoven's other sonatas.) At first sight the movement appears to be all *"innigste Empfindung"*—tenderest feeling—and to be thrown off, like a *Phantasiestück* of Schumann's, with the freedom of an improvisation. Actually however it is as firmly constructed as any movement in classical music, though here the supporting pillars are disguised with exceptional skill. The exposition section contains thirty-three bars, in which the first and second subjects and the final phrase form one unbroken line, a line that can hardly have its equal in length, in wealth of expression, or in the mildness of its tension. No hard and fast line can be drawn between the three parts of the exposition; the final phrase unfolds itself in three repetitions, crescendo (bars 16 et seq.); it loses itself in a series of chords, five bars in which the strong beat is disguised by syncopation, and which thus almost remind us of the ambiguity of Schumann's rhythms. (In an apparent detail, however, we see the difference between Beethoven and Schumann: owing to the syncopation, the first beat of the bar is silent for five bars (30–34), but in bar 35 it is played by the right hand as well as the left; and the same occurs again after bars 36–37, and 39–40. At this passage, as at many others, Bülow's edition is not quite correct.) The entry of the recapitulation is also somewhat nebulous, owing to the fact that at its reappearance the first subject is in the minor. Thereafter, however, everything proceeds regularly, and a splendid coda of fifteen bars follows, in which the movement seems to take a deep breath. The second movement, 'Vivace alla marcia', with its sublimation of the march rhythm and its strangely reflective middle section in canon, might have formed part of one of the last Quartets. The short, pensive Adagio—it is only twenty bars long—is assuredly more than a mere introduction to the Finale. We expect a broad development, but in place of this the first movement makes a shadowy reappearance, after which, as if by a sudden decision, the work plunges into the pert and humorous Finale. The working-out, though it is in imitation, is not to be looked on as a strict fugue. The Finale contrasts strongly not only with the preceding Adagio but also with the other movements, yet inwardly the work forms one complete and homogeneous whole.

To say in a few words anything useful about the *Hammerklavier* Sonata, op. 106, is almost impossible. (The name, which was also intended for op. 101, has no particular meaning, but merely represents an attempt on Beethoven's part to render in German the word 'pianoforte'.) To this Sonata applies in the highest degree what must be said of so many of Beethoven's works: it is reminiscent of nothing that had previously been written. Once again the 'idea' of the sonata was embodied in

P

something entirely new—this time in such dimensions, and of such tension, as are hardly to be found even in Beethoven's symphonies. In it we can see indications of the standard by which he thought and created: it was written while he was engaged on the preliminary work on the Ninth Symphony and the Mass. It should never have been orchestrated and turned into a symphony—a process that Nietzsche suggested and Weingartner carried out; its style is that of the piano sonata, even though the piano does not exist that can bring out its sonority in full perfection. The first movement reaches out to far-off things, as if it would lose itself in the infinite. But that at the same time it is highly concentrated can be seen from the development section, whose hundred bars are almost entirely dominated by various transformations of the principal motive.

The Scherzo forms the sharpest possible contrast with the very resolute first movement. In the middle section it becomes altogether vague and shadowy, the melody simply consisting of a series of broken common chords of B flat minor and D flat major—the steps are B flat-D flat, D flat-B flat—now and then in canon. The 3/4 rhythm is twice interrupted by duple time.

The Adagio is not only the longest of Beethoven's slow movements, but also one of the most profound and affecting. The construction of the principal theme (bars 1–26) is most unusual, and is pure last-period Beethoven. The chord of the dominant with which the first phrase of the theme ends, at bar 5, is the basis of almost all that follows, for with the exception of the two very lovely changes to G major (in reality the Neapolitan sixth in F sharp minor), which are like a ray of sun falling into a dark place, the only harmonic event of importance is this repeated step to the chord of the dominant, or imperfect cadence (bars 5, 9, 11, 13, 19, 21, 26). Only on the first occasion is this chord reached from below, for each other time the step descends. As if enough had not been heard of the F sharp minor tonality, a second melody follows, with a still simpler harmonic basis; in this, bar 24 is developed into a broad and passionate, almost Chopinesque, fioritura passage. The ensuing modulation to D, (bars 36–45), again, is filled with passionate unrest, which however gives place for eight bars to a sense of sublime peace. The immediately following cadential passage, up to bar 67, is widely extended in compass; note that in the eleven bars 58–68 the treble drops more than three octaves and then rises again to the same height. The twenty bars leading to the return of the principal theme contain, in bars 68–84, twenty-four downward steps of a third, which however are again and again caught up, as it were, by rising sixths. The music seems to be feeling its way back to the principal key, though this is never far off; neither the changes of key-signature nor the numerous accidentals imply enharmonic modulations. At its return the main theme is hidden by figuration of a spiritual depth that Beethoven was capable of plumbing only in his last period. In the coda the principal theme returns, shortened to eight bars, and is followed immediately by a reminiscence of the second subject, now in F sharp minor. (Beethoven's own metronome mark, ♪ = 92, is important; it shows that he wanted the movement to be played with passionate emotion. The sketches published by Nottebohm (*Zweite Beethoveniana*, pp. 133 et seq.) are highly instructive, for they show how Beethoven "worked from the whole" and how "the idea gradually crystallized into notes.")

The fugal Finale is a movement of tremendous boldness and novelty, but overladen to the point of artificiality with all the arts of the fugue. It was said that he wrote it to prove that he was master of the form. In one place—at the entry of the B minor section—he introduces the very long subject 'cancrizans', i.e. in retrogression, a fact that cannot be heard, but only seen from the printed notes. What however is remarkable is that, no less than the rest of the movement, this passage is replete with the highest possible emotional tension. Here there is no trace of the static form of the fugue; apart from a few interludes, the main subject, it is true, dominates the whole movement in uninterrupted polyphony; but it is no longer, as was the case with Bach, inviolable within certain limits; it has to submit to all possible permutations and combinations—hence Beethoven's instruction 'con alcune licenze'; like all his sonata themes it has its vicissitudes, and these it is that ensure that in its organic structure the movement is a symphonic whole. In style also it fits perfectly into the organism of the whole work, and in spite of the impossibility of any really satisfactory performance on the piano, we could never wish for a Finale of a different kind. The Sonata is, in its four movements, perfectly balanced. After such a first movement, the climax in the last, which the 'idea' of the work demands, could only be realized by means of a fugue.

While he was composing the Mass he wrote the last three Sonatas, opp. 109, 110, and 111. Coming after op. 106, these show a return to more manageable dimensions, though their 'specific gravity' is not thereby any the less. In them sonata style has been so far sublimated that the strictness of their form, particularly that of the first movements, is often overlooked. Even the first movement of op. 109, in E, is in true sonata form and not a free fantasia. It is, to be sure, unusual for the rhythm and tempo of the second subject to be different from those of the first, and it is easy to mistake this for formless rhapsodizing until we realize that bars 4–6 of the Adagio are simply an ornamental variation of bars 1–3. What follows is a true working-out of the first subject, leading, ten bars before the return of the Adagio, to a normal recapitulation. In this the second subject appears, according to rule, in the tonic, though it is true that for a few bars it makes a harmonic digression; but thereafter it leads quite regularly into the very beautiful and expressive coda. It is especially necessary, in the case of this almost too fragile musical structure, clearly to understand its formation.

The second movement, a Prestissimo that is at once spectral and charged with daemonic energy, is also in strict sonata form. The only motive worked in the development section is the counterpoint of the first subject. At the beginning of the recapitulation a felicitous touch is added by the inversion of the parts, the subject being repeated in the bass while the counterpoint appears in the treble.

The theme of the variations is one of exalted beauty, and they themselves are among the most profound that Beethoven ever composed. On occasions they are very remote from the theme, but at the end this reappears as though it were returning from far-off regions. (Bach's *Goldberg Variations* also close with a restatement of the theme as an epilogue; but this is a different matter, for here the theme is present throughout.) In many passages, as for example the second part of Var. IV, the piano writing has something of the magic of Chopin.

It has been said that the A flat Sonata, op. 110, is a "return to old times"—*vide* Thayer and Bekker. Actually it is, as much as the preceding one, genuine last-style Beethoven; and this is the case even in the first movement, in spite of its song-like first subject (after the introductory motive), which would be unusual in this place even in early Beethoven. From the nature of this subject it seems at first as if we were about to hear a slow movement. But very soon a change takes place: the movement turns out to be in true sonata form, though the entry of the second subject is curiously disguised, for it opens, immediately after the demisemiquaver arpeggios, in what sounds like A flat but is really the subdominant of E flat. Only by degrees, after the series of trills in the bass, is the E flat clearly asserted. (This is an isolated case, and only possible in Beethoven's last period. In earlier works he often introduced the second subject through the dominant of the dominant, e.g. in the first movement of op. 31, no. 2, and only thence did he arrive at the dominant of the principal key, at the same time allowing the tension to relax.) It is just the transparent, almost immaterial texture, and the delicacy of contour and tenderness of expression of the smallest phrase of this second subject and the following passage, that is most truly representative of his last style. The working-out is very unusual; it is an eightfold repetition, devoid of all tension and with the simplest possible harmonization, of the first two bars of the introductory motive. In the recapitulation Beethoven very wisely refrained from allowing the 'song theme' to appear again with a definite close; instead it fades away in a mysterious modulation to F flat major, here written as E major. The twenty bars of the coda maintain the gently gliding character of the whole movement. The fifth bar before the end contains a surprising reminiscence of the first bar.

The scherzo-like second movement also, in spite of its somewhat naïve theme, is true 'last style', particularly in the figures of the middle section, which though expressive have little solid harmonic foundation. What follows is one of the most splendid inspirations of Beethoven in his last period. This is the 'arioso dolente', introduced by a most expressive recitative, which contains within itself every possible shade of feeling. Though its lay-out—four phrases of four bars—is very regular, its construction is unusual in that it has something new to say each time. Thus the tune is, so to speak, lacking in a germinal motive. It is succeeded without a break by a fugue, which, unlike those in opp. 102 and 106, is song-like, especially in the counterpoint. In spite of the climax towards the end, it is quiet and peaceful, but not static in the sense of a Bach fugue. The Arioso returns, this time 'wearily complaining', and no longer in A flat minor but in the gloomier key of G minor. The sense of weariness comes from the fact that the melody, this time slightly varied, is now broken by suspensions and rests. This continues up to the return of the fugue, which is marked 'poco a poco di nuovo vivente.' The theme is first presented in inversion and, as it gradually returns to the principal key (A flat), in augmentation, in diminution, and finally, in a shortened form, in double diminution. There is much here, perhaps, that is somewhat strained and artificial; but once the key of A flat is reached we have the feeling that we have fought our way into the open through a narrow defile: it is as if the theme had never until now been able to develop its full power, which hitherto had been latent and only hinted at towards the end of the fugue at its first appearance. In the last thirty-nine bars the theme seems to rise from triumph to triumph, fugal form being abandoned after the tenth bar for simple chords. There is no other example in Beethoven of a conclusion of this kind, in which the movement works up to an entirely unexpected climax at the very end. (It is not the same thing as in the case of last movements that from the beginning are seen to be the climax of the work as a whole, and have their own climax at the end.) It may be said that this close points to something outside the work itself, and that it is thus a case of 'open form'. Yet at the same time it points back to the beginning of the sonata: the introductory motive of the first movement is related to the closing theme, for the shape of the sequence A flat-D flat-B flat-E flat-C-F, the theme of the fugue, is undoubtedly foreshadowed in the first three bars of the Sonata. (There is also a structural similarity between the theme of this fugue and that of the fugue in the *Gloria* of the D major Mass. Evidence of this similarity, however, is not to be found in the identity of any given sequence of notes, but only in that of certain structural elements.)

In his last Sonata, op. 111, Beethoven, by a strange coincidence, returned for the first time to the structural principle of his first Piano Sonata, i.e. he developed the whole of the first movement out of a single theme. He preceded it with an introduction, maestoso, which in its rhythmic and harmonic pathos is a little reminiscent of the *Pathétique*, op. 13, but at the same time foreshadows very different things. It 'introduces' the movement in the truest sense of the word, more so than in the case of the *Pathétique*. Thus, if we see the B-C-D of bar 2 as related to the E-F-G of bar 4, and add the steps G-A-B-C of bars 11–12, which anticipate those of the up-beat with which the principal theme opens, then the force and purpose of this introduction will be clear. The Allegro is exceptionally tense and concentrated, even for Beethoven; perhaps the tension would be almost unbearable if it were not frequently relaxed for a moment by the bars marked 'ritenente'. (Here again we see the 'other side'.) The figuration of the unusually fine transition is derived from the principal theme, which also, as Schenker was the first to observe, is the basis of the second subject, in A flat.

simplified: Principal motive

The final phrase combines the principal theme with the inversion of a figure derived from the second subject. In the short development section only the principal theme is worked, the first bar being repeated five times, forte, immediately before the recapitulation. The coda, only thirteen bars in length, opens with a sequence derived from the heart of the principal theme:

of which we are also reminded by the semiquaver figures of the bass. (The principal theme had 'occurred' to Beethoven twenty years earlier, for it is to be found in almost exactly the same form, in F sharp minor, among the sketches for the Violin Sonata op. 30, no. 1. It was not by chance that he did not use it until so late in life, for the diminished fourth, B-E flat, an interval that gives a strong effect of tension, is typical of his last-period style.)

Something has already been said about the theme of the second and last movement. That the Sonata is not, as Schindler thought, unfinished, need not be emphasized. It is as complete, as finished, as any other composition, even though the contrast between the moments of tremendous concentration in the first movement and the balance and serenity of the second are not united in a Finale. This enormous concentration of the first movement called for complete relaxation, which here, however, led to regions from which there was no return. The second movement at once carries us into the infinite: from the fourth variation, in which the theme is presented alternately in the bass, in shadowy syncopated chords, and high in the treble, in demi-semiquaver figures, it is indeed clear that from here there is no possibility of return. The following passage opens with a series of trills from which fragments of the theme, particularly bar 7, seem to detach themselves, after which the theme twice reappears in its original form but accompanied by arpeggios and semiquaver figures—the highest degree of spiritualization.

Much could be said about Beethoven's farewell to the pianoforte, the *Thirty-three Variations on a Waltz of Diabelli*, op. 120, written a year later. (These came after the Bagatelles, opp. 119 and 126, miniatures that are now and then of astounding depth.) These Variations are undoubtedly Beethoven's greatest work in that form. In them his power of invention is inexhaustible; the theme, itself entirely insignificant, is expounded with incredible versatility; and the work embraces a world of forms and feelings. As Hans von Bülow, its real discoverer, said, it may be looked upon as "an epitome of the whole world of music." Though August Halm, in his *Beethoven*, gives a valuable analysis in outline of the Variations, there is still room for an exhaustive description of this powerful work.

Beethoven's only compositions during the last three years of his creative life, 1824–1826, are the five string Quartets, opp. 127, 130, 131, 132, and 135, and the Great Fugue, op. 133, which he originally wrote as the Finale of op. 130. That this should be so—that he carried out none of the many other plans that occupied his mind—is certainly not due to chance or to external circumstances. The String Quartet was the true means of expression for all that he had to say after he had completed his two greatest works.

It is Paul Bekker who, following up hints thrown out by Nottebohm, first drew attention to certain thematic similarities and inward associations between these last Quartets. The sketchbook shows that Beethoven composed the subject of the closing fugue of op. 130 while he was at work on the first movement of op. 132, to the opening phrase of which it bears a family likeness; and also that the opening theme of op. 131, in C sharp minor, reappears in the Scherzo of op. 132, towards the end of the Trio. Yet it would be wrong to scent in these similarities anything in the nature of a leading motive or of programmatic associations. It is merely that in his last period Beethoven had a partiality for motives in which the step of a semitone is combined with other intervals creating an effect of tension, such as the diminished seventh, the augmented second, and the diminished fourth. (In the same way the line C sharp-B sharp-

A-G sharp in the last movement of op. 131 is comparable with
that of the principal theme of the first movement of op. 132,
A-G sharp-F-E.) It is also known that the *Danza tedesca* of op.
130 was originally intended for op. 132.

Op. 131
 1st Movement   Finale
       a   b

Op. 132
 2nd movement, Trio
                              a

 1st Movement   *Allegro*
       c   b

Op. 133 (Great Fugue)
       c

Thus it may certainly be said that these last Quartets no
longer have the individuality that from the very beginning was
so typical of Beethoven's works. In one respect or another they
'belong together', though not, as in the case of Haydn's and
Mozart's series of quartets and symphonies, as different species
of one class whose basic form is laid down once for all. The
reverse is, in fact, the case: the form of these works and of their
separate movements is more multifarious than ever before,
thanks to a hitherto unexampled versatility and differentiation
of feeling. In opp. 130, 131, and 132, this versatility leads, indeed,
to an increase in the number of the movements, something
entirely new to Beethoven; and now we find short movements
such as are only very seldom to be met with in his earlier works.
Yet it cannot be said that they are any the less pregnant; nor is
their organic growth—more difficult though this may be to
follow—any the less vigorous, in spite of often strikingly abrupt
contrasts such as we find in the sequence of movements of

op. 130, viz., *Danza tedesca*, Cavatina, and, originally, the Great
Fugue—or even the Finale that replaced it. What however does
not appear so clearly and impressively is the individuality of
the work as a whole. The three Quartets of op. 59, though all
written in one year, are as distinct from each other as three
sharply defined personalities. It is true that there is a clear line
of demarcation between these three late Quartets, in as much as
each work in itself is perfectly balanced, the sequence of
movements assures to it a certain 'wholeness', and, particularly,
the first and last movements respectively 'begin' and 'end' the
works in the truest sense of the words. But there are threads
that cross these lines of demarcation and connect one Quartet
with another; and this not only because they are the creations of
one man, or because, having been composed at the same time,
they 'belong together' stylistically, or even because of the thematic similarities to be found in them; but because the 'world-
background' permeates each note of them so intensely that the
bounds that separate one work from the other no longer have
the power to withstand it that they formerly had.

This phenomenon, hardly expressible in words but familiar to
all those who are capable of 'hearing' these works, is perhaps
best explained by reference to that of 'contrast'. Beethoven's
contrasts, significant and expressive as they were from the very
beginning, have now acquired an altogether unparalleled profundity. Movements are juxtaposed in seeming incompatibility
—in sharper contrast than ever before; and there are 'surprises'
of astounding magnitude, such as the sudden unison in the Trio
of op. 132, which comes in the midst of the unconstrained ease of
the dance-like measures, or—and this is far more important
from the point of view of the construction of the movement as
a whole—the major phrase that twice appears (bars 56 and 216)
in the tempestuous minor of the Finale of op. 131, only to fade
away each time in gentle sighs. Not only this, but there are even
whole movements in which contrasts prevail without interruption, such as the first of op. 132, in the first forty bars of which,
and later also in long passages, there are continual changes of
mood—contrasts even occurring simultaneously—without the

homogeneity of construction, which in spite of all is very strict, being in the least impaired. (This movement as a whole has a further contrast in its song-like second subject, which appears, like a gracious vision, three times—in exposition, recapitulation, and coda—almost unchanged except in key.) The 'transparency' of this music is incomparable. And the impossibility of any verbal interpretation is obvious: Helm, in his book on Beethoven's String Quartets, which otherwise contains many thoughtful and subtle observations, does not help when he suggests two possible interpretations of the powerful close: either "I refuse to yield—I will not bow my head!" or "The enemy's cause has prevailed—all is lost!" The spiritual content of this music has its roots in depths wherein no question of such alternatives has yet arisen.

In the last Quartets, it is true, there are structures that are quite different from this first movement of op. 132—movements in which a thought, a feeling, a rhythm, is obstinately maintained through long periods, and which therefore seem to lack this 'transparency'. Typical examples are: the second movement (Scherzo) of the A minor Quartet, and the Presto of the C sharp minor, which, with its twice repeated Trio, has both the form and the character of a scherzo. Throughout long passages of this Presto the crotchets rush ahead at uniform speed; but later they are held up by ritardandos and unexpected pauses, as a sign that there is something else in the world than their self-sufficient, bustling activity. The square-cut regularity of the eight-bar phrases, too, is almost unparalleled in any other than folk music. What is most remarkable is that in two places (bars 109 and 275) Beethoven expressly ensures this regularity by marking them 'ritmo di quattro battute' (Rhythm of four bars); though here the phrasing does not coincide with the melody, since there is an overlap of two bars. As a result of this conflict between phrasing and melodic line the music seems to falter for a few moments. In the Scherzo of the A minor, the main section of which is throughout dominated by two strongly contrasted two-bar phrases, not only is the Trio, with its two sections—the one a Musette, a swaying, somewhat shapeless tune, and the

other similar in type to the Ländler, the old German slow waltz—
in the sharpest contrast to the main section, but it is itself interrupted, without preparation or transition, by the unison passage that appears from out the void. Similar interruptions
occur also in the Scherzos of opp. 127 and 130.

Hans von Bülow relates (*Schriften*, Vol. III, p. 445, note)
that Brahms once referred to the point in conversation and
observed that "Beethoven nowhere submits to the laws of
musical form with such Spartan rigour as in his individual and
strongly imaginative last Sonatas and Quartets." It cannot be
said that this piece of wisdom has been very widely assimilated,
for we still read that Beethoven's last works entirely lack real
form, and that its place is taken by a "succession of visions."
"Form no longer exists, but only a framework that holds together the substance of the music." (Mersmann) This may perhaps apply to some of Schumann's works, for with him sonata
form is indeed simply a framework that holds the release of the
emotions within due bounds, but remains outside the actual
musical substance and is thus always clearly in evidence. It is
the opposite with Beethoven's latest works, for there framework
and content are so entirely one that the former is not seen, with
the result that the impression might arise that these works are
beyond all external form. As compared with his earlier ones
this is nothing fundamentally new, but only a step—decisive,
no doubt—further along the path he had followed from the
beginning; and thus it is a fresh proof of the perfect consistency
and homogeneity of his development. He began by animating
the dead framework of form with the living breath of melody:
he ended by concealing it.

A few examples must suffice. The first movement of op. 127
is an outstanding case of this concealment of the framework.
The opening maestoso reappears twice, as in the first movement
of op. 13, in which the 'grave' is to be found at structurally important points, viz., at the opening of the movement, as the introduction to the development section, and, now only as a
reminiscence, at the beginning of the short coda. In op. 127 the
second appearance of the maestoso introduces the development

section; the third, however, does not introduce the recapitulation, as might be expected, but divides the development section into two, and the recapitulation does not begin until later, at a point that is only distinguishable by a very attentive listener, eight bars after the final return of the E flat key signature. Now, however, the recapitulation is unusually regular. It repeats the exposition bar for bar, with only one addition of six bars in the second part of the first subject. (It is followed by a coda of forty-three bars.) There is, it is true, considerable interchange of voices, and the melodic line is now and then disguised by figuration. This is the natural consequence of the inward animation and vivacity that dominate the movement throughout; it is like a close-woven fabric with a pattern that is not immediately discernible. Moreover, the bounds between the different themes are blurred: in particular the first (G minor) part of the second subject contains certain elements of the first.

The first movement of op. 130, though marvellously complete in itself, is still less easy to fathom. The frequent change of tempo is more noticeable when reading the score than when hearing it played, for a quaver of the introductory Adagio, which reappears several times, is equivalent to a crotchet of the Allegro. This introduction contains much of thematic importance, in particular the step of a second in bars 4 and 5. The second subject (bar 54) is in G flat, and is similar in character to an Adagio theme; but it is related to the first subject by the semiquaver figures. The most surprising thing is the D major section of the working-out, which in three of the parts is connected with the exposition: first through the step of a second, already noted in the introduction; second through the accompanying motive of the first subject; and third through the semiquaver figures. The fourth voice is provided by the Cello, with its cantilena. As Helm says, "the polyphony of quartet style can be carried no further." The accompanying motive is heard twelve times in its original form, and then leads straight into the recapitulation. The whole movement consists almost entirely of simultaneous contrasts; and it is throughout entirely dominated by different emotional strata. It is the same in the 'andante poco scherzoso', though here the melodies hover between jest and earnest, pensiveness and graceful charm. Only in the *Danza tedesca* and the Cavatina are these strata perceptible apart from one another; a chasm opens, which it was Beethoven's first intention to close by the tremendous Fugue, op. 133. The present Finale is not, as is often maintained, a mere make-shift, forced upon him by his publishers' opposition and lack of understanding on the part of the public. Two possibilities are inherent in the previous movements: to increase the tension to the limit of human endurance and shift the climax to the end of the whole work, or to relax it and finish in a mood of quietness and serenity, which often, to be sure, hardly conceals the "abysses of the world." Both endings are 'organic', and both are in keeping with the 'idea' of the work, for it is this that is open to the 'world-background'. It should be noted that the case is entirely different to that of op. 30, no. 1, whose original Finale was used for the *Kreutzer* Sonata, and of the 'Andante favori', which was originally the middle movement of op. 53. In these Beethoven, so to speak, made good an error—an offence against the 'idea' of the work, which he had lost sight of in the process of composition.

As was usually the case in his earlier works, so now his last movements are more straightforward and spacious in their development, less tense and close-packed in their thematic work, than his first movements; and thus in style they are often somewhat reminiscent of the Rondo. The Finale of op. 132 has for its first subject an almost nervously impassioned tune thirty-six bars long—how difficult to realize that it was once intended for the Finale of the Ninth Symphony!—out of a short extension to which (bars 40 et seq.) the second subject grows. This hovers indeterminately between G major and E minor and at last leads back by imperceptible degrees to the principal key, A minor. A repeat of the first subject (bar 90) leads to the working-out (bars 124–163), the thematic heart of which is a figure consisting of the last three quavers of the principal theme. The transition to the recapitulation, which, contrary to custom, is reached by vay of the subdominant, is wonderful. The recapitulation itself is quite regular, but it is immediately followed at bar 244 by a remarkable and very long coda—almost double the length of any of the other three sections. The theme, played by the Cello in the highest part of its compass, is passionately accelerated, but before the end tension is suddenly relaxed. A passage of over a hundred bars follows, still full of restless motion, but in an indecisive major; in this nothing is heard of the various themes, and the melodies grow more and more formless until they fade away altogether. (Structurally bars 302–350 correspond exactly to bars 351–399.) We are reminded of the close of the op. 95 Quartet, but here the music, though more incorporeal, is larger in form.

The superficial listener, carried away by the wild energy of the dance rhythm that dominates long passages of the movement, is apt to regard the Finale of op. 131 as in the nature of a rondo, in which, except for two very abrupt contrasts, the note that was struck at the opening is maintained throughout. Actually however it is in sonata form, not only externally but also in its essence—a movement of vigorous but admittedly unusual inner growth. The principal theme, in the complete and self-contained form in which it first appeared after the short but impressive introductory motive, only returns once, fairly soon, at the beginning of the development section, (bars 78 et seq.). It reappears with its second part attenuated, at the opening of the recapitulation (bar 160); here its entry is given special prominence by the introductory motive, greatly extended and played fortissimo. Later, even in the very long coda (bars 262 et seq.), only fragments of the principal theme appear. It is interesting to note that the proportions of the movement gradually increase: the exposition contains seventy-seven bars, the development eighty-two, the recapitulation a hundred and three, and the coda a hundred and twenty-six. It is as though the tension of the principal theme were being reduced by degrees; and the same impression is created by the way in which, in the working-out, the harmony gradually flattens from C sharp minor to F sharp minor, and so to B minor. On the other hand, vigorous counter-themes make their appearance, thus: in the working-out there is one consisting of rising seconds; in the recapitulation another, C sharp-A-G sharp; in the coda there is one consisting of descending seconds; and a fourth, C sharp-F sharp-E sharp, appears seven times at the end of the movement and dominates it in its last bars. (In this last theme may be heard a transformation of the subject of the fugue with which the work opens.) The end of the movement is led up to by a succession of minor cadences in which the subdominant side of the key, as well as the dominant, constantly appears, and which formed the harmonic basis of the coda. The close is a plagal cadence, i.e. it moves from the subdominant, F sharp minor, to the tonic, C sharp major.

Harmonically the first entry of the second subject, which dies away in a whisper, is introduced with perfect regularity, but otherwise it comes as a complete surprise.

At its second appearance, in the recapitulation, this subject is expanded to twice its former length; that it is prepared in an entirely different manner is due to what has happened meanwhile.

It is a well-known fact that in the big works of his last period Beethoven made use of variation form, particularly for slow movements, far more than in his earlier ones. Examples are:

q

the Ninth Symphony, the Piano Sonatas opp. 109 and 111, and the String Quartets opp. 127, 131, 132, and 135. It was not so much that he derived pleasure from the free play of his synthetical imagination, as that he felt the need for a certain measure of relaxation, for which this form offers special opportunities. Here it is a case not of opposition but of juxtaposition; and the length and structure of the theme itself very largely determine all that is to follow. In this form it is a question more of coordination, and less of subordination than in any other that Beethoven employed; but it is remarkable how he floods each variation with light from the depths and how even here he extracts the full value of each contrast and each significant point. This is to be seen at its finest in opp. 127 and 131, while in opp. 111 and 132 he confines himself to an ever fuller and more inspired figuration. (In op. 132 the contrast comes in the episode, which is also varied once.)[15]

But this desire for relaxation, which is evident even in some of the most impassioned movements of his last period, does not indicate a failure of strength. This is shown clearly by such a movement as the Great Fugue, op. 133, in whose power there is even to-day almost something breath-taking, and which, owing to the terrific energy with which it spends its force, is not only almost unplayable but also hardly possible to 'hear' correctly. It is true that the 'motive power' of this music is of a different kind to that of the earlier works; it is not, to the same extent, directed, under great tension, towards a goal, but discharges itself in full force at the very beginning, and maintains this force over a long period. For a hundred and twenty-nine bars the first section of the Fugue storms along in an unremitting fortissimo and with the same intensity of expression, to be succeeded by a second section in which a pianissimo is similarly maintained from beginning to end. In all the seven hundred and forty bars of the work there are only very few crescendos, which in the case of other forms used by Beethoven were a structural element of great importance. When they do occur, this is only in certain passages outside the actual Fugue itself. The case of Bach's organ fugues presents itself to the mind, for in these too

there is neither crescendo nor diminuendo, but only an alternation of loud and soft sections. Apart from this, however, Beethoven has never been so far from Bach as here. On this battle-
field it is not a question, as is so often the case with Bach, of the
victory of the angels over the spirits of evil, or of God's majesty
speaking through the music; here the demons are raging
furiously together, and even the iron law of the fugue has
difficulty in asserting itself against their tumult. But this
tumult is of a different kind from that of the Finale of the
Seventh Symphony; the music does not storm headlong forward, rather does it stamp about in wild ecstasy, like a savage
as he performs some orgiastic dance. Yet in this case the fugal
form is still perceptible beneath all the tumult; in another—in
the Scherzo of the F major Quartet, op. 135—the tumult comes,
divested of all art, like a bolt from the blue into the calm and unconstrained ease of the movement, which is only now and then
disturbed by moments of tension. This is at the passage in the
Scherzo where a short figure that has already been heard in the
middle section suddenly falls into a frenzy. It is repeated forty-
eight times fortissimo in the three lower octaves, while the first
violin, with its dance-like motive, climbs higher and higher.

Many timid people thought, even when they first heard the
Finale of the Seventh Symphony, that Beethoven must have been
drunk or out of his mind when he wrote it: when they heard this
passage, and other similar ones, they were certain of it. Oulibisheff discusses the point in considerable detail in his book on
Beethoven, and ridicules his contemporary, Wilhelm von Lenz,
for finding in such passages traces of Beethoven's genius. With
an astonishing depth of insight Lenz made a remark that
Oulibisheff quotes with a sneer: "Beethoven is all things at all
times. He is the very nature of things under unchanging conditions." This is perfectly true: even when Beethoven seems to
have lost all self-control, and to have worked himself up into the
wildest frenzy, he sees the world with eyes that are as clear as
ever. But he is not afraid to draw aside the curtain that veils the
abyss. He knows no fear of chaos, out of which matter is made
form, because he is aware of his power to give form to all that

his eyes have seen. To quote a saying of Romain Rolland that expresses admirably a thought of Kant upon the subject of genius, he is

"the creative power of Nature herself."

APPENDIX

EROICA SYMPHONY, FIRST MOVEMENT

AN ATTEMPT AT AN ANALYSIS OF THE ORGANIC STRUCTURE

(Note. In the counting of the bars, the four at the double bar that lead back to the repetition are omitted.)

A. FIRST SECTION (EXPOSITION)

I. FIRST SUBJECT

The first movement of the *Eroica* has no 'principal theme'. It is probably the only classical movement in sonata form in which this is the case. There can however be no doubt about its 'principal motive'. This appears at the very beginning of the movement (bars 3–6), compact and pregnant, and returns again and again in the same or a slightly different form. But nowhere is a complete and self-contained musical period evolved from it (except the very simple phrases towards the end of the coda, which were indeed only possible at this place); nor is there any other phrase, in addition to or connected with the principal motive, that can be described as a 'principal theme'. The passage that immediately follows the motive at its first statement (bars 7–15) does not reappear in the same position anywhere else in the movement, even at the opening of the recapitulation. And apart from this, the first period, though it is brought to a decisive close by means of a broad cadence, is as a whole structurally of a highly unusual type, and for this reason alone is quite unsuited to the function of a principal theme.

The principal motive (which, as is well known, is to be found in the Overture to Mozart's *Bastien und Bastienne*, written when he was twelve years old) consists simply of a broken common chord, such as was used again and again as a motive from the late baroque period onwards. Here it is, so to speak, the melodic 'unfolding' of the notes

247

already heard simultaneously in the form of chords, those two mighty hammer-blows with which the movement opens and which give us a hint of its 'heroic' character. In itself the motive is decidedly static: it begins on the key-note, and returns to it three times, at the beginning of each succeeding bar. The third and fifth of the chord 'turn' about the key-note, as it were, and it is only the rhythm that gives the figure that significance that is the essential quality of a 'motive'. In other cases in which such motives occur, they are usually repeated several times on different degrees of the scale (e.g. the tonic followed by the dominant, or by the supertonic and then by the dominant); and often contrasting phrases are inserted, as in Mozart's great Piano Sonata in C minor, or Beethoven's in D minor, op. 2, no. 2, so that the motive forms part of a broad musical sentence. But what happens here?

The bass, to which the motive is given, proceeds by two downward semitone steps to c♯—or possibly d♭,* we do not yet know which. Meanwhile the violas and second violins continue their throbbing beat on b♭ and g′ respectively. The resultant harmonic ambiguity is

---

*In order to show the pitch of the notes and the shape of the figures quoted in this analysis, the names of the notes in the various octaves are differentiated as follows:

C — B   c — b   c′ — b′   c″ — b″   c‴ — b‴

further emphasized by the syncopation of the first violins, crescendo, which in its turn gives rise to rhythmic ambiguity. After two bars, however, the syncopation ceases, and the basses rise from c♯ to d. (Only now do we know for certain that it is c♯ and not d♭.) Yet the harmonic ambiguity has only apparently been resolved; or rather we are deluded into thinking that the key is G minor—though only for one bar, it is true, for the a♭ of the first violin brings us back to E flat major. In the next five bars this key is confirmed by a perfectly straightforward cadence, and not only the harmonic but also the rhythmic and melodic ambiguity is brought to an end. The melodic element in particular now comes into its own for the first time with a tender and expressive tune given out by first violins and violas. Though this has a very definite close, it has no real beginning, for it grows gradually out of the first violins' g″ in the syncopated bars. From its melodic line it sounds as if it were an answer to an earlier phrase; it is, as it were, the second half of a complete musical period. But to what is it the answer? We can only relate it to the four bars of the principal motive in so far as it 'turns' about a central point—the note g″—from which it started and to which it comes back. But here the line moves by steps of a second and not, as in the case of the principal motive, by skips of a third, fourth, or fifth. In the immediately preceding bars, however, there is yet another 'turning' figure, and with this the connexion seems to be closer. It consists of the chromatic progression of the bass after the end of the principal motive, viz.: e♭–d–c♯–d–e♭; and the crucial step, c♯–d, is given the same prominence by the dynamic marking (crescendo leading to a sforzato) as is given a bar later to the crucial step in the treble, g″–a♭″. Thus the 'turning' figure—we shall meet with similar cases again and again—raises itself out of the twilight of the bass into the bright regions of the treble, and only there becomes a clearly defined entity. The 'turning' motion influences the following quaver figures.

Thus by means of certain hidden analogies these twelve eventful bars become one homogeneous whole, as the hearer probably feels without being able to account for it. But the homogeneity is of a very special kind. It is certainly not that of a normal period such as might serve for the statement of a principal theme; rather is it that of a phrase that we might expect to find as the preparation for it. And at the moment when the motive reappears (bar 15) we do indeed have the impression that the movement is only now about to get under way. It is as if hitherto everything had been merely an introduction, though certainly one of an unusual kind, since the tempo is laid down, and it is with the principal motive itself that the movement opens. When the motive is next heard, at bar 15, it at once assumes an entirely new 'solidity', and we take it for granted that this time it will not immediately vanish again. Nor are we disappointed: the expected developments now take place. The second half of the motive is twice repeated higher in the scale—the parts extending over five octaves—at the same time passing from the tonic by way of the supertonic to the subdominant of E flat. The original skip of a fourth at the up-beat becomes a step of a semitone, with the result that at each repetition the connexion is drawn closer. Thus there arises a line, eb–e–f–g–ab, extending over eight bars; but this is certainly not a period such as might convert the principal motive into a theme. Even in this form the motive remains a motive, and in the truest sense of the word—it is the 'motive power' that alone gives life to the harmonic development of the movement. But this harmonic development cannot possibly come to an end with the ab, and so the line is carried on, in the eighth bar, by way of a♮ to bb. With this the immediate aim, the dominant of the principal key, is reached. But now, since the motive could hardly reappear a fourth time, and in order that the hearer should not be led to expect this, the bass takes a different line. It steps down from c (with the first inversion of the subdominant triad) to C♭ and on to B♭, thus heightening the effect of the upward chromatic steps ab–a–bb of the upper and middle voices. As a result the dominant, as befits its greater importance, is emphasized far more strongly than the supertonic and the subdominant, which were the intermediate stages of the ascent. In the following passage this emphasis is still more marked: for six bars the Bb is held as a bass pedal-point, while in the treble the melodic step a–bb is broadened out and strongly accented. In bars 27–28 we seem to be firmly established in Bb; but the descent of the bass to Ab in the next bar makes it clear that we have not yet quitted the principal key, which is confirmed in a broad passage of eight bars. (Note here the weight of the bass line B♭–A♭–G–A♭–G–F–B♭–E♭.) That B flat major was deceptive, giving as it did the impression that we were approaching the second subject, though in that case the modulating passage would

have been a very short and indecisive one. Actually the fourteen bars
23–36 merely affirm the dominant of E flat, and the B flat is only the
first hint of what awaits us.

Yet other events of the greatest importance happen in these fourteen bars. Until towards the end, it is true, they are kept piano. But in
them there are no less than twelve sforzatos, all against the beat; that
is to say that from bar 25 to 32 (with the single exception of 27, which
corresponds to 23) they accentuate every other beat. The passage is
thus syncopated, and the four bars 29–32 consist of a series of
'hemiolias', or in other words they are arranged in six groups of two
crotchets instead of four groups of three crotchets. In bars 33–34

"Hemiolias"

the rhythm is skilfully brought back to 3/4 by the accentuation of the
last beat in each bar. Now we are back in the rhythmic ambiguity of
bars 7–8; the value of the syncopated notes is doubled, and the effect
of the syncopation is heightened both by the sforzatos and by the
expressive line of the first violin part. This part is obviously related to
the principal motive: the gradual descent in bars 23–24 and 27–28
is like the answer to the equally gradual threefold ascent of the
motive, which is now twice repeated in broken triads (b♭′–d″–f″–
b♭″, and e♭″–g″–b♭″). But here the upward path seems beset with
obstacles; it is as if it were a question of again attacking and conquer-
ing the heights, or rather as if the music had to force its way through
a narrow defile and only then were free to take the topmost heights by
storm (bars 35–36). At the summit the principal motive makes its
third appearance, now for the first time fortissimo and in all the
splendour of the full orchestra. Again we have the impression that
everything up to this point has been an introduction. Only now, as a
result of the broad preparation in which the dominant has played so
great a part, is the principal key fully displayed. In many respects the
third appearance of the motive corresponds to the second. In both
cases, for instance, the eight bars are similarly arranged. But now the
harmonic progression is different: previously the direction was upwards, from the tonic by way of the supertonic to the subdominant;

now the motive, given to the bass strings and wind, takes two resolute downward steps of a third, from the tonic to the submediant (C), and thence to the subdominant (A♭), while the first violin—the highest part and so the arbiter of the proceedings—holds the e♭''' for seven bars. A further important difference is that the motive is not repeated when at bar 43 the subdominant is reached, but that the bass remains on the A flat, and indeed emphasizes it with its six throbbing quavers. From here it moves down by way of G flat, on which it also remains for a bar, to F. These steps correspond to the upward progression e♭–e–f in the treble. What happens therefore is almost the same as in bars 22–23, though it is now broader and more powerful; but though in each case the starting-point (the subdominant) is the same, and though the transitional chords (augmented sixths—in the first instance c♭–e♭–f–a, here g♭–b♭–c–e) correspond, the harmonic aim is now different. Previously it was the dominant, B flat; this time it is F major, and with this the principal key is obviously quitted. This is because the starting-point of the bass was not, as before, C (the third of the chord) but the root, A flat. But it is the melodic side of bar 44 that gives this transitional chord its importance, viz., a very expressive quaver figure, which is heard in three octaves. The figure itself is new, but its line is similar to that of the melody in bars 11–13, for it too turns about a central point, this time in steps of a second, so that it gives an impression of unusual intensity.

1st theme of Transition

etc.

It will be seen that this bar is exceptionally eventful, as indeed is only to be expected when we realize that in it the highly important step is made from the subdominant of the principal key to the 'dominant of the dominant', that is, of the key of the second subject. In the works of his maturity Beethoven almost invariably approached this latter key by way of its dominant. But hardly anywhere else does he do it so concisely, and with such tremendous tension, as here. This could be possible only by means of a climax such as this that he here builds up, and of the compactness and concentration of the principal motive— which now even less than at its second appearance is expanded into a theme. Here more than ever its function is confined to that of a motive; and it is significant that it disappears altogether when the subdominant is reached. Bar 43, consisting only of the common chord of A flat, and in which the motive does not appear, has no other function than to prepare for the very tense discord in the next bar. (Note for conductors: these two bars, 43 and 44, must be given their full value as the peak point of all that has hitherto been heard, and in particular the melodic quaver figure of bar 44 must be clearly audible.)

II. TRANSITION

With bars 44 and 45 the principal key and, as the hearer immediately feels, the sphere of influence of the principal motive, are for the time being quitted. This does not however imply that we have reached the point at which the second subject may be expected to appear. First the position that has been gained outside the principal key must be consolidated. This consolidation is effected by the following passage, which at the same time bridges the gap between what we have already heard and what, in its significance for the whole, is now to be revealed.

The harmonization of the next passage is as simple as possible: above the bass F, which, though not always sounded, dominates it in spirit, the harmony alternates between F and B flat. At first it is doubtful whether these harmonies are to be regarded as the tonic and subdominant in F or the dominant and tonic in B flat. In bars 55–56 the question is finally decided in favour of the latter, a decision that accords with Beethoven's custom, already referred to, and with the expectation to which the e♭ in bar 46 gave rise in our minds. The close that is reached after twelve bars marks the end of a self-contained period, the tonality of which only lacks 'full weight', so to speak, owing to the absence of subdominant harmony. For this reason alone—quite apart from what happens in the way of motive and melody—it cannot be called the second subject, though in comparison with the principal motive it is more like a full-grown musical period. The structure of the motive is above all rhythmic; and now for the first time we hear dotted rhythm. This recurs ten times in the same metre, beginning on the second beat of the bar. This metre is, indeed, not entirely new, for there was a hint of it in the syncopated passage (bars 25–34); this time, however, there is no syncopation, the 3/4 beat being, in fact, emphasized by the even tread of the bass. Moreover the melodic line of the motive—or better, of that which develops from the motive and is distributed among the various instruments—is only apparently new. In it we find, at any rate at the beginning, that 'turning' motion about a central point that we heard in bars 11–13 and 44. If we do not feel a break at bar 45, in spite of the new material introduced there, this is partly because the turning quaver figure bb–a–bb–c–bb–a (bars 44–45) is carried on in the figure g–f–e–f–eb in bars 45–46, though the latter, it is true, has a different rhythm. It may perhaps even be said that the melodic line of this first theme of the transition (bars 45–56) is developed from the quaver figure of bars 44–45; and that its emphasis on the second beat reproduces and heightens the effect of features already heard, while its dotted rhythm enriches the movement with a new element. Bars 53–56 bring this period to an end with three repetitions of the motive of its first bar, on the first two occasions in the minor, but on the third in the major again, *ff*, with almost the whole orchestra playing in unison for the first time.

This B flat major close is emphatic enough to raise expectations of the second subject, especially since at bar 57 all motion ceases for the space of a minim. But it is soon clear that the transition is not yet finished. In contrast with the harmonic breadth of the previous passage, the harmonies of this second theme change at each bar. As the basis of quite simple melodic figures, we twice hear the sequence: tonic—subdominant (long awaited!)—tonic—dominant. On the second occasion a quaver figure appears that seems, as in bars 13–14 and 35–36, about to reach a full close. But this is still delayed: for eight bars the motion, owing to the semiquavers that now make their first appearance, becomes more and more agitated; and the same tension is felt in the harmony, which, avoiding for the time being the expected full close in B flat, first touches the submediant (G minor)—an interrupted cadence—which however is prepared by an 'intermediate dominant'. With this a cadential passage of great breadth is commenced, each individual step of which is also further broadened and enriched by 'intermediate dominants',* until at bar 75, where the

---

*The term 'intermediate dominant' seems to me a better designation for these harmonic progressions than any other. The inter-

melodic line reaches its highest point with the subdominant, straight-forward quaver motion returns. This quaver passage is closely related to the previous ones, whose function was the same (i.e. cadential), though here it is greatly extended and its expression heightened. And so, in a downward rush of eight bars, over two and a half octaves, with the orchestra playing in unison over five octaves, it at last arrives at a perfect cadence. The whole cadential passage takes eighteen bars, and is thus several times longer than any earlier passage of the same kind. Now the fulfilment of our expectations can no longer be postponed; the second subject must surely be at hand.

III. SECOND SUBJECT

Is what now comes a true 'second subject', such as we are acquainted with in the symphonies of Haydn and Mozart, and in those of Beethoven's first period? The spiritual contrast with what we have already heard is clear enough: the music seems for a time to be reposing, with the wood-wind chords that gradually work their way upwards and whose expression is for the present derived only from their (melodically important) chromatic passing notes. In the second half of the period (bars 87 et seq.) this expression becomes more intense, and the upward pressure of the violins more urgent. The harmonic progression is simple and regular: tonic–subdominant–supertonic–dominant–tonic; and the melodic line, which until the last bar has been upward, regains its balance, as it were, with the run down from g to b♭ in the last bar. But although the theme apparently marches ahead in straightforward crotchet motion, its structure depends upon a rhythmic point: not only the theme, but also each separate phrase of which it is composed, starts on the second beat of the bar; and this is the case also in the latter half of the theme, with the ascending line of the violins. Here also, therefore, we find that accentuation of the second beat that we have so often noticed before, and at the same time we observe a connexion with what we have previously heard. This connexion is, indeed, extremely close. When the theme begins,

---

polated chords undoubtedly stand in the relation of dominant to those immediately following them. Without these interpolations, which help to broaden the passage and to increase the tension, the bass line would simply be G–E flat–F–B flat.

at bar 83, it at first sounds like an echo of the fortissimo blasts from the horns and trumpets in the two previous bars. These also begin on the second beat of the bar, and not for the first time, for the same occurred in bars 73–74, and also, in the violins, in bars 59–60. Further examples are to be found in the rhythm of the horns in bars 48 and 52; there is an earlier hint of it in the horn part in bar 36, and even a first premonition in the corresponding passage for the basses in bar 14.* Truly this is proof of an almost superhuman power of 'seeing the work as a whole', and at the same time a warning to all superficial listeners and performers to disregard nothing—not even an inner part whose sole purpose is apparently to fill in the harmony.

Rhythm of 2nd Subject
First Hint

Regular eight-bar periods such as this, which return to the tonic, usually have a more or less varied 'after-phrase' leading to the dominant. Here also, the dominant is reached after eight bars, though by a very unusual road. Beethoven evidently chose this road to avoid interrupting the forceful symphonic development of the movement, and so dividing it up, like a song, into self-contained sections. The

---

*This, however, is perhaps doubtful. The copy of the score corrected by Beethoven shows no tie between bars 13 and 14. (See also Breitkopf and Härtel's Complete Edition.) In the old parts published by Haslinger, and in the old Simrock Edition, on the other hand, the tie is shown. When did it first appear?

'after-phrase' opens like a minor variation of the first period, and similarly works its way up in three stages, beginning each time on the second beat of the bar. But its harmonic development is more pronounced, opening as it does with a modulation that seems about to lead to some remote key. With the fourth bar the dominant of D flat is reached. This bar is given special prominence by the fact that it is the only one in all the sixteen bars in which the second beat is not accented. The melodic step db–c, which corresponds with the step d–c in the fourth bar of the first phrase, decides the course of melodic events in the following bars, for this descending semitone recurs three times, each time as the resolution of a passing note. Twice this is approached by an expressive downward step of a third, the first time in the bass (f–db, bar 95), and without any supporting harmony. This lack of harmonic support is, however, only apparent; actually the step has a purely harmonic basis; it is in fact due entirely to the demands of the harmony, for the f is the resolution of the gb of the previous bar, while the db is the key-note itself. In the next bar (96) we find a very striking chordal formation, which is only to be understood by reference to the resolution of the accented passing note, c, in the bass (which of course is melodic). Its root, though unheard, is clearly G, so that it is actually a chord of the dominant seventh, with ab, the minor ninth. Thus we have a notional skip of a fifth in the bass, db to G. This is followed in the next bar by a further notional skip of a fifth to C, above which again we find the passing note f resolving on e; and to make still clearer the connexion with the previous resolution, it is again preceded by a downward step of a third, bb–g (here purely melodic) for the oboe. Thus the bass C dominates two bars—very significantly, for a further skip of a fifth is made from it to F, with which the dominant of B flat, to be expected at the end of the second half of this sixteen-bar period, is reached. With this, however, the period does not come to a definite close—it was just this that had to be avoided—for the chord is a dominant seventh, with eb, and points forward to what is yet to come. This follows without a break.

But the D flat major of bar 94 is certainly not an independent key, reached by normal modulation. It is merely a stage on the road taken by the bass from the B flat in bar 91 to the F in bar 99. This road is a true 'cycle of fifths'—from bb it leads in bar 92 to eb, which owing to

r

the melodic structure of the theme is shifted to the treble, and from there on to ab. The following progression, db–g–c–f, we have already noticed. It is possible that Beethoven was prompted to describe this cycle by the progression of the bass in the previous bars, for in bar 89 it had already moved from c to f, and from there, in bar 91, to bb. The change to the minor made three more skips of a perfect fifth possible; one more still, to G flat, might even have been made— and indeed, as the sketches show, Beethoven originally intended it. From there the next step was to have been straight to F, evidently in the same way as in bars 44–45, and Beethoven, no doubt in order to avoid repetition, decided to proceed further by way of G–C. The sketches also show that the bass notes Db and Gb were originally to have been sounded. (From these sketches (Nottebohm-Mies, p.16) it is also clear that at one time he intended the descending third in bar 95 for the treble, where it was to appear as part of the melody. The sketches also throw valuable light on other points relating to this part of the movement.) The final form of the subject, wherein the framework is concealed, and even the music itself almost dies away for one bar, was a true inspiration. This passage, indeed, is one of the most inspired in the whole movement.

IV. CLOSING PASSAGE

With that bass step to F a goal was reached that had long been in sight; and now the seventh, eb, reinforced by the minor ninth gb, at once points ahead towards another. To this the next ten bars press on. The final bass step from F to B flat, is not taken until the end of this passage; and, as is soon to appear, the latter key is not fully defined even there. The passage begins in the rhythm of the second subject, and even in the melody of bars 101–103, there is an echo of bars 88–90. At the fifth bar, however, one of those quaver figures enters whose function is purely cadential and whose aim in this case is the B flat of bar 109. Here the top note, f''', is heard throughout eight bars; similarly in the middle voices and the bass the F reigns supreme; and it is also the lowest note. The result of this predominance of F is to deprive the close in B flat of much of its effect; we have not yet, in fact, arrived at a true full close in that key. These eight bars play a similar part in the growth of the movement to that of bars 45–53; and they remind us of these in other ways as well, for the bass F dominates both passages, the second beat of the bar is always accented, and the harmony in each case vacillates between dominant and tonic. And even the dotted rhythm returns in bars 113–116 exactly as before; though here the melodic line is different, for it approximates more to that of the principal motive. The connexion is undoubted, and of the greatest importance to the organic growth of the movement as a whole. The reason for this is that here there is no mere repetition of something already heard: neither the 'expression' of the motive nor the manner in which the passage is linked up with the preceding and succeeding ones, is the same, or even similar; yet the mysterious laws of the 'whole' result, in two separate passages, in very similar structures. It should be noted that there is a very definite reminiscence of the rhythm of the second subject in the horn and trumpet parts in bars 112 et seq.; this corresponds to the first premonition of that rhythm in the horn part in bars 47 et seq., to which attention has already been drawn.

That in bars 109–116 the true bass note is really F is made quite clear by the transition to bar 117. Here the bass moves from F by way of E flat to D; and on this is a chord of the sixth out of which grows one of those rushing cadential quaver passages that we have so often met with. This time however there is a difference: the passage is very fully harmonized (at each quaver there is a different chord—'intermediate dominants' and their resolutions); while from the third bar onwards the rhythm is against the beat, i.e. it consists of 'hemiolias', the sforzatos coinciding with the beat on which the parts are in unison and forming an ascending line c–d–e♭–f. But here the figure does not lead direct to the close; it culminates in a chord of D major (the 'intermediate dominant' of G minor, which is the submediant of B flat), and resolves itself into a series of chords. For five bars the first beat is silent (note the reminiscence of the rhythm of the second subject), and with the sixth bar the chords, 6/5 on E♮, are arranged as 'hemiolias'. As a result the tension is heightened to an almost unbearable degree. This is the most powerful syncopated passage in all music up to that time, though it is to be excelled later in this same movement. The bass note of the chord, E♮, is chromatically sharpened from E♭ and is therefore still within the ambit of B♭ harmony. It leads immediately (bar 132) to a 6/4 chord on F—that is, the crucial chord for the perfect cadence in B flat. But—and here we see a remarkable thing—after this violent outburst from the full orchestra, it is given to the lower strings only, piano, and it is spread—in other words it is related to the principal motive. Violins and flutes answer with another chord, the augmented sixth on g♭, similarly spread; the sequence is repeated, and from the last note of the answering figure grows a tune that gradually swells to a fortissimo.

This tune is a new one, but it again has a somewhat similar motion to the 'turning' figures that we have so often noticed. At the same time the bass, after moving from f to g♭ and back to f, resumes the upward line over g, a♭, and a♮, to b♭; while the cellos, violas, and second violins accompany the tune with a succession of broken chords in quavers, thus preparing us for the quaver motion of the last four bars, 140–143, which lead to the full close. So at last, with bar 144, the tension that has dominated the music for forty-six bars is broken. The cadential passage that brings the exposition to a close is broader by far than any of the previous ones. Yet it reminds us of them and points back to them; and by borrowing and expanding much of their material, it gives unity to all that we have yet heard.

The exposition is brought to an end with a series of heavy chords that are reminiscent of the two with which the movement opens. These strongly emphasize the beat; but even they are answered three times by the violas and second violins with sforzatos on the second beat of the bar.

B. SECOND SECTION (WORKING-OUT)

The exposition is so tremendously rich in musical ideas that we are now eager to see which of them are to be 'worked' according to the laws of symphonic form. It may be said at once that, apart from figuration, the only one besides the principal motive to be so treated is the first theme of the transition (bars 45 et seq.). For this reason alone, the working-out gives the impression of greater simplicity and spaciousness than the exposition, in which new and unexpected things were constantly appearing; but this does not mean that the former is any less fertile than the latter, nor, provided we take the trouble to probe it to its full depth, shall we find it any easier to 'understand'.

The bridge passage leading to the working-out (and also to the repeat of the exposition) opens, at bar 148, with a reminiscence of the principal motive, which we have not heard for more than a hundred bars. But the time for this motive to come into its own once more has not yet arrived. It therefore disappears again, or rather it is transformed into a mysterious figure that leads us from the B flat major of the close of the exposition away into new harmonic regions. With the working-out we have entered the domain of shifting tonalities. The first step, from B♭ over A♭ to G, is often found at the opening of this section, as for instance in the first movement of Haydn's last E flat Sonata. But we have already heard it in bars 43–45 (A♭–G♭–F), and this time it aims at the same goal as before, for the passage beginning at bar 45 corresponds exactly, both in motive and harmony, to that beginning at bar 166. This time however the goal is not reached without some delay; but the passage that causes this delay (bars 150–166) is of the greatest importance. In it the music seems to be taking breath after the impassioned outpouring of the exposition; it is too exhausted yet to rally its strength or to concern itself with the next stage of its journey. At the same time a faint stirring can be heard—as it were a premonition of further adventures.

It is significant that the step b♭–a♭ (bars 149–150) should be given first to the upper parts over the bass B♭, and that the bass should only gradually be drawn in; so also is the hesitating repetition of the step a♭–g in the bass (bars 154–160), while in the treble the last echo of a figure derived from the principal motive is heard three times unchanged. This consists of the notes g–e–f, and is thus another 'turning' figure, the central point being the f that later, as the seventh above G, is to dominate five bars, and in the end, to our surprise, to move up over f♯ to g. This is a reminiscence of the step e–f of bars 44–45, and as in those bars it leads to an apparent tonic (G major). As a bridge leading to the working-out the whole passage is as inspired, as delicate, and at the same time as prophetic, as can be conceived.

What follows is the first theme of the transition. It is almost unchanged, but such variations as there are must not be overlooked. From the outset two horns hold the g, and emphasize the rhythm of the second subject more strongly than on the previous occasion. Secondly, a playful quaver figure now makes its appearance in counterpoint with the motive, which as before appears now in one voice and now in another; it flits from instrument to instrument, and to some extent takes the place of the bass crotchets, with their ascending broken chords, that had previously helped to maintain the 3/4 rhythm against the syncopation of the motive. The third, and most important and surprising change, is that the bass emphasizes not only the dominant, in this case G, but also the C (bars 170 and 173), as if the key were really C major and this the tonic. As a result the passage is now more static than at its first appearance, and it is therefore only logical that the vigorous close of bars 55–56 should here be wanting—even an increase in tone would be out of place. Accordingly the dynamic marking returns from p to pp, and instead of a new motive, as before, the principal motive follows, now for the first time in the minor. After twelve bars of very definite major, the appearance of the minor is unexpected; our ears however still retain the impression that the introductory bars of the working-out point rather to the minor than the major, so that the sudden change at bar 178 seems like a reference to the opening of the section, and bars 166–177 like a gracious but fugitive vision.

Here for the first time the music is definitely in the minor, which hitherto has only been touched upon in passing. This continues for some time—actually, more than forty bars. The effect of this sudden change is all the more striking since it coincides with the first reappearance of the principal motive. This is in C minor, and the form of the motive itself is substantially altered. Thus, in the fourth bar, instead of returning to the key-note, it rises from dominant to submediant (a♭), thus in itself giving effect to the music's upward impulse—a purpose that in bars 18–19 was served by an 'intermediate dominant'. Here the fourth bar of the motive itself becomes an 'intermediate dominant'; and the motive is at once repeated (the first time in full) a semitone higher, i.e. in D flat (C sharp) minor. A second rise of a semitone, C♯ to D, following that from C to C♯, makes it quite obvious that the passage is not to be regarded as in C minor. And now at last it is clear why the bass has been different from that in bars 45 et seq., and why the close in bars 55–56, which so strongly emphasized the 'dominant' character of the whole passage, is omitted. Here, in the working-out, the function of this passage cannot be to prepare for a key that is later to be defined, as was the case in the exposition; the passage has, in fact, itself been prepared by the preceding one in such a way that the harmony seems to be leading up to a definite C major, though the progression is diverted for a moment by the step f♯–g in bars 165–166. But with this bass the key cannot be, as it were, of full weight, for subdominant harmony is wanting. The position, which it is difficult to explain in words, becomes clearer if we ask ourselves what would be the effect here of the cadence of bars 55–57. The answer is that it would be entirely unsuitable, and for two reasons. First, the bass note C need not be so heavily emphasized if it has already been heard clearly as the bass of the tonic chord in root position; and secondly, there is no point in insisting so strongly on the C major tonality if it is to be abandoned again immediately. As Beethoven decided the question, the music proceeds imperceptibly to the entry of the motive in C minor, on one harmonic plane, so that there is no question of 'transition', but merely of 'progress'; and the hearer feels the two semitone steps, to C♯ and to D, as a further gradual ascent on the same plane.

It is true that the scene changes once the D minor is reached, in bar 186, or rather when with the last crotchet of bar 185 we come within the ambit of this key. The crescendo (at first *pp* followed by *p*), now suddenly culminates in a fortissimo in which almost the full orchestra is united. The violence of this sudden crescendo is emphasized by the fact that on the last crotchet of bar 185 the clarinets, bassoons, and violas add an f to the a and c♯ of the 'intermediate dominant', thus anticipating the following third with a dissonance. What now follows, viz., two fortissimo passages of eight bars each, divided by four bars piano, is of the simplest possible construction. With the first two bars of the principal motive, the harmony changes from tonic to dominant of D minor (four bars of tonic followed by four bars of dominant harmony). The last bar of the passage (193) repeats the first bar of the motive, evidently to avoid a too square-cut formation. The wind gives out the familiar rhythm of the second subject, and in the violins we hear the lively figure of bars 65–70. In the four interpolated piano bars, the motive is heard in diminution, first in straightforward rhythm and then in 'hemiolias'; and at the same time the key modulates, by the sharpening of the f, from D minor to G minor. Bars 198

–205 repeat bars 186–193 a fourth higher, in G minor, and are followed by the four interpolated bars, 194–197, likewise a fourth higher. This raises expectations of a third appearance of the eight-bar phrase, this time in C minor, which however is not forthcoming, and necessarily so if tiresome monotony is to be avoided. But—the C itself is heard, in a repetition of the four-bar phrase (bars 210–213), so that it may be said that the eight-bar phrase in C minor is simply left out. From this point the harmonies proceed in the same way, though not to a repetition of the motive in F minor, or even to an exact repetition of the four-bar phrase. The F appears, however, with the seventh in the bass as at all the previous corresponding points. But the upper part now follows a different course. It proceeds in straightforward quavers, and, in place of the two bars with the 'hemiolias', the B flat minor (bar 215) that has been prepared by the dominant seventh on F is at once quitted again. The music now changes key bar by bar, by way of E♭ and A♭, to D♭ (bar 218), the first inversion of whose common chord is followed by the augmented sixth, which, as before, leads by an upward and downward semitone step to a strongly accented triad, in this case that of E flat major (bar 220). Here again we have a 'cycle of fifths', from D (bar 186) by way of G (199), C (210), F (214), B♭ (215), E♭ (216), and A♭ (217), to D♭ (218). This cycle differs from the previous one (bars 91 et seq.) in that it does not return to its starting-point, since it contains no diminished fifth. This progression would have been impossible on the previous occasion: here it stresses the 'shifting tonalities' that are characteristic of the working-out. While in the exposition the cycle starts in B flat and returns to it, and while each step is relevant to that key, there is here no question of any definite tonality. (It is only for the sake of clarity and simplicity that chords are here referred to as belonging to any given key.) This in no way detracts from the 'tonal' clarity of the individual harmonic steps, all of which lead from dominant to tonic. (It is significant that subdominant harmony, which is essential for key-definition, is nowhere touched upon. All the harmonic progressions are direct from dominant to tonic.)

But merely to have traced these harmonic progressions through does not mean that we have discovered the full significance of this powerful passage. It has already been pointed out that in bars 194–197 and 206–209 the motive appears in diminution, and the 'hemiolia' bars in double diminution. This connexion with the motive is maintained until bar 217, though in the last four bars, since the harmony now changes with each bar, the motive is different in form. But apart from this connexion the growth of the section as a whole is not overlooked. It is by no means far-fetched to see a line of ascending seconds leading from the g'' of the oboe in bar 179 to the eb''' of the flute and violins in bar 220—a line by which the connexion is drawn closer even than by the harmonic progressions.

It was not at first Beethoven's intention that the A flat tonality that, though not of 'full weight', is in force from bar 220 onwards, should come at this place. He can indeed only be said to have had any definite harmonic scheme for the working-out in so far as he had decided upon the key (E minor) of the much discussed episode, which is the very heart of the section. As the sketches show (Nottebohm-Mies, p. 30 et seq.), he always intended to use the first theme of the transition as the bridge leading to the episode, but it was originally to have opened in D major instead of A flat major as in its final form. (In the sketches it only appears once.) It was only as the dimensions of the section grew greater and greater that Beethoven decided upon the present arrangement, and conceived the idea of approaching the E minor from such remote harmonic regions. He evidently considered it better first to establish contact with the principal key once more by means of its subdominant.

What now follows—the preparation for the episode—is unexampled both in boldness and in genius. The first theme of the transition has previously always pointed forward to, and introduced, something new; now it comprises this new thing in itself. That is to say, it does not this time come to an end after ten bars, but changes to the minor (F minor)—for the first four bars without any alteration either in structure or in the distribution of parts. Eight more bars with the same motive immediately follow, but without the quietly murmuring accompaniment. Instead, the character of the writing changes altogether, and a passage in imitation now starts, at first in two voices only. Gradually more and more join in, and the whole works up to a high pitch of animation. At the same time the F minor is quitted; C minor and G minor are entered one after the other, and D minor is reached at the moment the shape of the motive changes. It is essential for our understanding of all that follows to realize that the germ of the motive—i.e. the second crotchet of the bar, which is dotted and stressed by sforzatos, is still in command, and remains so to the end of the tremendous passage that forms the transition to the episode. Thus the delicacy of expression that previously characterized this motive gradually but surely gives way to savage defiance.

With the chord of the diminished seventh in bar 248 the harmony approaches the ambit of A minor, and a series of six-bar phrases begins (down to bar 271), each phrase identical in structure and containing the same 'hemiolias' that we have already met in bars 25 et seq. For twenty-eight bars this rhythm obstinately persists, and at the same time the E minor, in which the episode is to open, is prepared in a series of broad harmonic progressions. Up to bar 259 we are in A minor; but the chord of the seventh on B natural in bar 260 gives the impression of a definite move from subdominant to dominant harmony—the first of its kind since the beginning of the working-out and therefore also the first real modulation to a fully defined key. Actually what happens between bars 254 and 283 is nothing but a very broad and resolute cadential passage in E minor, with transitional chords interpolated (bars 266–271). The expression of this passage increases in intensity as it approaches the end, the submediant taking the place of the tonic in bars 274–275, and the subdominant appearing in bars 276–279 in the form of the 6/5 chord, a–c–e–f (with the Neapolitan sixth), a very strident discord. And when for four bars the chord of the dominant seventh, at first with c, the minor ninth, is sounded (in crotchets, and in what is obviously the rhythm of the second subject), there can no longer be any doubt that we are now within the ambit of E minor. This is confirmed by the fact that the key was approached by perfectly 'legitimate' ways, and without the use of enharmonic modulation.

The episode that now follows, which August Halm calls a "foreign body", has always been the subject of surprise and speculation, and often, indeed, something of a stumbling-block.

How comes this tune, which apparently has no thematic connexion

with the rest of the movement, to be here? Why should it have had
that magnificent preparation? And what is its purpose, seeing that
the movement is already overflowing with musical ideas, and that the
working-out (a section in which, it is true, new material often makes
its appearance) has already exceeded the usual span allotted to it? The
structure of the episode is of course determined by the highest part,
given first to the oboe, and not, as Halm and Schenker consider, by
the counterpoint, which to begin with is in the hands of the cellos and
first violins. We cannot therefore explain its connexion with the rest
of the movement by pointing out that the line of the counterpoint,
e'–g'–b, corresponds to the first two bars of the principal motive, and
that of the melody, e''–g''–b'', with bars 3–4. This explanation is so
artificial that, as Halm admits, it does nothing to help the impression
created by the passage.

And yet no hearer capable of appreciating the infinite breadth of
this movement feels the episode as "foreign" to the whole; nor in
fact is it difficult to indicate the true basis of its connexion with the
rest of the movement. It is simply that the new theme is one of those
'turning' figures of the kind that from the very beginning of the movement we have so often met with. If we compare the first four notes
with the corresponding ones of the quaver figure in bar 44, or the
third to the sixth notes with the f–g–ab–g of bars 12–13, and (to
anticipate a later transformation of the 'turning' figure) the fifth to
the ninth notes with the corresponding ones of the quaver figure in
bar 627, we must at once admit the relationship. This however by no
means implies that the new theme is simply put together from scraps
taken from other phrases; it is only that in the tendency to this 'turning' motion, and thus also in 'expression', the figures bear at least a
family likeness to each other. It is true that the principal motive also
has something in common with these figures, so that we are even
justified in tracing a connexion between that motive and the figure of
the episode; though this, to be sure, is a relationship of the second degree, for there is an essential difference: in one case the 'turning'
figure is a broken triad, in the other it proceeds by steps of a second.
In the episode most of the steps are, moreover, not only seconds but
minor seconds; and their poignant and passionate expression is
heightened by the dotted rhythm of the second bar, and (though the
passage is kept piano) by the sforzatos. (It should not be overlooked

by the conductor that the markings are at first *sfp* and later *sf*; that is to say, the expression increases in intensity.) In any event, it is hardly possible to imagine a sharper contrast than that provided by the immediately following unison entry of the principal motive in C major, at bar 300. In this uncompromising juxtaposition the whole range of forms and feelings that the movement encompasses is immediately made manifest.

The next twenty-two bars form one of the most remarkable passages in the whole movement, and, in spite of its simplicity, one of the most enigmatic. Here we have twenty-two bars of almost complete unison in strings and wood-wind, which is only broken by the horns and trumpets with their insistent g (again in the rhythm of the second subject). The passage is composed entirely of the principal motive, which at first appears complete and in its original form. It opens in C major, the common chord of which is as much within the ambit of E minor as that of the A minor in the episode. After eight bars it darkens into C minor, and thence proceeds by chromatic steps to E flat major and so to E flat minor, upon which it comes to a sudden end. What is the significance of this passage in the organic growth of the movement as a whole? The answer is evidently that Beethoven felt the need of striking back boldly and energetically from the remote regions of the episode to the principal motive, and of reminding the hearer of this latter as vividly and emphatically as possible. But he did not want to return by the same circuitous and ingenious harmonic road that he had taken to reach the E minor, as Mozart had done in the Finale of the G minor Symphony. And so he chose the most direct itinerary available without recourse to enharmonic modulation, viz., a series of ascending chromatic steps, in unison. But the moment the episode reappears, in E flat minor, it becomes clear that this passage does not represent the definitive return to the sphere of the principal motive—such would be altogether too summary, not to say crude, a proceeding!—but is merely a connecting link. Originally Beethoven intended to repeat the episode in its entirety, i.e. to let the theme appear four times, twice in E flat minor and twice in A flat minor. Had he done so, the significance of the part it plays in the working-out as a whole would be still further emphasized, with the result that that of the unison passage would be decreased. As it is, however, the theme of the episode is repeated once only without alteration, as a mere reminiscence. Yet it does not immediately disappear altogether; it is subjected to a remarkable transformation, which once more opens up the prospect of new things to come. Suddenly the counterpoint, which up to now has been given to the lower parts, comes to the top:

the theme itself disappears; and the counterpoint of the first two bars is followed, not as before by descending semitones, but, as naturally as if it had always been so, by the quaver figure of bar 44—proof positive that the melody of the episode is akin to those familiar 'turning' figures. At the same time the E flat minor brightens into G flat major, in which key this melodic phrase, now docked of the 'turning' figure, is three times repeated. It returns to E flat minor, and from there proceeds, in a half close, to B flat major, with which, as will soon be seen, a crucial point is reached.

In these last eight bars (330-337), in which only the first two bars of the counterpoint appear—this time in the major—there is a definite link with the principal motive. This link is of the greatest importance for what is to come. The inner relationship of the 'turning' figure with the principal motive is now for the first time made clear by the figure g♭–a♭–b♭–a♭–g♭; and so what is now to come joins with what has just passed to form a perfect unity. Superficially, what happens in bar 338 is the same as what happened in bar 300: the principal motive follows the episode. But whereas previously the two phrases were juxtaposed in sharp contrast, the one now grows out of the other as though the two had always been a single whole. And looking back from this point at the earlier passage, it seems almost as if it had been a first experiment, or at most a temporary, and not a final, solution of the problem of how to return from the distant regions of the episode to those of the principal motive. In spite of its apparent robustness, there is something spectral about the unison passage; and once the E flat minor is reached, the principal motive vanishes like a ghost to make way for the only solid reality—the episode. But now, as the tune of the episode gradually dies away, it enters into a mystic union with the principal motive, which itself is now divested of all its robustness and is half veiled by a fabric of many colours.

In bar 338, the chord of B flat is again reached with a half close in E flat minor; and all that happens during the rest of the section—the bridge leading to the recapitulation—is within the ambit of the latter key. From now onwards the whole burden is borne by the principal motive, and this is presented with a wealth of imitation hitherto un-paralleled. The first bassoon, which opens the proceedings, gives out the motive five times in different positions, but repeats the high-est note in the fourth bar—a variation that afterwards reappears with still greater significance. The bassoon is answered each time at the second and third bars by other instruments, with a resultant overlap between the end of each answer and the next entry of the motive. Thus the bassoon's is the only part in which the motive is played through without change of harmony. But this instrument alone is not strong enough, even with the help of the complete motive, to safe-guard the four-bar structure; and it is therefore accompanied by the basses with an apparently new and very conspicuous figure, which however is actually nothing but a modification of the principal motive Bb–d–Bb–f–bb–d'–f', the fourth bar being stressed by a sforzato (*sfp*). (In this bar the first violins also emerge from their temporary obscurity with the third bar of the motive; and the rhythm of the second subject is suggested by the third horn.) Thus on the one hand the four-bar arrangement is strongly emphasized, and on the other the risk of monotony due to too great insistence on this square-cut formation is avoided by the entry of the other parts in imitation. It is a fabric of the finest texture that is here woven from the principal motive; and, significantly enough, the piano is only abandoned when, instead of the complete motive played by the wind, the first bar is re-peated four times, with the first beat sforzato. And now, the music having worked up to a fortissimo at bar 362, the only hint of the motive is to be heard in the bass figure, which now ends in a different but very significant way, while the whole of the wind band and the tympani combine to give out the rhythm of the second subject. We are now in C flat (the submediant of E flat minor); and the fact that this key remains in force for eight bars, or twice as long as before, only results in a postponement of the perfect cadence, by means of an exploration of the wider possibilities of the tonality of E flat, which had previously been expanded in the direction of D flat. The bass, having moved from B flat by way of c, db, and d♮, to eb (bars 338–358) now moves down again to C flat. From there, in bars 370–377, it repeats the steps c–d–eb, only to return in bar 378 to Bb, the crucial note for the final cadence, on which it remains for twenty bars. Meanwhile the activities of the other voices have almost ceased; but the part they play is still of importance and takes its place in the general organic growth of the section. The strict four-bar arrangement persists, now principally evidenced by the dotted minim chords of the wind band, though to start with the strings continue to emphasize the fourth bar with the third bar of the motive. With bar 374 the harmonic progression is speeded up, and at the same time the third bar of the motive appears in diminution in each bar, but with the beat displaced so that syncopation results. And even when at bar 378 this last reference to the principal motive ceases, there still remains the syncopated accentuation of each third beat by pizzicato chords. From bar 382 onwards a further effect of syncopation is given by the shifting of the wind chords to the second half of each four-bar period, the first two bars being filled by a shadowy tremolo in the strings. The first violins descend from cb to bb, with the minor ninth still emphasizing the E flat minor tonality that had also dominated the wind chords. At last also the syncopated pizzicato ceases, and for four bars the tremolo of the strings is heard alone. And now we hear, as from afar, that famous and much discussed horn passage, with its E flat major in sharp dissonance with the ab and bb of the violins, that has so often been censured and was even 'corrected' by Wagner. True it only lasts for two bars, pianissimo (the strings, for the first and only time, are even marked *ppp*); and then the full orchestra bursts in with the chord of the dominant seventh, first forte, then fortissimo, and with it at last breaks the tension and brings the working-out to a close.

How is this horn passage to be explained from the purely musical point of view? Of one thing we may be sure: it has not its like in all classical music. Even the famous passage towards the end of the first movement of the op. 81a Sonata (*Les Adieux*) is different, though there too tonic and dominant harmonies are sounded together. This, indeed, happens elsewhere also; but the point is that only here is the third of the scale sounded simultaneously with the fourth, i.e. the seventh of the dominant—and that without any preparation. With

some degree of artifice it is perhaps possible to construe the g–e♭ as
the second of three parallel thirds of which the first, a♭–f, is given to
the second clarinet and third horn, and the third, f–d, to the second
clarinet and first bassoon. But apart from the four bars' rest in between, the a♭–f is an octave higher than the horn's g–e♭. We must
content ourselves with looking upon the entry of the tonic, while
dominant harmony is sounding, as an unusually bold and striking
unprepared dissonance. Such cases we find often enough in Beethoven, but effected in a very different way, the most outstanding examples being the preparation for the Finale of the C minor Symphony, and the very similar passage soon after the start of the Allegro
of the *Leonora* Overtures 2 and 3. Here the bass suddenly bursts in,
ff, with the tonic, in the midst of the full chord of the dominant
seventh; and it is some time before the resultant discord is resolved.
The horn passage in the *Eroica* is harsher since the third is sounded
as well as the key-note; but on the other hand the passage is pianissimo and the dissonance is over in a fraction of a second, for it lasts
only for the space of a crotchet. Yet however we look at it, and firmly
as its foundations are established in the musical context of the whole,
it remains unparalleled in its audacity. Evidently Beethoven wanted
to prepare for the final return of the principal key by means of this
first shadowy reappearance of the g♮, after the E flat minor had held
sway for more than seventy-two bars.

A few words on the general form of the working-out.—As the
sketches show, this section, with its wonderful clarity and ample
proportions, was not composed in accordance with a plan whereby
the general lines of its evolution were already laid down. (See Nottebohm-Mies, p.27 et seq., in which however not all the variants—and
by no means all the important points—are dealt with.) It may be
said with certainty that very early in the proceedings, before he had
settled the general form of the section, Beethoven had decided upon
two details, viz., the E minor episode—or in other words the introduction of a new musical idea that had not appeared in the exposition,
and for which he had from the beginning fixed upon that key; and the
horn passage at the end, which he discarded during composition but
soon reinserted. From the very beginning—which however does not
mean the beginning of the work on the *Eroica* as a whole—this

appears again and again in the sketches, and always, without hesitation, as a dissonance. Clearly this was a spontaneous inspiration of Beethoven's—not thematic but structural. So too, the E minor melody was a true inspiration, and we may take it that from the very beginning Beethoven intended it for this movement, "foreign" as it may seem in its surroundings; that is to say that he very early felt the need of creating the greatest possible emotional contrast within the movement. Apart from these two passages, the remainder of the section only gradually evolved into the organic structure that to-day we so admire and that so fully repays close study.

What it is essential to understand, or at least to feel, in order to grasp the general form of the working-out is something like this: we must realize that the function of the first theme of the transition at its return (bars 166 et seq.) is to prepare the way for what is to come; we must be able to hear what is new both in the bass—i.e. its static nature—and in the forward-driving quaver figure; we must realize that the principal motive, which now at last has made its reappearance, dominates the whole of the long passage from bar 178 to bar 219, and fully grasp the points of concentration, the abbreviations, the figuration, and the gradual but insistent upward impulse that are in this passage. We shall then feel the return of the first theme of the transition at bar 220 not only as the reappearance of something we have already heard—that is to say, as a frame for the intervening passage—but, in spite of the almost note-for-note repetition of eight bars, as something new, that takes place on a higher level. And it will seem to us perfectly natural that this motive, which originally tripped along so demurely, should now be worked gradually up to an overpowering passion and intensity of expression. (Failure to see, or realize the importance of, the thematic unity of development in bars 220–279, implies failure to grasp one of the most important features of the working-out.) But it is also essential for the understanding of the E minor episode to have consciously travelled the long road that the harmony has taken to arrive at that key, and to see the repetition of the tune in E flat minor as an integral part of the episode—that is, not to look upon the unison passage of the principal motive, bars 300–321, as the definitive return to the principal key. This does not take place until bar 338, and it is again essential for our understanding of the section that we should hear all the rest of it, down to the re-

s

capitulation, as one single prolonged cadential passage in E flat, starting out from the dominant, B flat.

Comparing the general form of the working-out with that of the exposition, we shall find that the customary difference between the structure of the two sections is in this case especially noticeable. Apart from its unusual wealth of ideas, a characteristic feature of the exposition is that the cadential and transitional quaver figures are very strongly emphasized, and also that they gradually increase in length as the movement progresses. It is significant that in the working-out these cadential figures are altogether lacking. They would, indeed, be out of place, for here there can be no question of the definition of keys that are to remain in force for long periods. And Beethoven appears deliberately to have constructed the only broad cadential passage in the development section (except that which prepares the way to the recapitulation)—i.e. the preparation for the E minor episode—in an entirely different way; for here it was a question of consolidating a road that leads far away from the ruling tonalities (E flat-B flat) of the movement.

But though here the broad cadential figures by means of which the exposition is so distinctly articulated are wanting, this by no means implies that the articulation of the working-out is any the less clear. This section, on the contrary, gives the effect of being laid out even more spaciously, and on even broader lines than the first—though to be sure it is by his treatment of the thematic material, and not by figuration, that he effects this. Only with the greatest possible mastery could Beethoven have succeeded in building up a structure of the grandeur and dimensions of this section out of two already familiar motives (the principal motive and that of the first theme of the transition) and one new melody, and have articulated it with such incomparable clarity. Of the two hundred and fifty bars of which the section consists (including the eighteen bars of bridge passage from the exposition) a hundred and forty-two are dominated by the principal motive, seventy-two by the first theme of the transition, and thirty-six by the episode. But it must not be overlooked that here too, in spite of the prominent part played by the principal motive, this is nowhere developed into a complete and self-contained 'theme', of whatever shape or kind—many and various as are the forms in which it makes its appearance.

C. THIRD SECTION (RECAPITULATION)

This 'premature' entry of the horn with the principal motive anticipates, and so masks, the actual opening of the recapitulation. But once this starts, it sounds as if it were going to be an exact repetition, both in position and in instrumentation, of the opening of the movement. So decided is its tone, indeed, that we are the more surprised when after no more than six bars a change takes place, as a result of which it almost seems as if we had not yet left the domain of shifting tonality. In the first of the two syncopated bars (in which the violins are now reinforced by the violas at the octave) we already hear signs that the harmony is about to take a different course. The second violins sound an e♮, thus preparing the way for the bass to move from c♯ (or rather d♭) to c♮. A bar later, in the treble, the melody imitates this downward step by moving from g″ to f″, and so establishes the key of F major. The melodic phrase in which this modulation occurs is two bars shorter than that at the opening of the movement, but, like the former one, it is a 'turning' figure. The horn now gives out the principal motive, in F major, but slightly modifies it by repeating the penultimate note, as in bars 338 et seq. It remains on this note for four bars, hints at the rhythm of the second subject, and finally moves up to d♭″, in which key the passage is repeated with the motive given to the flute. The whole course of proceedings between bars 398 and 422 seems to belong more properly to the harmonically freer working-out. The following bass progression, D♭-C♭-B♭, below the tied a♭, is reminiscent of that at the opening of the working-out (B♭-A♭-G). But when the principal motive is repeated once more on the chord of B♭, with the seventh, a♭, and passes into a cadential quaver figure, we realize that an end is now to be put to the 'shifting tonality'. And indeed, at bar 430, the principal motive now enters in full majesty, *ff*, in E flat major, over a tonic pedal. As at bar 18, it moves to the supertonic——but thereafter the chromatic upward impulse is more urgent, as according to the sketches was Beethoven's original intention for the exposition; that is to say, the line e♭″-e″-f″ is carried on over f♯″ to g″ and a♭″, which is followed by the step d‴-e♭‴. Thus a simple musical period (ten bars, arranged 4+2+4) is built up from the principal motive; and this is immediately succeeded by the second powerful statement of the motive, which corresponds to that at bars 37–43. In these sixteen bars the motive is given out with full emphasis; and though, as is now nearly always the case, it is shorter than in the exposition, its weight and importance are even greater. (Bars 430–445 correspond to bars 15–43; but it must be remembered that even in the exposition the first fifteen bars sounded as if they were merely an 'introduction'.) And it is a proof of the importance Beethoven himself laid upon the 'turning' figure of bar 44 that he not only introduced it here, where the harmonic progression is different (in the bass we find A♭–A♮–B♭ instead of A♭–G♭–F), but even repeated it so as to bring out the full structural significance of the progression from the A♭ of bar 446 to the B♭ of bar 448. The latter, as the dominant of the main key, here prepares the entry of the second subject in the tonic, as the F of bar 45 had prepared its entry in the dominant.

What now follows is, broadly speaking, a bar-by-bar repetition of the corresponding part of the exposition (bars 448–551 =bars 45–148). Such a repetition, coming after wide variations in those passages that are dominated by the principal motive, is the rule in Beethoven's symphonies. What is unusual is that here the two themes of the transition also reappear unchanged, with the result that we now hear an almost exact repetition of an eventful passage of over a hundred bars. Evidently Beethoven felt the need, after all the vicissitudes through which the music had passed in the working-out, of once more emphasizing the original structure of the whole as ordained by its inherent organic laws. Such variations as we find are mostly in the instrumentation, and so do not actually concern the subject-matter, but only the orchestral colour, of the music. The few other variations are in no way founded in necessity; rather are they to be explained by reference to the law of 'freedom of development' that is proper to all organic growth. As in nature every leaf of a plant, though subject to the general laws governing the organic structure of its species, has a vast potentiality of particular development, so also in art there is never only one available means of attaining organic perfection. And Beethoven particularly, even in those cases in which he followed a second time almost exactly the same course of development that he had previously adopted, was concerned to show that there were other ways of attaining that perfection. Fundamentally there is only one difference of any importance, although experience shows that this generally passes unnoticed: the explosive 'hemiolias' of bars 531 et seq. are not as before, 6/5 chords, but diminished sevenths (i.e. a–c–e♭–g♭ instead of a–c–e♭ f), which, while just as 'logical', creates a feeling of still greater suspense. And these are followed, not by the 6/4 chord (which here would be b♭–e♭–g), but the triad in root position (e♭–g–b♭). Thereby, it is true, the harmonic function of the chord is not so significantly emphasized; but on the other hand the connexion with the principal motive is brought out more clearly, and this is maintained in the following violin figure (e♭–g♭–a etc.). Connexion with the bass line leading to the cadence is only established again with the C flat of the cellos. Beethoven evidently did not think it necessary to make the bass progression (here A–B♭–C♭–B♭) so clear the second time. For the same reason, probably, the wind does not emphasize the rhythm of the second subject in bars 484–485—this after all had been brought out prominently again and again during the movement.

D.   FOURTH SECTION (CODA)

The recapitulation closes at bar 551 exactly as the exposition had closed at bar 148, i.e., with the first two bars of the principal motive. But this time they are repeated, and for six bars the chord of E flat major, as it dies away from piano to pianissimo, sounds as if it were to be the close of the movement. We are the more surprised, therefore, when we hear the same bars repeated a tone lower, i.e. in D flat, and once again in C major. It is like a breathing space after a period of deep emotional stress; but that this cannot be the end is shown clearly enough by the harmonic progression, which leads far away from the main key. And indeed we are yet to experience a multitude of new adventures in a coda whose length is commensurate with that of the movement as a whole.

The progression E flat–D flat–C is not new to us, for a corresponding one forms the basis of the bridge passage from exposition to working-out (B flat–A flat–G). But here things are different, and certainly both unusual and surprising. On the previous occasion the bass had descended, in a melodic line derived from the principal motive, from B flat over A flat to G, while an f in the treble had established the harmonic connexion between A flat and G. But now the triads of E flat major, D flat major, and C major, both in the form of chords and broken (in the rhythm of the principal motive), are heard one after the other, without any connecting link—a progression that entails consecutive fifths and octaves. For the time all growth seems to have ceased; the music confines itself to emphasizing as definitely, but as simply and unmistakably, as possible, its remoteness from the main key, which had not been quitted for over a hundred bars. Hence this insulation of each repetition of the motive. No harmonic connexion, such as was established in the bridge passage to the working-out, is required here.

But once this progression is completed, the growth of the movement begins again, and in the same harmonic direction as before; but this time it is slower, for the C major remains in force for eight more bars, whereas previously the seventh had at once appeared. But this comes in due course; and as it had formerly prepared the entry of the principal motive in C minor, so now it prepares that of the episode, this time in F minor. Thematically, the sixteen bars up to the F minor are dominated by the first two bars of the principal motive, as in bars 186 et seq., except that here the whole passage is kept pianissimo and thus has the effect of a shadowy reminiscence. This effect is strengthened by a new quaver figure for violins, in which the impetuous semiquaver motive, of bars 65–72, 186–218, etc. is now only hinted at. (It is perhaps permissible to see in this motive the embryo of the 'turning' figure.) But, as is shown by bars 570–571, which correspond exactly to bars 79–80, these quavers form one of those cadential figures that are always heard when a passage is about to reach its immediate goal. But here it too is shadowy, especially in the last four bars leading to the F minor cadence.

Now comes the episode. It opens with all the poignancy of expression that is derived from its accentuation and instrumentation; but after the sixth bar the melody breaks off, and only the counterpoint in the bass carries on to the repetition in E flat minor. This also is not completed; again the melody breaks off after six bars, and it is not heard again. Thus even here the shadows do not fully materialize. Now follows a remarkable passage. That the bass part had something very special to say at the last appearance was to be guessed from the fact that, for the first time, the counterpoint is given to a horn as well as to the bassoon and cellos. With the first beat of the seventh bar (595) both melody and counterpoint stop short; or rather, instead of proceeding in crotchets as before, bassoon and cellos proceed in

dotted minims, from d, the note upon which the counterpoint had
ceased, to d♭ and c. So the bass continues the line that the counterpoint would have taken. In the upper parts, however, all melodic
connexion with the episode is abandoned; only the semiquaver
motive already referred to is heard, like a reminiscence of the opening
of the coda. The cellos do not move direct to B flat as before, but
first touch C flat. This is probably partly due to the continued influence of the chromatic progression, and partly to the demands of
rhythm, a fourth bar being required to complete the phrase. And
probably it is also for this latter reason that the bass proceeds by
further semitone steps from B flat over A to A flat, with the quaver
figure continuing in the treble. The whole constitutes an eight-bar
period of which the general trend is downward. In it no harmonic
developments of any importance take place; the bass line started with
B flat (the dominant of E flat) and thither it returns, but with the
difference that it is now heard with its seventh, a♭, and so prepares
the way for further developments.

In the following passage the influence of the dominant, of which
we have been conscious since bar 595, becomes stronger and stronger.
Two figures contribute towards the creation of this effect. In the
bass we again hear that expressive transformation of the principal
motive that we heard in bar 338; here, however, it is aided in its
forward and upward impulse by another figure, in the treble, that
pushes its way chromatically up from b♭, first over b♮ to c, and then
over c♯ to d. Although this is its first appearance in this form, it has
its roots in the past and indeed gives the impression of being the final
fulfilment of long-indicated tendencies. Semitone steps occur
throughout the movement; and we underrate their importance if we
pay attention only to their transitional function. Schenker rightly
speaks of an "upward impulse", and finds evidence of it as early as in
the bass progression c♯–d of bars 7–9, which is answered in the treble
by the g–a♭ of bars 7–10. He also finds it in the e♭–e–f of bars 18–19,
the g–a♭–a–b♭ of bars 20–23, the e♭–e–f of bars 43–45, the g–a♭(g♯)–a
of bars 179–185, the d♭–d–e♭ of bars 218–220, the g–a♭–a–b♭ of bars
312–315, and the e♭–e–f–f♯–g–a♭ of bars 433–437. But nowhere is
this upward impulse so strongly in evidence as in bars 605–613 of the
coda, where, in answer to the chromatic descent of the previous bars,
the ascending steps from b♭ to e♭ are emphasized, thematically and

melodically, by the wood-wind. Out of these, and out of the answer
to the bass motive, grows a new and expressive tune, which rises
higher and higher and at last, in bar 623, passes into the 'turning'
quaver figure of bar 44, which here, and only here, is repeated four
times, in a descending line, to be followed by one of those cadential
quaver figures that are so familiar to us. Meanwhile, the horns softly
give out fragments of the principal motive, and gradually the rhythm
of the second subject is heard more and more clearly in the inner
parts. Fundamentally, this whole passage of thirty-six bars (595–
630) is nothing but the preparation for what is about to come—an
extended and elaborately adorned cadential passage leading from the
dominant to the tonic of E flat major, filled with a mysterious feeling
of suspense, and new in every bar even where there are allusions to
motives already known to us. Seen in relation to the movement as a
whole, this passage is very similar to, indeed almost identical with,
that at the end of the working-out, after the return of the episode in
E flat minor. On both occasions, after the melody of the episode has
broken off, the harmony progresses from E flat minor to a half-close
on B flat, which is followed only by a passage in which the wider
possibilities of the tonality are explored. Thematically the two passages are related through the bass motive and the unobtrusive
references to the principal motive. But apart from this, everything is
different; in the coda the whole of the music is more incorporeal,
more evanescent—as after all is only natural seeing that here we do
not look forward, as we did after the working-out, to further high
adventures.

But it was impossible that a movement of such power and heroic
achievement should end in this mood. And so this bridge passage
leads to one last soaring flight, which, if not the most impassioned, is
the most brilliant of all. Now at last, after six hundred and thirty
bars, the principal motive seems to be fully deployed—and not
merely in its capacity as the mainspring of the movement. It makes a
last effort, more determined even than at the opening of the recapitulation, to expand into a true symphonic 'theme'. Four eight-
bar periods, thematically identical, follow one another. In each of
them the motive appears in the same shape as at the close of the
working-out, bars 338 et seq., i.e. with the fourth bar altered, first
in tonic and then in dominant harmony. The accompaniment, in

which fresh instruments gradually join in, is dominated by a semi-quaver figure, based on that of bars 65 et seq. and 186 et seq. and alluded to early in the coda, which now, however, for the first time ascends energetically instead of descending. At the same time the rhythm of the second subject is given out by the wind. In spite of the gradual increase of tone, which is due mainly to the entrance, one after another, of additional instruments, the dynamic marking does not yet exceed forte; not until the end of the following cadential passage does it rise to a fortissimo. The last bars of this passage (bars 663–673) fully define the key of E flat, after the repeated alternation of tonic and dominant. It is easy to overlook the presence in this passage of parts of the principal motive:

Bar 663

etc.

In the bass figure of bars 663–664 we hear the third and fourth bars of the motive (G–B♭–d♭), and in each of the succeeding bars the third bar of the motive in diminution. Only if this reference to the motive is brought clearly out—that is, if the bass figures are not overwhelmed by the noise of the chords in the upper parts—does this passage come into its full rights, apart from its function as a powerful, though purely formal, extended cadence. For it is only in these bars that the principal motive may be said to be rounded off as a full period, or a self-contained 'theme'.

The movement might have closed with this triumphant flight, but Beethoven decided otherwise. Gentler tones return once more with an exact repetition of the second theme of the transition, which we have not heard since bars 57–64. After all the excitement and agitation, this comes like a sigh of relief; but when in bar 681 the chord of the dominant seventh is heard, and continues for eight bars, we realize that the relief can only last for a moment or two. The distorted rhythm reappears: two bars with the second beat accented, then six bars in which 'hemiolias' dominate, first in chords and then in a quaver figure for the first violins founded on the bass figure of bar 338, while the basses, tympani, and wind band emphasize the rhythm of the second subject. The movement ends, as it began, with two mighty hammer-blows on the common chord of E flat major.

NOTES

Page 54

[1]Thus, L. W. Neuling, an opera composer of Darmstadt, wrote on 15th July, 1825, from Vienna: "I have heard a Quartet (op. 127), composed perhaps three months ago. I can only say of it that it is one of the greatest masterpieces of our time."

Page 65

[2]The powerful impression created by Beethoven's personality and compositions is not due to the 'popularity' of any of his particular tunes or works, as is the case with Mozart, Weber, Schubert, Schumann, and Wagner. The only tune with which his name was connected and that ever became truly popular was not in fact by him but by Schubert. This, the so-called *Sehnsuchtswalzer*, was published as a composition of Beethoven's as early as 1826, that is, during his and Schubert's lifetime.

Page 76

[3]Riemann's theory that the "Mannheimers" were the true forerunners of Haydn, and thus also the parents of the classical symphony, is generally rejected. The connexion of the Mannheimers, who all came from Austria, with the Viennese School and its Masters, Wagenseil, Monn, and others, must not be overlooked. It should also be noted that many of the new ideas that sprang up at that time in Vienna and Mannheim had been foreshadowed by the old Italian Masters. In particular, sonata movements of a fairly developed form are to be found in Pergolesi, who died in 1736, that is before the period of the Mannheimers' activity. It must be admitted, however, that certain peculiarities of the later classical symphony are to be

found in the works of the Mannheimers earlier than anywhere else, in particular the presence of passages of tension or climax, the sole purpose of which is to prepare for what is to come. Unfortunately, however, it is precisely in these works that the true subject matter of the music—the melodic and thematic material—is quite insignificant, more so than in the case of the contemporary Viennese and C. P. E. Bach, the chief Master of the North German School.

Page 87

⁴That Beethoven, at every stage in the process of composition, was guided by his 'inspiration', is strongly emphasized by Romain Rolland in his remarks on the sketches for the first movement of op. 31, no. 2: "From the first sketch onwards the opening movement of the Sonata is a fully developed, living entity . . . Where microscopic examination of the 'cellular tissue' merely shows the germination of a motive consisting of a few notes, the 'idea' of the whole work is in fact already present. The oak is latent in the acorn. True, the creator cannot behold his creation until the process of birth has been accomplished. It is not a question of a work of development after conception, but a matter of procreation, which is first and foremost a function of the life-force."

Page 92

⁵It is unfortunately impossible to render fully and precisely the word *Gestalt* in English, and for this reason it has itself been adopted for use in the latest philosophical works in that language. I do not use it in my book in the comprehensive sense that it bears in the current *Gestaltsphilosophie*, the chief exponents of which are Max Wertheimer and Wolfgang Köhler. In this sense it denotes the idea of 'the Whole to which all detail is subordinated'—an idea that is to-day gaining ground more and more not only in philosophy but also in natural science and biology. When I speak of the *Gestalt*—here rendered by 'organic structure'—of a work of Beethoven's, I refer to its special significance and 'completeness in itself', and so emphasize the crucial difference between the works of Beethoven and other Classics and those of the Romantics.

Page 95

⁶Why in minor movements the second subject is generally not
in the dominant but in the relative major (although the function of
the dominant is the same in a minor as in a major key) may perhaps be
explained thus: the normal modulation from C major to G major
requires the alteration of one note only, F, which becomes F sharp.
But in modulating from C minor to G major, three notes must be
altered, i.e., F becomes F sharp, A flat A natural, and E flat E natural.
Here the interval of the augmented second, E flat–F sharp, ob-
trudes itself upon the ear. The resultant feeling of tension seems to
have been disliked, especially where, as is usually the case with minor
movements, the second subject has the effect of relaxing tension.
Beethoven only wrote the second subject in the key of the dominant
in movements in which the tension of that subject is greater than, or
at least as great as, that of the first, e.g. the Finales of op. 2, no. 1,
and op. 27, no. 2; the first and last movements of op. 31, no. 2 (reached
in the first movement after more than usually tense modulation, with
the augmented second appearing twice—F–G sharp and C–D
sharp); the first movement of op. 47; the last movement of op. 57;
and the first movement of op. 90.

Page 101

⁷Wagner, in one of the last articles he wrote (*Ueber das Opern-
dichten und Komponieren im besonderen*, published posthumously)
quotes the theme in the following form:

Freu-de schö-ner Göt-ter-fun-ken, Tochter aus E - ly - si - um

He evidently had not the score at hand, and it is characteristic that in
his memory the phrase should have become changed in this way. In
the unbroken crotchet rhythm he missed the close correspondence
with the words, which is precisely what Beethoven wanted to avoid.
In this form the tune sacrifices much of its depth and grandeur.

Page 104

⁸On the subject of contrast I would refer readers to Kurt Riezler's books *Parmenides* and *Traktat vom Schönen* (Klostermann,

Frankfurt a/M) and to an article by the same author, *Homer und die Anfänge der Philosophie*, in the journal *Die Antike*, 1936.

Page 120

[9]A popular German colloquialism, meaning roughly "it is something extra-special."

Page 198

[10]Among the sketches for the Mass in D that are preserved in the Berlin Library is a sheet that is of the greatest importance in tracing the history of the *Dona*. (This is reproduced in facsimile in *Musiker-handschriften*, by G. Schünemann, Atlantis-Verlag.) On it Beethoven wrote: "*Dona nobis pacem* still in the minor, for after all they are praying for peace therefore only peace dealt with as if it had already come." This shows that from the very beginning Beethoven's intention was to contrast peace with strife. But at first he evidently wanted to do it the other way round, that is, with the prayer of the chorus for peace, which was still far off, in the more plaintive minor mode. Only the orchestra was to depict peace "as if it had already come." Not until later did he hit upon the solution as we know it, viz., the transfer of the image of 'strife' to the orchestra, which was of course more correct. Now the thought of peace dominates the picture from the beginning of the *Dona*. Yet even there the troubled world is hinted at; like a sinister apparition it appears in the two episodes, temporarily blinding us to the image of peace, though it remains nothing but a background before which the peace in which the close of the Mass is steeped stands clearly out. The other way round, it would have been impossible to create this effect in such stupendous form; and in particular the effect of the first *Dona*, with its bright-toned major, would have been altogether lacking.

Page 202

[11]The harmonic procedure is exactly the same as in the Adagio of the B flat Piano Sonata, op. 106 (the *Hammerklavier*). In this we are suddenly aware, in the midst of the very definite F sharp minor tonality of the principal theme, of a passage apparently in G major (including the subdominant of that key). In both cases the return to

the original tonality is effected by a simple step of a semitone, B (i.e., C flat) to B flat, and G to F sharp respectively.

Page 204

[12]So far as I am aware, the basso ostinato in this passage is the only one of a 'static' nature to be found in Beethoven. In older music its function always was static, i.e., to support a repeated and self-contained harmonic development, as for instance in Bach's C minor Passacaglia. An earlier instance is a Passacaglia of Buxtehude, and a later one the Finale of Brahms's Haydn Variations. In other cases in which Beethoven used a ground bass—especially in the codas of the first and last movements of the Seventh Symphony—it forms an integral part of the general harmonic development, and its repetition delays the relaxation of the tension, so that its function is in the highest degree dynamic.

Page 205

[13]Beethoven's marking is not to be taken too literally. He evidently wanted the same tempo as that to which the stringendo has worked up in the first 'alla breve' bar. The speed of the crotchets cannot possibly be reduced again to less than it was in that bar. The passage shows that Beethoven's metronome markings are not absolutely binding. In many cases he inserted them at a later date, probably in accordance with his 'feeling'. It is possible also that 'feeling' for tempo has undergone a change in the course of time. At least it may be said that blind obedience to Beethoven's tempo indications is in many cases impossible. Toscanini's attempt to play the first movement of the Ninth Symphony at the speed indicated ($\flat$=88) can hardly be considered a success. Even this conductor, so famous for his fidelity to the composer's indications, takes the Adagio substantially slower than Beethoven prescribed. The importance of Beethoven's tempo indications lies in the facts that they show the ratio that he wanted between two tempi (e.g. in the slow movement of the Ninth, in which he intended the Andante to be only slightly speeded up), and that they ensure the correct interpretation of the spirit of the music, as in the Adagio of op. 106.

Page 222

[14]Beethoven was particularly drawn to the Lydian mode. As is shown by a note, he wanted to write "Chöre in der lydischen Tonart." This cannot have been due to his study of Palestrina's music, for as Jeppesen, the authority on Palestrina, has ascertained, the Lydian mode is to be found in none of that Master's music, and only occurs, in fact, in unison Gregorian plain-song. (This, it is true, applies only to the period before 1600; Heinrich Schütz's *St. Luke Passion*, written about 1650, contains several movements in pure Lydian.) What particularly charmed Beethoven in this mode was its "incorporeity," which is due to the lack of the perfect triad on the subdominant.

Page 242

[15]As is shown by the sketches, Beethoven originally wanted the sharpest possible contrast in the variations of op. 127. The lofty A flat theme was suddenly to appear in quick time in C major. In the sketch-books a considerable part of this variation with the heading 'la gaieté', is worked out. (Nottebohm doubts, in my opinion wrongly, whether this piece has any connexion with the Quartets; in the sketches, however, the return to A flat is expressly provided for.)

GLOSSARY

(NOTE. The use of technical terms is unavoidable in any serious discussion of musical matters; and since it is improbable that even the most musical layman has a complete knowledge of these, a short explanation of the most important terms used in this book is appended.)

BASSO OSTINATO (or GROUND BASS). A figure (q.v.) or melody used as the bass of a passage or movement, repeated several times to the accompaniment of different figures, often with varying harmonies.

CADENCE (or CLOSE). The last two chords of a musical phrase, answering approximately the same purpose as that of stops in language, and conveying a sense of more or less complete repose. There are four main kinds of cadence:

(1) *Perfect Cadence* or *Full Close*. The dominant chord leading to the tonic.

(2) *Plagal Cadence*. The subdominant chord leading to the tonic. (This is sometimes known as the *Amen Cadence*.) Beethoven, following the example of ancient Church music, uses it in the *Benedictus* of the D major Mass; and it is frequently found in minor movements of sonatas etc., e.g. Finales of op. 10, no. 1, op. 18, no. 4, and op. 131, and first movement of op. 111.

(3) *Imperfect Cadence* or *Half Close*. The dominant led up to by the tonic, the subdominant, or some other chord.

(4) *Interrupted Cadence*. The dominant chord leading to a chord other than the tonic, usually the submediant.

CADENTIAL PASSAGE (or CADENTIAL PHRASE). That more complicated form of phrase-ending in which other chords besides the dominant —particularly the subdominant and the so-called "intermediate dominant" (see note, p. 254)—are employed, with the object of providing a broader basis to the harmonic developments that lead finally to the perfect cadence.

DOMINANT. The fifth degree of the scale counting upwards.

ENHARMONIC.

(1) *Enharmonic Notes* are those that differ in notation but have, in our modern system of tuning known as 'equal temperament', the same pitch, e.g. C sharp and D flat, C flat and B natural.

(2) *Enharmonic Modulation* is modulation effected by means of this change of notation. Sometimes however, for the sake of convenience, the note B is written instead of C flat (or F instead of E sharp, and so forth); in such cases, which are recognizable by return to the original notation, there is no actual enharmonic modulation. This only takes place when the whole scale, and not merely certain notes, are changed in this manner, and the original key is definitely quitted. Examples are to be found in the Andante of Mozart's great B flat Violin Sonata, and in the Funeral March of Beethoven's op. 26 Sonata, in which C flat major is written as B major, whence it modulates back, by way of B minor and D major, to E flat major and A flat minor.

FIGURATION. The use of scale and arpeggio figures or passages, e.g. in the variation of a theme.

FIGURE. A short succession of notes forming a more or less complete musical idea. A figure may be used either melodically or as the accompaniment to a melody, and may consist of two or more notes.

LEADING NOTE. The seventh degree of the scale counting upwards.

MEDIANT. The third degree of the scale counting upwards.

MODULATION. The process of passing from one key to another.

MOTIVE. A figure (q.v.) that owing to its significance is susceptible of organic development. It provides, as it were, the 'motive power' of the whole or part of a musical composition.

PEDAL POINT (also PEDAL or ORGAN POINT). A note or notes held or repeated by one or two parts while other parts move in changing, often dissonant, harmonies. The Pedal point is usually, but not necessarily, in the bass, and normally consists of tonic or dominant or both.

RONDO FORM. Rondo Form and Sonata Form (q.v.) are both derived

t

from Song Form, which may be represented by the formula a-b-a. In the Rondo, this simple formula is developed into a-b-a-b-a, or a-b-a-c-a-b-a, the themes represented by 'b' and 'c' being called 'episodes'. A movement in Rondo Form is one of repetition and not, like a movement in Sonata Form, of development, for the themes generally recur without essential alteration and there is no 'working out'.

SONATA FORM (or FIRST-MOVEMENT FORM). This is the form in which the great majority of first movements of sonatas, symphonies, quartets etc., are written. It consists of three main sections, to which an Introduction and a finishing section (or coda) may be added:

(1) *Introduction* (optional), which is usually in slower time than the main body of the movement.

(2) *Exposition*, in which the subject-matter of the movement is given out. It comprises:

(a) the *first subject*, which opens and closes in the principal key but may be subjected to transient modulation during its course. It consists of the *principal theme*, or occasionally of that and a subsidiary theme. It is connected by

(b) the *Transition*, or *Bridge Passage*, with

(c) the *second subject* in a related key—in major movements usually the dominant and in minor movements usually the relative major. In early sonatas, up to the time of Haydn and Mozart, the place of the second subject is often taken by a varied repetition of the first subject.

Following the perfect cadence at the end of the last of this group of themes is:

(d) the *Codetta*, which consists of a passage further establishing the key and connecting with the repeat of the Exposition or the beginning of

(3) the *Development* (or *Working-out*) *Section*, in which the themes or motives from the Introduction or Exposition are developed or 'worked out', i.e. treated by any means that the composer's skill and imagination may suggest. This section may also contain an 'episode', i.e. material that has not appeared in the Exposition. (An example is in the first movement of the Piano Sonata op. 10, no. 1.) This section leads to

(4) the *Recapitulation*, in which the themes given out in the Exposition are restated, often in a varied form, and with the Transition so arranged harmonically as to lead to the second subject in the main key instead of the dominant or other key.

(5) *Coda* (optional, but since the time of Beethoven usual and often of considerable extent and importance). The coda serves to give added emphasis to the end of the movement.

Sonata Form is a form of continuity and development, and is based upon thematic and harmonic contrast.

SUBDOMINANT. The fourth degree of the scale counting upwards.

SUBMEDIANT. The sixth degree of the scale counting upwards.

TONALITY. "Tonality is the element of key ... Upon the clearness of its definition the existence of instrumental music in harmonic forms of the sonata order depends. It is defined by the consistent maintenance for appreciable periods of harmonies, or passages of melody, which are characteristic of individual keys." (Grove's *Dictionary of Music and Musicians*, 1st Edn.)

All harmonic progressions within one tonal context are dominated by the attraction exerted between each of the three primary triads, i.e. tonic, subdominant, and dominant. (A simple and very striking example is the opening solo passage of Beethoven's E flat Concerto.) These triads do not always appear undisguised; in particular the subdominant triad is often replaced by the supertonic. The dominant triad, whether in a major or a minor key, must always be a major chord on account of the leading note, which is its major third; but the subdominant, even in a major key, may be a minor chord. In place of this minor chord (i.e. in C major or minor, the triad F–A flat–C) there may be one on the flattened supertonic (D flat–F–A flat, usually with the F in the bass—the so-called 'Neapolitan Sixth'). This chord bears exactly the same relation to that of the true minor subdominant (F–A flat–C) that the supertonic triad (D–F–A or F–A–D) bears to the major subdominant triad (F–A–C). An example is to be seen in the fifth bar of the illustration on p. 154. Here the normal subdominant triad (A–C sharp–E, with the sixth, F sharp, added) is followed by the chord A–C–F (the Neapolitan Sixth), which in its turn is followed directly by the dominant triad (B–D sharp–F sharp).

TONIC. The key note, or first degree of the scale.

TRIAD. A chord consisting of a note with its third (major or minor) and fifth (perfect, augmented, or diminished). A triad is either a 'major or minor common chord' (e.g. C–E–G or C–E♭–G), or an 'augmented or diminished triad' (e.g. C–E–G♯ or C–E♭–G♭).

CHRONOLOGICAL LIST
OF THE MORE IMPORTANT WORKS
(The numbers in brackets refer to the pages on which the works are mentioned.)

BONN

1782–4   Variations on a March by Dressler.
Three Piano Sonatas, E flat major, F minor, D major.
Two-part Fugue for Organ.
Two Rondos for Piano, C major, A major.
Piano Concerto, E flat major.
Songs: *Schilderung eines Mädchens* and
An einen Säugling.

1785   Three Piano Quartets, C major, E flat major, D major.

1787–9   Prelude, F minor.
Two Preludes through all the major and minor keys.
Two Piano Trios, C major, E flat major.
Songs. (181, 183)

1790–2   Two Cantatas (on the death of Joseph II and the Accession of Leopold II). (26, 83, 84)
Songs (principally from op. 52).
Variations on a Theme from Mozart's *Figaro*, and other
Variations.
Ritterballett. (84)
Allegro and Minuet for two Flutes.

VIENNA

OP.

1792–5   1   Three Piano Trios, E flat major, G major, C minor.
(27, 29, 90, 113)

293

OP.

2 Three Piano Sonatas, F minor, A major, C major.
(90, 113, 114)

3 String Trio, E flat major.

87 Trio for Two Oboes and English Horn.

103 Octet for Wind Instruments (possibly composed at
Bonn). (88)

19 Piano Concerto in B flat major, no. 2. (134, 160)

46 Song: *Adelaide*. (181, 182)

Songs: *Seufzer eines Ungeliebten* and *Gegenliebe*.

1796–7 4 String Quintet, E flat major. (88)

5 Two Sonatas for Piano and Cello, F major, G minor.
(126)

6 Sonata for Piano, for four hands, D major.

7 Piano Sonata, E flat major. (115)

8 Serenade for String Trio, D major.

25 Serenade for Violin, Flute, and Viola, D major.

16 Quintet for Piano and four Wind Instruments, E flat
major (also published as Piano Quartet, with
Strings). (128)

71 Sextet for Wind Instruments, E flat major.

71a Sextet for Strings and Wind Instruments, E flat major.

15 Piano Concerto no. 1, C major. (134, 160)

65 *Scena* and *Aria: Ah, Perfido!*

51 No. 1. Rondo for Piano, C major.

1798–9 9 Three String Trios, G major, D major, C minor.

10 Three Piano Sonatas, C minor, F major, D major.
(116-118)

11 Trio for Piano, Clarinet, and Cello, B flat major. (127)

12 Three Violin Sonatas, D major, A major, E flat
major. (127)

13 Piano Sonata (*Pathétique*) C minor. (99, 118, 119)

14 Two Piano Sonatas, E major, G major. (120)

20 Septet for Strings and Wind, E flat major. (127)

21 First Symphony, C major. (134-135)

1800–1 17 Sonata for Piano and Horn, F major.

OP.

18 Six String Quartets, F major, G major, D major, C minor, A major, B flat major. (81, 83, 94, 127-128, 134)

22 Piano Sonata, B flat major. (120, 121)

23 Violin Sonata, A minor. (127)

24 Violin Sonata, F major. (127)

26 Piano Sonata, A flat major. (121, 122)

27 Two Piano Sonatas *quasi una fantasia*, E flat major, C sharp minor. (99, 122-124)

28 Piano Sonata, D major. (124-126, 152)

29 String Quintet, C major.

37 Third Piano Concerto, C minor. (134, 160)

43 Ballet: *The Men of Prometheus*. (36, 137)

85 Oratorio: *The Mount of Olives*. (183)

51 No. 2. Rondo for Piano, G major.

49 Two small Piano Sonatas, G minor, G major.

1802   30 Three Violin Sonatas, A major, C minor, G major. (100, 131-132, 239)

31 Three Piano Sonatas, G major, D minor, E flat major. (100, 129-131, 159)

33 Seven Bagatelles for Piano (some dating from earlier).

34 Variations for Piano, F major.

35 Variations for Piano on a theme from *Prometheus* (the so-called *Eroica Variations*). (137)

40 Romance for Violin and Orchestra, G major.

50 Romance for Violin and Orchestra, F major.

36 Second Symphony, D major. (134-135)

1803   44 Variations for Piano, Violin, and Cello.

47 Violin Sonata in A major. (132-133, 239)

48 Six Sacred Songs, poems by Gellert. (182)

55 Third Symphony (*Eroica*), E flat major. (37, 38, 134-139, 200, 247-281)

1804-5 32 Song: *An die Hoffnung*, first setting. (182)

53 Piano Sonata, C major. (164-165)

'Andante favori' for Piano, F major. (165, 239)

OP.

54 Piano Sonata, F major.
57 Piano Sonata, F minor. (90, 92, 99, 164-166)
56 Triple Concerto for Piano, Violin, Cello, and Orchestra, C major.
72 *Fidelio*, Opera, first and second versions; *Leonora* Overtures nos. 1, 2, 3, C major. (162, 179, 184-187)

1806   58 Fourth Piano Concerto, G major. (92, 160-161)
59 Three String Quartets, F major, E minor, C major. (168-172)
60 Fourth Symphony, B flat major. (140-141)
61 Violin Concerto, D major. (161)
     Thirty-two Variations for Piano, C minor.

1807-8 62 Overture to *Coriolanus*, a play by H. J. von Collin, C minor. (163)
67 Fifth Symphony, C minor. (90, 142-149)
68 Sixth Symphony (*Pastoral*), F major. (81-82, 149-152)
69 Sonata for Cello and Piano, A major. (174-175)
70 Two Trios for Piano, Violin, and Cello, D major, E flat major. (175-176)
80 Fantasia for Piano, Chorus, and Orchestra. (183)
86 First Mass for Solo Voices, Chorus, and Orchestra, C major. (188)
     Four settings of Goethe's *Nur wer die Sehnsucht kennt*. (182)

1809-10 73 Fifth Piano Concerto, E flat major. (161)
74 String Quartet, E flat major. (172-173)
76 Variations for Piano.
77 Fantasia for Piano. (122)
78 Piano Sonata, F sharp major. (167)
79 Piano Sonata, G major.
81a Piano Sonata (*Les Adieux*), E flat major. (81, 167)
84 Overture and Incidental Music to Goethe's *Egmont*. (164)

75
and 83 } Seven Songs, words by Goethe. (180, 182)

u

OP.

119   Bagatelles for Piano (some composed earlier).

121a Variations for Piano, Violin, and Cello on the song
      Ich bin der Schneider Kakadu.

124   Overture, *Die Weihe des Hauses*, C major.
      Rondo for Piano, *Die Wut über den verlorenen Gros-
      chen*, G major. (218)

120   Thirty-three variations on a Waltz by Diabelli, C
      major. (232-233)

1822-3   126   Bagatelles. (108, 220)

1817-23 123   Mass in D major (*Missa Solemnis*) [1818-22].
               (180, 187-198, 218, 222)

         125   Ninth Symphony, D minor [1817-18 and 1822-4].
               (199-216, 218, 223)

1824-5   127   String Quartet, E flat major. (221, 233-242)

1825-6   132   String Quartet, A minor. (81, 233-242)

         130   String Quartet, B flat major (with the Great Fugue,
               op. 133). (233-242-243)

         131   String Quartet, C sharp minor. (233-242)

1826   135   String Quartet, F major. (57, 81, 218, 233-243)
               Finale to op. 130. (57, 218, 239)

BIBLIOGRAPHY

I. SOURCES

(a) Beethoven, L. van: *Sämtliche Briefe*. Kritische Ausgabe ed. by A. C. Kalischer. 5 vols., Berlin and Leipzig, 1906–8. English trans. by J. S. Shedlock, 2 vols. London, 1909. 2nd Edn revised by Th. von Frimmel, 1909–11.

(b) Wegeler, Franz, and Ries, Ferdinand: *Biographische Notizen über L. van Beethoven*. Coblenz, 1838. Supplement, 1845. New Edn by Kalischer, Berlin and Leipzig, 1906.

(c) Breuning, Gerhard von: *Aus dem Schwarzspanierhaus*. Erinnerungen an L. van Beethoven aus meiner Jugendzeit. Vienna, 1874. New Edn by Kalischer, Berlin and Leipzig, 1907.

(d) Kerst, Friedrich: *Die Erinnerungen an Beethoven*. 2 vols., Stuttgart, 1913. 2nd Edn, 1925.

(e) Leitzmann, Albert: *Beethovens Persönlichkeit*. Urteile der Zeitgenossen. 2 vols., Leipzig, 1914. New Edn, 1921.

(f) Frimmel, Theodor von: *Beethoven im zeitgenössischen Bildnis*. Vienna, 1923.

(g) Nottebohm, Gustav: *L. van Beethoven*. Thematisches Verzeichnis sämtlicher im Druck erschienenen Werke. Leipzig, 1851. 2nd and enlarged Edn, Leipzig, 1868 etc.

(h) Nottebohm, Gustav: *Beethoveniana*. Aufsätze und Mitteilungen. 2 vols., Leipzig and Winterthur, 1872–88. New Imp., 1925.

(i) Nottebohm, Gustav: *Zwei Skizzenbücher von Beethoven aus den Jahren* 1801 *bis* 1803, beschrieben und in Auszügen dargestellt. New Edn with Preface by Paul Mies, Leipzig, 1924.

(j) Frimmel, Th. von: *Ed. Beethoven-Jahrbuch*. 2 vols., Munich and Leipzig, 1808–9.

(k) Sandberger, A.: *Ed. Neues Beethoven-Jahrbuch*. 6 vols. have appeared. Augsburg, 1924–35.

II. BIOGRAPHIES AND GENERAL DESCRIPTIONS OF WORKS

(a) Schindler, Anton: *L. van Beethoven*. Münster, 1840. 5th Edn, ed. F. Volbach, 1927.

(b) Marx, Adolf Bernard: *L. van Beethoven*. 2 vols., Berlin, 1859. 5th Edn, Leipzig, 1902.

(c) Nohl, Ludwig: *Beethovens Leben*. 3 vols., Vienna and Leipzig, 1864–77. 2nd Edn, ed. by P. Sakolovski, Berlin, 1909–13.

(d) Thayer, Alexander Wheelock: *L. van Beethovens Leben*. First appeared in Germany in 3 vols., trans. and ed. by Herm. Deiters. 2nd Edn ed. by H. D. and Hugo Riemann, 5 vols. Berlin, 1901–11. New Edn, Leipzig, 1917–23. The original English Edn, revised and amended by H. E. Krehbiel, appeared in 3 vols., New York, 1921.

(e) Bekker, Paul: *Beethoven*. Berlin, 1911 etc. English trans. by M. M. Bozman, London, 1925.

(f) Thomas-San Galli, W. A.: *L. van Beethoven*. Munich, 1913.

(g) Ernest, Gustav: *Beethoven. Persönlichkeit, Leben und Schaffen*. Berlin, 1920 etc.

(h) Schiedermair, Ludwig: *Der junge Beethoven*. Leipzig, 1925.

(i) Rolland, Romain: *Beethoven. Les grandes époques créatrices*. Paris, 1928.

(j) Herriot, Edouard: *La vie de Beethoven*. Paris, 1930.

(k) Turner, W. J.: *Beethoven*. London, 1927.

III. BOOKS UPON THE WORKS (ANALYSES &C.)

(a) Lenz, Wilhelm von: *Beethoven et ses trois styles*. St Petersburg, 1852. New Edn, ed. M. D. Calvocoressi, Paris, 1909.

(b) Lenz, W. von: *Beethoven. Eine Kunststudie*. 5 Pts, Hamburg, 1855–60. New Edn, ed. Kalischer, Stuttgart, 1923.

(c) Oulibisheff, Alex. von: *Beethoven, ses critiques et ses glossateurs*. Leipzig, 1857. German trans. by L. Bischoff: *Beethoven, seine Kritiker und seine Ausleger*. Leipzig, 1859. (A criticism disparaging the majority of the later works of Beethoven, written in opposition to W. von Lenz.)

(d) Kretzschmar, Hermann: *Führer durch den Konzertsaal*. 3 vols., Leipzig, 1888–90 etc. Revised and continued by H. Engel, H. Mersmann and others. Leipzig, 1930 etc.

(e) Schenker, Heinrich: Analyses of various instrumental works in

Der Tonwille, 10 Nos., Vienna 1921–4; and in *Das Meisterwerk in der Musik*, Munich, 1925–30.

(f) Grove, Sir George: *Beethoven and his Nine Symphonies*. London, 1896 etc. German trans. by M. Hehemann, London, 1906.

(g) Evans, Edwin (Senr.): *Beethoven's Nine Symphonies fully described and annotated*. 2 vols., London, 1923–4.

(h) Nef, Karl: *Die neun Sinfonien Beethovens*. Leipzig, 1928.

(i) Schenker, Heinrich: *Beethovens 3. Sinfonie zum erstenmal in ihrem wahren Inhalt dargestellt*, in *Das Meisterwerk in der Musik*. Munich, 1930.

(j) Schenker, H.: *Beethovens 5. Sinfonie*. Vienna, 1925.

(k) Schenker, H.: *Beethovens 9. Sinfonie*. Vienna, 1912.

(l) Tovey, Sir D. F.: *Beethoven's Ninth Symphony*. Edinburgh, 1922.

(m) Helm, Theodor: *Beethovens Streichquartette*. Leipzig, 1885 etc.

(n) Wetzel, Justus Hermann: *Beethovens Violinsonaten nebst den Romanzen und dem Konzert analysiert*. Vol. 1. Berlin, 1924.

(o) Bülow, Hans von: *Beethovens Werke für Pianoforte solo von op. 53 an*. Kritische und instruktive Ausgabe. 2 Pts. Stuttgart, 1877–8.

(p) Reinecke, Carl: *Die Beethoven'schen Klaviersonaten*. Briefe an eine Freundin. Leipzig, 1895. 9th Edn, 1924. English trans. of 1st Edn by E. M. T. Dawson, London, 1898.

(q) Nagel, Wilibald: *Beethoven und seine Klaviersonaten*. 2 vols. Langensalza, 1903–5. 2nd Edn, 1923–4.

(r) Schenker, Heinrich: *Die letzten 5 Sonaten für Klavier*. Erläuterungsausgabe, Vienna, 1913–16 (excl. op. 106).

(s) Riemann, Hugo: *L. van Beethoven's sämtliche Klavier-Solosonaten*. 3 vols., Berlin, 1918 etc.

(t) Volbach, Fritz: *Die Klaviersonaten Beethovens*. Cologne, 1919. 3rd Edn, 1924.

(u) Braunstein, Josef: *Beethovens Leonore-Ouvertüren*. Leipzig, 1927.

(v) Jahn, Otto: *Zur Entstehungsgeschichte des Fidelio*, in *Leonore*. Piano arrangement by O. Jahn. Leipzig, 1851.

(w) Prieger, Erich: *Zur Entstehungsgeschichte des Fidelio*, in *Leonore*. Piano arrangement by E. Prieger. Leipzig, 1905.

IV. GENERAL AND PHILOSOPHICAL

(a) Wagner, Richard: *Beethoven*, 1st Edn, Leipzig, 1870. English trans. by E. Dannreuter. London, 1880.

(b) Mersmann, Hans: *Beethoven*. Die Synthese der Stile. Berlin, 1922.

(c) Cassirer, Fritz: *Beethoven und die Gestalt*. Stuttgart etc., 1925.

(d) Krug, Walter: *Beethovens Vollendung. Eine Streitschrift*. Munich, 1925.

(e) Halm, August: *Beethoven*. Leipzig, 1927.

(f) Schmitz, Arnold: *Beethoven*. Bonn, 1927.

(g) Engelsmann, Walter: *Beethovens Kompositionspläne*. Augsburg, 1931.

(h) Rolland, Romain: *Goethe et Beethoven*. Paris, 1930. German trans. by A. Kippenberg, Zürich and Leipzig, 1928.

(i) Engelsmann, Walter: *Goethe und Beethoven*. Augsburg, 1931.

V. MISCELLANEOUS

(a) Schmitz, Arnold: *Beethovens "zwei Prinzipe"*. Berlin and Bonn, 1923.

(b) Schmitz, Arnold: *Das romantische Beethovenbild*. Berlin and Bonn, 1927.

(c) Mies, Paul: *Die Bedeutung der Skizzen Beethovens zur Erkenntnis seines Stils*. Leipzig, 1925.

(d) Aerde, Raymond van: *Les ancêtres flamands de Beethoven*. Malines, 1928.

(e) Schweisheimer, Waldemar: *Beethovens Leiden*. Ihr Einfluss auf sein Leben und Schaffen. Munich, 1922.

(f) Bilancioni, Guglielmo: *La sordità di Beethoven*. Considerazioni d'un otologo. Rome, 1921.

(g) Leux, Irmgard: *Christian Gottlob Neefe*. Leipzig, 1925.

(h) Nohl, Walther: *Goethe und Beethoven*. Regensburg, 1929.

INDEX OF WORKS DISCUSSED

WORKS FOR PIANO

SUBJECT INDEX

GENERAL INDEX